MW00658721

CompTIA Network+:

Get Certified Get Ahead

N10-006 Practice Test Questions

By Darril Gibson

CompTIA Network+ Get Certified Get Ahead
N10-006 Practice Test Questions
By Darril Gibson

YCDA, LLC,
1124 Knights Bridge Lane,
Virginia Beach, VA, 23455

YCDA, LLC, books may be purchased for educational, business, or sales promotional use. For information, please contact Darril Gibson at darril@gcgapremium.com.

Technical editor: Steve Johnson
Copy editor: Karen Annett
Quality control: Jaena Nerona
Book cover: Denise Kelly

ISBN-13: 978-1-939136-04-6
ISBN-10:1-939136-04-0

About the Author

Darril Gibson is an accomplished author and professional trainer. He has authored or coauthored more than 35 books and contributed as a technical editor for many more. He holds many current IT certifications, including CompTIA A+, Network+, Security+, CASP, (ISC)2 SSCP, and CISSP.

He is the CEO of YCDA, LLC, (short for You Can Do Anything) and actively writes, teaches, and consults on a wide variety of IT topics, including CompTIA A+, Network+, and Security+. Darril is active on the Internet:

- Posts blog articles at *http://blogs.getcertifiedgetahead.com*
- Tweets daily tips for CompTIA certifications at *http://twitter.com/darrilgibson*
- Posts daily practice test questions on the Get Certified Get Ahead Facebook page *https://www.facebook.com/GetCertifiedGetAhead*
- Sends out periodic updates on the Get Certified Get Ahead Newsletter *http://eepurl.com/g44Of*

Darril lives in Virginia Beach with his wife and two dogs. Whenever possible, they escape to a small cabin in the country on over 20 acres of land that continue to provide peace, tranquility, and balance. You can send him an email at *Darril@gcgapremium.com*.

Acknowledgments

A single person can't do books of this size and depth, and I'm grateful for the many people who helped me put it together. First, thanks to my wife for putting up with my long days as I worked on this project. She has provided me immeasurable support throughout this project. Thanks also to my dogs that help me remember to get up and go for walks regularly.

I want to extend my sincere appreciation to Jaena Nerona for the work she did helping me prepare material. In addition to doing a significant amount of formatting and editing, she also provided some valuable insight that helped make this resource better for you. I'm extremely grateful for all the skills and expertise of Karen Annett. She's an awesome copy editor and I'm glad she was able to help with this project.

While I certainly appreciate all the feedback everyone gave me, I want to stress that any technical errors that may have snuck into this book are entirely my fault and no reflection on anyone who helped. I always strive to identify and remove every error, but they still seem to sneak in.

Table of Contents

Introduction

Congratulations on your purchase of this book. It includes over 300 practice test questions with in-depth explanations to help you take and pass the CompTIA Network+ exam the first time you take it.

I learned that many people were using the *Microsoft Windows Networking Essentials* (MTA exam 98-366) book to study for Network+ exam. While there is a lot of crossover between the two exams, the MTA book doesn't cover all of the Network+ objectives. To help people succeed, I wrote this practice test questions book for the Network+ exam. You can use it as a supplement to the Microsoft Windows Networking Essentials guide, or as a supplement to any Network+ material you are using.

While I've received some great feedback on this book, I've also received many requests to write a full Network+ book similar to the popular *CompTIA Security+: Get Certified Get Ahead: SY0-401 Study Guide*. Due to a variety of reasons, I wasn't able to do the Network+ study guide right away, but I'm now focused on it. I'm trying something new and releasing chapters of the Network+ study guide as they're completed with the goal of helping people review some key topics based on what they need.

This book is organized into five chapters with each chapter covering one of the Network+ domains. The chapters have different numbers of questions, based on the percent of examination content and the topics covered. The five Network+ domains are:

- **Network architecture:** 22 percent of examination content

- **Network operations:** 20 percent of examination content
- **Network security:** 18 percent of examination content
- **Troubleshooting:** 24 percent of examination content
- **Industry standards, practices, and network theory:** 16 percent of examination content

CompTIA publishes a listing of the objectives on its website. At this writing, this information is accurate, but CompTIA includes the following disclaimers:

- *"The bulleted lists below each objective are not exhaustive lists. Other examples of technologies, processes or tasks pertaining to each objective may also be included on the exam although not listed or covered in this objectives document.*
- *"CompTIA is constantly reviewing the content of our exams and updating test questions to be sure our exams are current and the security of the questions is protected. When necessary, we will publish updated exams based on existing exam objectives. Please know that all related exam preparation materials will still be valid."*

You can verify that the objectives haven't changed by checking on the CompTIA site: *http://certification.comptia.org/getCertified/certifications/network.aspx.*

About the Exam

CompTIA first released the Network+ exam in 1999 and it has quickly grown in popularity. They revised the exam objectives in 2002, 2005, 2009, 2011, and in 2014. The 2014 exam is numbered as N10-006 (or JK0-023 for the academic version of the exam). CompTIA retired the N10-005 exam on August 31, 2015.

A summary of the details of the exam includes:

Number of questions: Maximum of 90

Time to complete questions: 90 minutes (does not include time to complete pre-test and post-test surveys)

Passing score: 720

Grading criteria: Scale of 100 to 900

Question types: Multiple choice and performance-based

Exam format: Traditional—can move back and forth to view previous questions

Exam prerequisites: None required but A+ is recommended along with nine months of networking experience

Exam test providers: Pearson Vue

You can get a discount code, which gives you 10% off any CompTIA exam here: *http://gcgapremium.com/discounted-comptia-vouchers/*. The page includes instructions on how to redeem the code at the CompTIA marketplace.

Question Types

Expect many of the questions on the exam to be straightforward. For example, what's 5 X 5? Either you know the answer is 25 or you don't. The exam questions test your knowledge of the material, not necessarily your ability to dissect the question so that you can figure out what the question is really trying to ask.

I'm not saying the knowledge is simplistic, only that the questions often are worded so that you can easily understand what they are asking. At least most of the time.

As a comparative example, Microsoft certification questions can be quite complex. Microsoft questions often aren't just testing your knowledge of the topic but your ability to analyze the material and logically come to the right conclusion.

Here are two examples of questions—the first shows how Microsoft may word the question on a Microsoft certification exam, and the second shows how CompTIA may word it for the CompTIA Network+ exam.

- **Microsoft:** You are driving a bus from Chicago to Atlanta at 55 mph with 22 passengers. The bus is painted blue. At the same time, a train is traveling from Miami to Atlanta at 40 mph. The train has a yellow caboose. What color are the bus driver's eyes?
- **CompTIA Network+:** What color are your eyes?

Notice the first question adds a lot of superfluous information. Two pieces are critical to answering the first question. It starts by saying, "You are driving a bus…" and then ends by asking, "What color are the bus driver's eyes?" You're required to put the two together and weed through the irrelevant information to come to the correct answer.

The second question is straightforward. "What color are your eyes?" There's very little analysis required. Either you know it or you don't. This is what you can expect from most of the CompTIA Network+ questions.

CompTIA has begun a trend of adding multiple-choice questions that are more complex and these are often in the Network+ exam. However, because you only have about a minute for each question, don't expect to see them very often. The Network+ exam is not intended to be a reading comprehension exam.

As a more realistic example, consider the following one-sentence question.

"What port does HTTPS use?"

In this case, you'd need to know that Hypertext Transfer Protocol Secure (HTTPS) uses port 443.

Compare this to the following question. It asks for the same level of knowledge, but requires a deeper level of comprehension.

"Lisa is configuring a firewall and she needs to ensure that the firewall allows outgoing secure web traffic. What port should she open on the firewall to meet this need?"

In this case, you'd need to know that a web server uses HTTPS for secure web traffic, and HTTPS uses port 443. You would need to allow outgoing traffic to the Internet on port 443.

You may also see questions that use phrases such as "BEST choice," "BEST description," "MOST likely," "FIRST," or "LAST." In these examples, don't be surprised if you see two answers that could answer the question, but only one is the best choice. For example, which one of the following numbers is between 1 and 10 and is the highest: 2, 8, 14, 23. Clearly 2 and 8 are between 1 and 10, whereas 14 and 23 are outside this range. However, only 8 is both between 1 and 10 and is the highest.

Here is a more realistic, network-related question that shows this:

Question: On which layer(s) of the OSI model do wireless protocols operate?

A. Physical

B. Physical and Data Link

C. Data Link

D. Data Link and Network

There are actually three correct answers, but only one is most correct. Wireless protocols operate on both the Physical and Data Link layers. If you chose A or C, you'd be technically correct because they do operate on the Physical layer (answer A) and on the Data Link layer (answer C). However, you would get the question wrong because B is most correct. When you see key words like best, most, or highest, be careful not to jump on the first answer. There may be a more correct answer.

Multiple Choice

Most questions are multiple-choice types where you choose one answer or multiple answers. When you need to choose multiple answers, the question will direct you to choose two, choose three, or choose all that apply.

Performance-Based Questions

You can expect as many as between three and ten non–multiple choice questions. CompTIA refers to these as performance-based questions and instead of picking from a multiple-choice answer, you're often required to perform a task. CompTIA's goal is to provide more accurate testing to verify people have a full understanding of a topic. I've written a couple of blogs on this, including this one directly related to Network+ performance-based questions:

http://blogs.getcertifiedgetahead.com/network-performance-based-questions/. I've also created a demo here: http://gcgapremium.com/performance-based-question-demo/.

Some of the different types of questions you can expect are:

- **Identify.** In this type of question, you might be asked a question but instead of having a list of multiple-choice answers, you have a group of pictures. For example, consider this question: "What tool would you use to identify an open or short in a cable?" You would need to know that a cable tester easily identifies shorts and opens and has a setting to easily identify shorts and opens, and you'd need to identify a picture of the cable tester. Further, although a multimeter can also identify opens and shorts, it isn't the best choice to identify opens and shorts in a cable.
- **Matching.** Matching type questions might require you to identify words with pictures. For example, the words might be "Fiber connectors" and "Coaxial connectors" combined with pictures of various connectors. You'd be required to identify the pictures of fiber connectors by sight and the pictures of coaxial connectors by sight. Here's a demo I created for a Security+ practice test question: http://gcgapremium.com/performance-based-question-demo/.
- **Simulation.** In a simulation, you're expected to perform an action as if you are operating in a realistic environment. For example, most wireless routers are configured via a web page. A simulation might require you to configure a wireless router with specific settings using a simulated web page.

- **Drag and drop.** In some questions, you might need to drag items from one location on the screen to another location to answer a question. For example, you might see an out-of-order list of the seven items in CompTIA's troubleshooting model. You would need to drag and drop these items in the correct order.
- **Data entry.** Some performance-based questions might ask you to analyze a scenario and then enter appropriate data. For example, when configuring a wireless access point, you might need to enter specific data into the access point. A related question might ask you to configure an access point to work with WPA2 Enterprise mode. The Configuring a Wireless Router Lab available online (http://gcgapremium.com/labs/) shows you the steps to do this. Similarly, I wrote a series of blog articles on creating rules for routers and firewalls. The second post showed an example of a performance-based question and the last post provided the solution. You can read the posts here:
    - **ACLs and Security+.** *http://blogs.getcertifiedgetahead.com/acls-and-security/*
    - **Firewall Rules and Security+.** *http://blogs.getcertifiedgetahead.com/firewall-rules-and-security/*
    - **Firewall Rules Solution.** *http://blogs.getcertifiedgetahead.com/firewall-rules-solution/*
- **Command prompt.** CompTIA has provided several examples of how a simulation can require a test taker to execute commands at the command prompt. As one possible example, you might be tasked to identify the media access control (MAC) address of a system by entering a command. You'd need to know how to enter

ipconfig /all, and be able to recognize that the MAC address is the physical address.

It's common for people to be nervous when thinking about these performance-based questions. However, the majority of people who take the test say that they really aren't that difficult. As long as you understand the concepts from the exam objectives, you won't have any problem. I do recommend you check out the blog though, and see if I've posted any updates.

A question people often ask about these questions is if they get partial credit. CompTIA has verified that you get partial credit for some questions. However, other questions may not give you partial credit. Do the best you can with each question.

Performance-Based Questions Strategy

You'll see the performance-based questions first and they take much longer than typical multiple-choice questions. If the answer is clear to you, then by all means, take the time to answer it. However, if the question isn't clear, mark the question and skip it. You can come back to it later. It's entirely possible that the question is a poorly worded beta question that doesn't even count. However, if you spend 45 minutes on it, you might run out of time before you finish the multiple-choice questions.

Performance-based questions have occasionally caused problems for the test systems. A common problem is that instead of displaying the question, the screen is mostly blank. If this happens, you can often just use the reset button for the question. This allows you to move past the problem and continue with the test. However, resetting the question erases any answer you've entered so make sure you answer it after resetting it.

Number of Questions and Duration

You have 90 minutes to complete as many as 90 questions. This gives you about one minute per question. Don't let this scare you; it's actually a good thing. With only about a minute to read and answer a question, you know the questions can't be very long or complex. Individuals who live in a non-English-speaking country and for whom English isn't their native language are given a 30-minute extension.

You might have as many as 10 performance-based questions and as few as 70 multiple-choice questions. The performance-based questions are typically first and you might spend more time on these than the multiple-choice questions. That's normal. If a question has you stumped, you can skip it and then come back to it later. If you skip a question, mark it so that you can easily find it when you've finished the other questions.

Exam Format

You start at question 1 and go to the last question. During the process, you can mark any questions you want to review when you're done. Additionally, you can view previous questions if desired. For example, if you get to question 10 and then remember something that helps you answer question 5, you can go back and redo question 5.

Passing Score

A score of 720 is required to pass. This is on a scale of 100 to 900. If the exam is paid for and you don't get a single question correct, you still get a score of 100. If you get every testable question correct, you get a score of 900. This gives a range of 800 points so you'll get an average of 8 points per question, though some questions may be weighted higher than others.

If all questions are equal and you get 100 questions, then you need to get 78 questions correct, or score 78 percent on the exam. $78 \times 8 = 624$ plus the 100 points you start with will give you a score of 724.

However, CompTIA doesn't say if all questions are scored equally or whether harder questions are weighted and worth more. A score of 78 percent is high so you shouldn't underestimate the difficulty of this exam. However, many people regularly pass it and you can pass it too. With this book, you will be well prepared.

Beta Questions

Your exam may have some beta questions. They aren't graded but instead are used to test the validity of the questions. If everyone gets a beta question correct, it's probably too easy. If everyone gets it incorrect, there's probably something wrong with the question. After enough people have tested a beta question, it's analyzed and may be added to the test bank or rewritten and retested.

The good news is that CompTIA doesn't grade the beta questions. However, you don't know which questions are beta questions and which questions are valid. You need to treat every question equally.

Exam Prerequisites

All that is required for you to take the exam is money. Other than that, there are no enforced prerequisites.

However, to successfully pass the exam, you're expected to have 9 to 12 months experience working with computers in a networking environment. Also, it's recommended you have the A+ certification or equivalent knowledge. If you have more than that, the exam materials will likely come easier to you. If you have less, the exam may be more difficult.

Exam Test Provider

You can take the exam at a Pearson Vue testing site. Some testing sites provide testing and nothing else. However, most testing sites are part of another company, such as a training company, college, or university. You can take an exam at the training company's testing site even if you haven't taken a course with them.

The Pearson Vue website includes search tools you can use to find a testing site close to you. Check them out at *http://www.pearsonvue.com*.

Voucher Code for 10 Percent Off

As of this writing, the CompTIA Network+ exam is $277 in the United States if you purchase it at full price. However, you can get a 10 percent discount using a discount code. This code changes periodically, so you'll need to go to this page to access the current code: *http://gcgapremium.com/discounted-comptia-vouchers/*.

When you purchase a voucher, you'll get a voucher number that you can use to register at a testing site. A word of caution: Some criminals sell bogus vouchers on Internet sites such as eBay. You won't know you've been ripped off until you try to use it and by that time, the criminal will probably have disappeared. In contrast, if you use the discount code, you buy the voucher directly from CompTIA.

Book Format

The book is organized in five chapters matched to the five Network+ domains. Each chapter includes two sections.

Practice Test Mode Section

This section includes the questions, but it doesn't have the correct answers and explanations readily available. This allows you to go through all of the questions in the section without seeing the answers as you go through them. You can use this format to prevent you from seeing and just memorizing the correct answers.

Use this section to test your readiness. Ideally, you should be able to look at the answers and know why the correct answer is correct, and why the incorrect answers are incorrect. Don't worry if you're not sure, though. The next section includes all of the same questions along with the correct answer and an explanation.

Review Mode Section

The Review Mode section shows a practice test question with the answer and explanation readily available. You can use this to check your answers from the Practice Test Mode section, or as a method of studying, if that's what you prefer.

Resources

The Get Certified Get Ahead blog page has a wealth of articles on different certifications. You can view the blogs that include Network+ related topics here *http://blogs.getcertifiedgetahead.com/network-blog-links/*. I regularly tweet certification tips on Twitter, so feel free to check them out here: *https://twitter.com/DarrilGibson*. If you want to get certification tips and news delivered to your inbox, you can subscribe to the Get Certified Get Ahead Newsletter. I also have an active Facebook page where I regularly post free practice test questions: *https://www.facebook.com/GetCertifiedGetAhead.*

Also, people have asked me for online resources such as practice test questions and flashcards. I've created some test banks that include performance-based questions that are available for purchase here: *http://gcgapremium.com/network/network-value-package/.*

Bonus - Online Resources

Things change and a paperback book isn't easy to update. To accommodate these changes, I have created some online resources. You can access them here. http://gcgapremium.com/network-bonus/.

Many resources, such as online labs and blog posts, are free. Additionally, because you purchased this book, you can also purchase some of the premium resources for half price.

»Get Certified »Get Ahead

Chapter 1 Network Architecture

Network Architecture topics are 22 percent of the CompTIA Network+ exam. The objectives in this domain are:

1.1 Explain the functions and applications of various network devices.

- Router
- Switch
- Multilayer switch
- Firewall
- HIDS
- IDS/IPS
- Access point (wireless/wired)
- Content filter
- Load balancer
- Hub
- Analog modem
- Packet shaper
- VPN concentrator

1.2 Compare and contrast the use of networking services and applications.

- VPN:
    - Site to site/host to site/host to host
    - Protocols
        - IPsec
        - GRE
        - SSL VPN
        - PTP/PPTP
- TACACS/RADIUS
- RAS
- Web services
- Unified voice services
- Network controllers

1.3 Install and configure the following networking services/applications.

- DHCP
    - Static vs dynamic IP addressing
    - Reservations
    - Scopes
    - Leases
    - Options (DNS servers, suffixes)
    - IP helper/DHCP relay

- DNS
    - DNS servers
    - DNS records (A, MX, AAAA,CNAME, PTR)
    - Dynamic DNS
- Proxy/reverse proxy
- NAT
    - PAT
    - SNAT
    - DNAT
- Port forwarding

1.4 Explain the characteristics and benefits of various WAN technologies.

- Fiber
    - SONET
    - DWDM
    - CWDM
- Frame relay
- Satellite
- Broadband cable
- DSL/ADSL
- ISDN
- ATM
- PPP/Multilink PPP
- MPLS
- GSM/CDMA
    - LTE/4G
    - HSPA+
    - 3G
    - Edge
- Dialup
- WiMAX
- Metro-Ethernet
- Leased lines
    - T-1
    - T-3
    - E-1
    - E-3
    - OC3
    - OC12
- Circuit switch vs packet switch

1.5 Install and properly terminate various cable types and connectors using appropriate tools.

- Copper connectors
    - RJ-11
    - RJ-45

  - RJ-48C
  - DB-9/RS-232
  - DB-25
  - UTP coupler
  - BNC coupler
  - BNC
  - F-connector
  - 110 block
  - 66 block
- Copper cables
  - Shielded vs unshielded
  - CAT3, CAT5, CAT5e, CAT6, CAT6a
  - PVC vs plenum
  - RG-59
  - RG-6
  - Straight-through vs crossover vs rollover
- Fiber connectors
  - ST
  - SC
  - LC
  - MTRJ
  - FC
  - Fiber coupler
- Fiber cables
  - Single mode
  - Multimode
  - APC vs UPC
- Media converters
  - Single mode fiber to Ethernet
  - Multimode fiber to Ethernet
  - Fiber to coaxial
  - Single mode to multimode fiber
- Tools
  - Cable crimpers
  - Punch down tool
  - Wire strippers
  - Snips
  - OTDR
  - Cable certifier

1.6 Differentiate between common network topologies.

- Mesh
  - Partial
  - Full
- Bus
- Ring
- Star

- Hybrid
- Point-to-point
- Point-to-multipoint
- Client-server
- Peer-to-peer

1.7 Differentiate between network infrastructure implementations.

- WAN
- MAN
- LAN
- WLAN
    - Hotspot
- PAN
    - Bluetooth
    - IR
    - NFC
- SCADA/ICS
    - ICS server
    - DCS/closed network
    - Remote terminal unit
    - Programmable logic controller
- Medianets
    - VTC
        - ISDN
        - IP/SIP

1.8 Given a scenario, implement and configure the appropriate addressing schema:

- IPv6
    - Auto-configuration
        - EUI 64
    - DHCP6
    - Link local
    - Address structure
    - Address compression
    - Tunneling 6to4, 4to6
        - Teredo, miredo
- IPv4
    - Address structure
    - Subnetting
    - APIPA
    - Classful A, B, C, D
    - Classless
- Private vs public
- NAT/PAT
- MAC addressing
- Multicast

- Unicast
- Broadcast
- Broadcast domains vs collision domains

1.9 Explain the basics of routing concepts and protocols.

- Loopback interface
- Routing loops
- Routing tables
- Static vs dynamic routes
- Default route
- Distance vector routing protocols
    - RIP v2
- Hybrid routing protocols
    - BGP
- Link state routing protocols
    - OSPF
    - IS-IS
- Interior vs exterior gateway routing protocols
- Autonomous system numbers
- Route redistribution
- High availability
    - VRRP
    - Virtual IP
    - HSRP
- Route aggregation
- Routing metrics
    - Hop counts
    - MTU, bandwidth
    - Costs
    - Latency
    - Administrative distance
    - SPB

1.10 Identify the basics elements of unified communication technologies.

- VOiP
- Video
- Real time services
    - Presence
    - Multicast vs unicast
- QoS
    - DSCP
    - COS
- Devices
    - UC servers
    - UC devices
    - UC gateways

1.11 Compare and contrast technologies that support cloud and virtualization.

- Virtualization
  - Virtual switches
  - Virtual routers
  - Virtual firewall
  - Virtual vs physical NICs
  - Software defined networking
- Storage area network
  - iSCSI
  - Jumbo frame
  - Fibre Channel
  - Network attached storage
- Cloud concepts
  - Public IaaS, SaaS, PaaS
  - Private IaaS, SaaS, PaaS
  - Hybrid IaaS, SaaS, PaaS
  - Community IaaS, SaaS, PaaS

1.12 Given a set of requirements, implement a basic network

- List of requirements
- Device types/requirements
- Environment limitations
- Equipment limitations
- Compatibility requirements
- Wired/wireless considerations
- Security considerations

**

Practice Test Mode Section — Practice Test Questions without Answers for Network Architecture

1. What type of connector is commonly used with an analog modem?

   A. RJ-11

   B. RJ-45

   C. ST

   D. F-connector

2. Users in the network are frequently downloading videos, which has been slowing down overall network performance. Management wants to reduce the effect of streaming video on the performance of the network, but not block video streaming completely. Which of the following would administrators implement to define how much bandwidth video streaming traffic can consume?

   A. Traffic shaping

   B. Proxy server

   C. Content filter

   D. Load balancer

3. Your organization has two remote offices and a main headquarters location. Each location has access to the Internet. What can you use to connect the locations together?

   A. VPN concentrators

   B. Client-to-site VPNs

   C. Load balancers

   D. Content filters

4. Which of the following devices uses an ACL to prevent unauthorized access into a network?
    A. Firewall
    B. Proxy server
    C. Load balancer
    D. VPN concentrator

5. A website is hosted on four different web servers. What would you use to ensure each web server had an equal amount of traffic?
    A. Load balancer
    B. Proxy server
    C. TDR
    D. Throughput tester

6. You need to add the capability to filter Internet traffic through a firewall based on keywords defined by a company. What would you use?
    A. An implicit deny firewall
    B. A content filter
    C. An ACL
    D. A stateful inspection firewall

7. A company wants to prevent users from visiting gambling sites. What can they use?
    A. VPN concentrator
    B. Protocol analyzer
    C. Content filter
    D. IDS

8. A user attempts to access a social networking site from a work computer. Instead, a web page appears displaying the company policy about visiting prohibited sites and indicates that the user's activity has been logged. What is the company using?
   A. A VPN concentrator
   B. A proxy concentrator
   C. A content filter
   D. A load balancer

9. What can be used to serve cached copies of website pages and reduce overall Internet bandwidth usage?
   A. DHCP
   B. Load balancer
   C. Proxy server
   D. Content filter

10. Internet access for users within a company is very slow during peak usage times. Employees commonly visit the same websites. What can improve the performance of Internet access?
   A. DNS
   B. DHCP
   C. VPN concentrator
   D. Caching engine

11. Of the following choices, what does a load balancer provide?
   A. Content filtering and web page caching
   B. Internet usage reports and web page caching
   C. Distribution of network requests and increased availability
   D. Remote access to an internal network by traveling employees

12. Which of the following is commonly used with Cisco network devices and includes authentication services?

    A. MS-CHAPv2

    B. RADIUS

    C. TACACS+

    D. ICA

13. Users in your organizations frequently work from home, but connect to the organization's network. Which of the following would the organization use to authenticate these remote workers?

    A. RADIUS/802.1x

    B. VPN

    C. VTP

    D. IPsec

14. Which of the following can be used for router management and provides AAA services?

    A. SNMP

    B. TACACS+

    C. RADIUS

    D. Kerberos

15. Which of the following provides AAA services and encrypts the logon process?

    A. Smart card with a PIN

    B. IPsec

    C. TACACS+

    D. VPN

16. You need to ensure a network-based printer receives the same IP address from a DHCP server. What would you create on the DHCP server?

    A. A lease

    B. A scope

    C. A reservation

    D. A CNAME record

17. A website is currently known as GetCertifiedGetAhead.com. You want it to also be reached using the name gcgapremium.com. What type of record should you create?

    A. A

    B. MX

    C. CNAME

    D. PTR

18. A company wants to ensure that other mail servers on the Internet can locate its company-based email server. What type of record should you create?

    A. AAAA

    B. MX

    C. CNAME

    D. PTR

19. An intranet web server within an internal network is rebooted daily and is automatically assigned an IP address. This IP address is often different from the previously assigned IP address. You want users to be able to reach the server using its FQDN. Of the following choices, what will meet your requirements?
    A. Use DDNS.
    B. Assign the IP address with DHCP.
    C. Manually assign the FQDN.
    D. Disable the firewall on the server.

20. You are configuring a DHCP scope on a DHCP server. DHCP clients must be able to access Internet resources. In addition to an IP address range, what else must you configure? (Choose TWO.)
    A. Reservations
    B. DNS address
    C. MX records
    D. Default gateway

21. You are configuring a SOHO network and need to ensure that four internal computers can share a single public IP address for Internet access. What feature should be enabled on the router connected to the Internet?
    A. DHCP
    B. PAT
    C. DNS
    D. QoS

22. Which of the following technologies combines multiple signals using different wavelengths, and can increase the bandwidth of an existing fiber network?

    A. Satellite

    B. DWDM

    C. SONET

    D. MPLS

23. What type of connector would you use with a T-3 leased line?

    A. RJ-11

    B. DB-9

    C. RS-232

    D. BNC

24. Which of the following protocols uses labels instead of addresses to direct traffic?

    A. Token Ring

    B. DWDM

    C. LTE

    D. MPLS

25. What type of media is used with SONET?

    A. Twisted-pair

    B. Coaxial

    C. Satellite

    D. Fiber

26. Of the following choices, what provides the highest bandwidth for a WAN?
    A. SONET
    B. POTS
    C. T-1
    D. E-1

27. Which of the following is a valid WAN technology that does not require a physical medium?
    A. WiMAX
    B. SONET
    C. SDH
    D. T-3

28. You need to purchase cabling for a LAN in a building your organization recently purchased and you're trying to determine if you should purchase plenum-rated cables. Which of the following should you evaluate to determine what cabling to purchase?
    A. Location of servers
    B. Location of access points
    C. Location of airflow from HVAC
    D. Location of lighting

29. How many pins are on an RS-232 connector?
    A. 4
    B. 6
    C. 8
    D. 9

30. What would you use to attach a cable to a wiring block?

    A. Crimper

    B. Certifier

    C. Punch down tool

    D. Butt set

31. What type of connection is RS-232 used for?

    A. Fiber

    B. Coaxial

    C. Serial

    D. Twisted-pair

32. What type of connector would an RS-232 cable use?

    A. F

    B. RJ-45

    C. DB-9

    D. RJ-11

33. You are using CAT5e cables in your network and recently added a 1-Gbps switch. However, several of the computers are not running at 1 Gbps. Of the following choices, what is the BEST choice to resolve the problem?

    A. Replace the cables with CAT6.

    B. Verify the cables with a cable certifier.

    C. Replace the NICs on the computers.

    D. Check the cables with a toner probe.

34. You just helped about 50 users move into a new building using existing equipment from the original location. Users begin complaining that the network is slow. What can you use to check the wiring in the new building?

    A. Cable tester

    B. Ping

    C. Tracert

    D. Cable certifier

35. You need to create two small patch cables to connect Ethernet switches in a network. What would you use to create the cables?

    A. RJ-11 connectors

    B. Crimper

    C. TDR

    D. OTDR

36. What would you use to connect a twisted-pair cable to a network jack?

    A. Snips

    B. Punch down tool

    C. Crimper

    D. Butt set

37. What type of cable would use an F-connector?

    A. Fiber

    B. Twisted-pair

    C. RG-6

    D. RS-232

38. Computers within a network are only able to transfer data when they have access to a logical token. What type of topology does this describe?

    A. Star

    B. Ring

    C. Bus

    D. MPLS

39. You manage a network that has multiple computers connected via a single Ethernet switch. What topology does this network use?

    A. Ring

    B. Mesh

    C. Bus

    D. Star

40. A network is configured with a topology that forces devices to wait before communicating on the network. What type of network topology is this?

    A. Ring

    B. Mesh

    C. Bus

    D. Star

41. Which of the following network topologies has a central device that is a potential single point of failure?

    A. FDDI

    B. Mesh

    C. Bus

    D. Star

42. Computers within a network are connected in a logical circle. What type of topology is being used?
    A. Ring
    B. Mesh
    C. Star
    D. Bus

43. You are able to transfer files between Bluetooth devices. What type of network are you using?
    A. LAN
    B. PAN
    C. VPN
    D. WAN

44. A company in Silicon Valley owns three buildings within walking distance of each other, and each of these buildings are connected via a single network. What is the BEST name for this network?
    A. CAN
    B. LAN
    C. MAN
    D. PAN

45. What is the BEST label for the IP address of ::1?
    A. EUI-64 address
    B. Link-local address
    C. APIPA address
    D. Loopback address

46. Which of the following is a valid IPv4 loopback address?

    A. ::1

    B. 127.0.0.1

    C. 1a-2b-3c-4d-5e-6f

    D. 169.254.75.91

47. Which of the following IPv6-related standards takes place on Layer 2 of the OSI model?

    A. MAC

    B. IP address

    C. EUI-64

    D. Zero compression

48. You are designing a network segment that only needs 2 IP addresses assigned. You need to conserve the IP address space. What CIDR notation is the BEST choice for this network?

    A. /26

    B. /28

    C. /30

    D. /32

49. You are designing a network segment that only needs 58 IP addresses assigned. You need to conserve the IP address space. What CIDR notation is the BEST choice for this network?

    A. /26

    B. /28

    C. /30

    D. /32

50. You are designing a network segment that only needs 24 IP addresses assigned. You need to conserve the IP address space. What CIDR notation is the BEST choice for this network?

    A. /25

    B. /26

    C. /27

    D. /28

51. You are designing a network segment that only needs 32 IP addresses assigned. You need to conserve the IP address space. What CIDR notation is the BEST choice for this network?

    A. /25

    B. /26

    C. /27

    D. /28

52. You are designing a network segment that only needs 12 IP addresses assigned. You need to conserve the IP address space. What CIDR notation is the BEST choice for this network?

    A. /26

    B. /27

    C. /28

    D. /29

53. Using ipconfig, you see a computer has an IP address of 169.254.4.23 with a subnet mask of 255.255.0.0. What type of address is this?

    A. IPv6

    B. APIPA

C. DHCP assigned

D. DNS assigned

54. You are troubleshooting a computer system and you determine it has been assigned an IP address of 169.254.45.83. What does this indicate?

A. DNS could not be reached.

B. DHCP could not be reached.

C. The default gateway could not be reached.

D. The computer's firewall is enabled.

55. Which of the following provides fault tolerance for DHCP?

A. Dynamic IP address assignments

B. Exclusions

C. APIPA

D. DNS

56. What can you use to dynamically assign the same IP address to a printer configured as a network device?

A. DNS

B. DHCP reservation

C. SNMP

D. DHCP exclusion

57. Of the following choices, what is an address that would be assigned if a DHCP client cannot reach a DHCP server?

A. 10.8.34.2

B. 169.254.45.98

C. 172.16.4.34

D. 192.168.1.45

58. Which of the following is a valid IPv4 address?

A. 192.168.1.200

B. 192:168:1:200

C. ::1

D. 1a-2b-3c-4d-5e-6f

59. What class of IP address is 224.100.200.3?

A. Class A

B. Class B

C. Class C

D. Class D

60. Which of the following is a Class B address?

A. 10.71.12.73

B. 172.16.34.67

C. 192.168.100.5

D. 224.54.23.12

61. Which of the following is an example of an IPv4 address using CIDR notation?

A. 127.0.0.1

B. 192.168.1.1

C. 192.168.5.1/30

D. 169.254.17.4/36

62. All routers in your network have learned the same routing information. What is the BEST name for this state?

A. Split-horizon

B. Convergence

C. High availability

D. Balanced load

63. Management wants to ensure that critical systems continue to operate in the event of a disaster. Which of the following is management trying to ensure?

A. Convergence

B. HSRP

C. VRRP

D. High availability

64. A network administrator has been creating a baseline of network performance. During this process, he realizes that one router is operating significantly slower than the other routers on the network, but it is handling about the same amount of traffic as other routers. What is the MOST likely cause for this issue?

A. Processor issues

B. Hop counts

C. Split-horizon problem

D. Expired hop count

65. Which of the following BEST describes the next hop within networking?

A. The routing table

B. The address of the next hub in a path

C. The address of the next router in a path

D. The broadcast domain

66. Which of the following choices can a router use to share information with neighboring routers?

    A. RDP

    B. RIPv2

    C. IMAP

    D. TFTP

67. An organization maintains a private cloud, which connects data from three different data centers. Each data center is located at a separate geographical location to maintain high availability even if a disaster eliminates network connectivity for any one of the data centers. Which of the following provides the BEST solution to meet this need?

    A. APIPA

    B. Hop counts

    C. BGP

    D. Codec

68. Which of the following is a routing protocol that uses the first open shortest path it can identify?

    A. RIPv2

    B. APIPA

    C. OSPF

    D. CIDR

69. A database server takes approximately 2 seconds to respond to database queries when going through a legacy router. What is another name for this?

A. Uptime

B. Redundancy

C. Interference

D. Latency

70. Which of the following are the most sensitive to latency?

A. Video teleconferencing

B. SSL VPN

C. HTTPS

D. Traffic shaping

71. What is the MOST likely result of misconfiguring the AS number on a network device?

A. BGP routing issues

B. Internal DNS issues

C. DHCP issues

D. OSPF issues

72. An organization is setting up video conferencing equipment to support better communication between separate offices. It will use VoIP. Which of the following will the organization MOST likely include with this deployment?

A. VRRP

B. BGP

C. SIP

D. HSRP

73. An organization is setting up video conferencing equipment to support better communication between offices in different cities. It will use VoIP. Which of the following will the organization MOST likely include with this deployment?

    A. CAN

    B. Codec

    C. VLAN

    D. MIMO

74. IT management is implementing several different QoS features. What benefit will this provide?

    A. Limit the amount of video streaming on a network

    B. Block malicious traffic from reaching a network

    C. Provide redundancy

    D. Ensure predictable network performance

75. What is a virtual switch?

    A. A switch used for a virtual LAN

    B. A switch used for VPNs

    C. A logical switch that functions like a physical switch

    D. A planned change

76. run multiple operating systems on a server within your network. What would you use?

    A. VLAN

    B. Virtual switch

    C. Virtual machines

    D. NaaS

77. The Costington Department store hosts an application via the cloud. Authorized employees can access the application to submit sales and marketing data. What type of model does this describe?
    A. Community PaaS
    B. Public SaaS
    C. Hybrid IaaS
    D. Private SaaS

78. The Springfield Nuclear Power Plant is a private company and it is sharing resources with the Springfield public school system via the cloud. No other organization can access these resources. What type of cloud deployment model is this?
    A. Community
    B. Hybrid
    C. Public
    D. Private

79. The Springfield Nuclear Power Plant has created an online application teaching nuclear physics. Students in the Springfield Elementary School access this application via the cloud, and teachers can monitor the students' progress. What type of cloud service model is this?
    A. IaaS
    B. PaaS
    C. SaaS
    D. Public

80. The database stored on a SQL server has grown to several terabytes in size. Backups to tape take too long and the organization wants to reduce the time it takes to do a backup of the database. Which of the following would meet this need at the LOWEST cost?

    A. iSCSI SAN

    B. FCoE SAN

    C. PaaS

    D. NAS

81. You are planning a SOHO network for a business owner. Which of the following is a logical first step?

    A. Purchase the equipment.

    B. Create the website.

    C. List the requirements.

    D. Run the cable.

82. You are planning a SOHO network for a business owner and need to identify the best location for a server. Which of the following should you consider first?

    A. Equipment limitations

    B. List of requirements

    C. Environment limitations

    D. Compatibility requirements

Review Mode Section — Practice Test Questions with Answers for Network Architecture

Objective: 1.1 Explain the functions and applications of various network devices.

1. What type of connector is commonly used with an analog modem?
   A. RJ-11
   B. RJ-45
   C. ST
   D. F-connector

Answer: **A** is correct. An analog modem uses Registered Jack-11 (RJ-11) connectors and RJ-11 connectors are also used with phone lines.

B is incorrect. RJ-45 connectors are used with network twisted-pair cables.
C is incorrect. A straight tip (ST) connector is used with fiber connections, but fiber is not used with analog modems.
D is incorrect. An F-connector is used with Radio Guide 6 (RG-6) coaxial cable, but RG-6 is not commonly used with Voice over IP (VoIP).

2. Users in the network are frequently downloading videos, which has been slowing down overall network performance. Management wants to reduce the effect of streaming video on the performance of the network, but not block video streaming completely. Which of the following would administrators implement to define how much bandwidth video streaming traffic can consume?

A. Traffic shaping

B. Proxy server

C. Content filter

D. Load balancer

Answer: **A** is correct. Traffic shaping can limit traffic on a network based on specific protocols or types of traffic, such as limiting the amount of audio or video streaming. It can also limit the traffic for specific users, or based on other needs for an organization. It is often used as part of a quality of service (QoS) solution.

B is incorrect. A proxy server can block access to sites that stream audio and video using content-filtering techniques. However, it can only allow or block the traffic, not allow a certain amount of bandwidth as traffic shaping does.

C is incorrect. A content filter can allow or block traffic based on the content, but it doesn't include the ability to shape the traffic by allowing a limited amount of bandwidth for any type of traffic.

D is incorrect. A load balancer can balance the load for multiple devices, but it cannot shape the traffic.

3. Your organization has two remote offices and a main headquarters location. Each location has access to the Internet. What can you use to connect the locations together?

   A. VPN concentrators

   B. Client-to-site VPNs

   C. Load balancers

   D. Content filters

Answer: **A** is correct. Virtual private network (VPN) concentrators can be used to create site-to-site VPNs between the locations.

B is incorrect. A client-to-site VPN is used if individual clients (such as traveling employees) need remote access. However, the scenario wants to connect the locations together, so it would be a site-to-site VPN, not a client-site VPN.

C is incorrect. A load balancer will balance the load among several systems, such as between several web servers hosting a single website.

D is incorrect. Content filters can filter traffic based on content, such as filtering access to specific website addresses or filtering traffic based on specific keywords.

4. Which of the following devices uses an ACL to prevent unauthorized access into a network?
    A. Firewall
    B. Proxy server
    C. Load balancer
    D. VPN concentrator

Answer: **A** is correct. A firewall uses rules within an access control list (ACL) to prevent unauthorized access into a network.

B is incorrect. A proxy server reduces bandwidth by storing copies of website pages in cache and then serving these cached pages to other users. It does not use an ACL.

C is incorrect. A load balancer can balance traffic among multiple servers. It does not use an ACL.

D is incorrect. A virtual private network (VPN) concentrator supports multiple VPN connections, but it doesn't use an ACL.

5. A website is hosted on four different web servers. What would you use to ensure each web server had an equal amount of traffic?

   A. Load balancer

   B. Proxy server

   C. TDR

   D. Throughput tester

Answer: **A** is correct**.** A load balancer can balance the amount of traffic (the load) among multiple servers. A load balancer can be a hardware appliance, or software installed on each of the systems.

B is incorrect. A proxy server provides Internet access to internal clients and includes website caching to improve performance.

C is incorrect. A time domain reflectometer (TDR) is used to identify the location of a break in a cable.

D is incorrect. A throughput tester measures how much data can be transferred between two systems to identify the bandwidth.

6. You need to add the capability to filter Internet traffic through a firewall based on keywords defined by a company. What would you use?

   A. An implicit deny firewall

   B. A content filter

   C. An ACL

   D. A stateful inspection firewall

Answer: **B** is correct. A content filter can filter traffic based on keywords or website addresses. Some firewalls include the ability to filter traffic with a built-in content filter.

A is incorrect. Firewalls use an implicit deny philosophy where they block all traffic except for traffic that has been explicitly allowed. An implicit deny philosophy does not provide content filtering.
C is incorrect. An access control list (ACL) on a firewall identifies traffic that is allowed or blocked based on IP addresses, ports, and protocols, but cannot be used to block traffic based on keywords.
D is incorrect. A stateful inspection firewall can block or allow traffic based on the state of a connection, but not based on keywords. For example, if a packet has been allowed into a network, a stateful inspection firewall will allow the returned traffic out of the firewall.

7. A company wants to prevent users from visiting gambling sites. What can they use?
   A. VPN concentrator
   B. Protocol analyzer
   C. Content filter
   D. IDS

Answer: **C** is correct. A content filter can be used to prevent users from visiting any websites that the company considers inappropriate, such as gambling sites, social networking sites, or any other sites based on a company policy. It will block the requests using the website addresses and will often show the users a page indicating that access to the site is prohibited and their attempt to access the site has been logged.

A is incorrect. A virtual private network (VPN) concentrator provides remote access to an internal network.
B is incorrect. A protocol analyzer (also called a sniffer) can capture packets traveling over the network for analysis.

D is incorrect. An intrusion detection system (IDS) is used to detect potential intrusions by attackers and raise alerts when they are detected.

8. A user attempts to access a social networking site from a work computer. Instead, a web page appears displaying the company policy about visiting prohibited sites and indicates that the user's activity has been logged. What is the company using?

   A. A VPN concentrator

   B. A proxy concentrator

   C. A content filter

   D. A load balancer

Answer: **C** is correct. A content filter can detect when users attempt to visit blocked websites. Instead of showing the user the blocked web page, it can redirect the users to another page showing the company policy. Some organizations include a statement indicating that user activity is monitored and logged, and display the user's name and computer on this redirected page. Security administrators sometimes use this log to identify when employees are deliberately trying to circumvent a company policy.

A is incorrect. A virtual private network (VPN) concentrator provides remote access to a company's internal network from remote locations.
B is incorrect. There is no such thing as a proxy concentrator. However, a proxy server will often have similar capabilities as a content filter and can block access to prohibited sites, redirect the user to a company web page, and log the activity.
D is incorrect. A load balancer will distribute traffic among several network devices in an attempt to balance the load between the devices.

9. What can be used to serve cached copies of website pages and reduce overall Internet bandwidth usage?
    A. DHCP
    B. Load balancer
    C. Proxy server
    D. Content filter

Answer: **C** is correct. A proxy server can store copies of website pages visited by one user in cache and then serve these cached pages to other users. Bandwidth usage is reduced because the same page does not need to be retrieved again.

A is incorrect. Dynamic Host Configuration Protocol (DHCP) is used to dynamically provide DHCP clients with an IP address and other TCP/IP configuration options.
B is incorrect. A load balancer balances the load among multiple network devices.
D is incorrect. A content filter filters requests based on keywords or website addresses, but it does not cache requests.

10. Internet access for users within a company is very slow during peak usage times. Employees commonly visit the same websites. What can improve the performance of Internet access?
    A. DNS
    B. DHCP
    C. VPN concentrator
    D. Caching engine

Answer: **D** is correct. A caching engine included with a proxy server will store web pages in cache when they are first visited and serve the cached page to clients when the page is requested again.

A is incorrect. Domain Name System (DNS) is used to resolve host names to IP addresses. DNS is a requirement for Internet access (unless users can memorize the IP addresses of all the sites they visit, which isn't realistic). DNS does not improve the performance of Internet access.
B is incorrect. Dynamic Host Configuration Protocol (DHCP) dynamically provides DHCP clients with an IP address and other TCP/IP configuration options. It will not improve the performance of Internet access.
C is incorrect. A virtual private network (VPN) concentrator provides remote access to an internal network by external clients and is not used by internal clients accessing the Internet.

11. Of the following choices, what does a load balancer provide?

A. Content filtering and web page caching

B. Internet usage reports and web page caching

C. Distribution of network requests and increased availability

D. Remote access to an internal network by traveling employees

Answer: **C** is correct. A load balancer will balance the load among several network devices (such as several web servers). It can also sense when any of the devices fail and stop sending traffic to the failed device, which increases availability.

A is incorrect. A content filter can filter traffic based on content such as specific website addresses or keywords. A proxy server can also filter traffic based on website addresses and will cache website pages to improve performance.

B is incorrect. A proxy server can track user statistics, such as website visits, and cache web pages.

D is incorrect. A virtual private network (VPN) concentrator can be used to provide remote access to an internal network.

Objective 1.2 questions. Compare and contrast the use of networking services and applications.

12. Which of the following is commonly used with Cisco network devices and includes authentication services?
    A. MS-CHAPv2
    B. RADIUS
    C. TACACS+
    D. ICA

Answer: C is correct. Terminal Access Controller Access-Control System Plus (TACACS+) was developed by Cisco and is commonly used with Cisco network devices. It provides authorization, authentication, and accounting (AAA) services and is also used with remote access solutions.

A is incorrect. Microsoft Challenge Handshake Authentication Protocol version 2 (MS-CHAPv2) is used for authentication, but it is more common with Microsoft systems than Cisco devices.

B is incorrect. Remote Authentication Dial-In User Service (RADIUS) is an AAA protocol, but it is used for remote access, not specifically with Cisco network devices.

D is incorrect. Independent Computer Architecture (ICA) was designed by Citrix systems and is use for remote desktop solutions for operating systems, not network devices.

13. Users in your organizations frequently work from home, but connect to the organization's network. Which of the following would the organization use to authenticate these remote workers?
    A. RADIUS/802.1x
    B. VPN
    C. VTP
    D. IPsec

Answer: **A** is correct. Remote Authentication Dial-In User Service (RADIUS) and/or 802.1x is the only option that provides authentication.

B is incorrect. Although the scenario describes a VPN, the virtual private network (VPN) doesn't provide authentication.
C is incorrect. The VLAN Trunk Protocol (VTP) is a Cisco protocol that transmits VLAN information to all switches on the network.
D is incorrect. Internet Protocol security (IPsec) is often used as a tunneling protocol for a VPN, but it cannot authenticate users.

14. Which of the following can be used for router management and provides AAA services?
    A. SNMP
    B. TACACS+
    C. RADIUS
    D. Kerberos

Answer: **B** is correct. Terminal Access Controller Access-Control System Plus (TACACS+) is an access control protocol that can be used for the management of network devices (including routers) and it provides authorization, authentication, and accounting (AAA) services.

A is incorrect. The Simple Network Management Protocol (SNMP) is used for managing devices such as routers, but it is not an AAA protocol.
C is incorrect. Remote Authentication Dial-In User Service (RADIUS) is an AAA protocol, but only for remote access, not for router management.
D is incorrect. Kerberos is a single sign-on authentication protocol using tickets and is not used for router management.

15. Which of the following provides AAA services and encrypts the logon process?

    A. Smart card with a PIN

    B. IPsec

    C. TACACS+

    D. VPN

Answer: **C** is correct. Terminal Access Controller Access-Control System Plus (TACACS+) provides authentication, authorization, and accounting (AAA) services and encrypts the entire challenge/response logon process.

A is incorrect. A smart card with a PIN provides multifactor authentication, but it does not provide authorization or accounting services.
B is incorrect. Internet Protocol security (IPsec) does not provide AAA services.
D is incorrect. A virtual private network (VPN) provides private access to a network over a public network and typically uses an AAA protocol, but the VPN doesn't provide the AAA services.

16. You need to ensure a network-based printer receives the same IP address from a DHCP server. What would you create on the DHCP server?
    A. A lease
    B. A scope
    C. A reservation
    D. A CNAME record

Answer: **C** is correct. A Dynamic Host Configuration Protocol (DHCP) reservation ensures systems receive the same Internet Protocol (IP) address. It matches the system's media access control (MAC) address with a reserved IP address.

A is incorrect. A DHCP lease refers to how long a device can keep the assigned IP address.
B is incorrect. A scope is a range of IP addresses assigned by the DHCP server.
D is incorrect. A CNAME (Canonical Name) record is created on a DNS server (not a DHCP server) and it creates an alias for an A record.

Objective 1.3 questions. Install and configure the following networking services/applications.

17. A website is currently known as GetCertifiedGetAhead.com. You want it to also be reached using the name gcgapremium.com. What type of record should you create?
    A. A
    B. MX
    C. CNAME
    D. PTR

Answer: **C** is correct. A CNAME (Canonical Name) record is used to give a host an alias so that it can be resolved with more than one fully qualified domain name (FQDN).

A is incorrect. An A (IPv4 host) record provides host name to IP address mapping. It is used for forward lookups where a query to Domain Name System (DNS) includes the name of a host and the DNS server responds with the Internet Protocol version 4 (IPv4) address of the host.
B is incorrect. An MX (Mail Exchanger) record is used to locate a mail server.
D is incorrect. A PTR (Pointer) record is used for reverse lookups where a query to DNS includes the Internet Protocol (IP) address of a host, and the DNS server responds with the name of the host.

18. A company wants to ensure that other mail servers on the Internet can locate its company-based email server. What type of record should you create?
    A. AAAA
    B. MX
    C. CNAME
    D. PTR

Answer: **B** is correct. An MX (Mail Exchanger) record is used to locate a mail server and would be configured on a Domain Name System (DNS) server.

A is incorrect. An AAAA (IPv6 host) record provides the name to Internet Protocol version 6 (IPv6) address mapping and is used for forward lookups. If you query DNS with the name of the host, DNS responds with the address of the host.

C is incorrect. A CNAME (Canonical Name) record is used to give a host an alias so that it can be resolved with more than one fully qualified domain name (FQDN).
D is incorrect. A PTR (Pointer) record is used for reverse lookups where a query to DNS includes the IP address of a host, and the DNS server responds with the name of the host.

19. An intranet web server within an internal network is rebooted daily and is automatically assigned an IP address. This IP address is often different from the previously assigned IP address. You want users to be able to reach the server using its FQDN. Of the following choices, what will meet your requirements?
    A. Use DDNS.
    B. Assign the IP address with DHCP.
    C. Manually assign the FQDN.
    D. Disable the firewall on the server.

Answer: **A** is correct. Dynamic Domain Name System (DDNS) allows a Dynamic Host Configuration Protocol (DHCP) client to automatically register its name and IP address with a DNS server after being assigned an IP address from a DHCP server. When a host is registered with DNS, other systems can resolve the fully qualified domain name (FQDN) of the host to the IP address by querying DNS. Although not included in the choices, two other solutions are (1) manually assign the IP address instead of using DHCP, and (2) create a DHCP reservation to always give the server the same IP address.

B is incorrect. Because it is being automatically assigned an IP address each time it is rebooted, it is already a DHCP client. However, just making

it a DHCP client doesn't allow clients to resolve the FQDN unless the record is dynamically being updated through DNS.
C is incorrect. The FQDN is the name of the server and it would always be manually assigned.
D is incorrect. Whether the firewall is enabled or disabled will not have an impact on resolving the FQDN of the server using DNS.

20. You are configuring a DHCP scope on a DHCP server. DHCP clients must be able to access Internet resources. In addition to an IP address range, what else must you configure? (Choose TWO.)
    A. Reservations
    B. DNS address
    C. MX records
    D. Default gateway

Answer: **B** and **D** are correct. In addition to setting up dynamic IP addresses and a subnet mask, you also need to add two options: the default gateway and the address of at least one Domain Name System (DNS) server. The default gateway is the address of a router that provides a path out of the network. The DNS server resolves host names to IP addresses and is required when accessing Internet resources.

A is incorrect. Reservations are needed if you want any specific system to get the same IP address, but this isn't required in this scenario.
C is incorrect. An MX (Mail Exchanger) record is on a DNS server and it identifies a mail server.

21. You are configuring a SOHO network and need to ensure that four internal computers can share a single public IP address for Internet access. What feature should be enabled on the router connected to the Internet?

    A. DHCP

    B. PAT

    C. DNS

    D. QoS

Answer: **B** is correct. Port Address Translation (PAT) is an extension of Network Address Translation (NAT) that allows multiple internal clients to share a single public IP address. It translates private IP addresses on the internal network to the public IP address on the Internet, and translates public IP addresses back to private.

A is incorrect. Dynamic Host Configuration Protocol (DHCP) will likely be running on the router, but it provides dynamic IP addresses to internal clients. It will not translate public and private IP addresses.

C is incorrect. Domain Name System (DNS) provides host name to IP address name resolution, but it does not translate internal private IP addresses with external public IP addresses.

D is incorrect. Quality of service (QoS) often refers to managing problems related to Voice over IP (VoIP) traffic, not IP address translation.

Objective 1.4 questions. Explain the characteristics and benefits of various WAN technologies.

22. Which of the following technologies combines multiple signals using different wavelengths, and can increase the bandwidth of an existing fiber network?
    A. Satellite
    B. DWDM
    C. SONET
    D. MPLS

Answer: **B** is correct. Dense wavelength division multiplexing (DWDM) is a technology that combines multiple signals using different wavelengths and transmits the multiplexed signals over a fiber-optic cable. Data within these different wavelengths can be transmitted at the same time increasing the bandwidth of the cable.

A is incorrect. Satellite signals don't use any type of cable when transmitted between Earth and satellites.
C is incorrect. Synchronous Optical Network (SONET) uses time-division multiplexing. Although it can increase the number of signals transmitted over a network, it doesn't increase the overall bandwidth.
D is incorrect. Multiprotocol Label Switching (MPLS) is a wide area network (WAN) protocol that uses labels for addressing. It might use fiber but might not. Similarly, it is not dependent on any specific protocol, so it might use a multiplexing signal or it might not.

23. What type of connector would you use with a T-3 leased line?

    A. RJ-11

    B. DB-9

    C. RS-232

    D. BNC

Answer: **D** is correct. A T-3 leased line, also called a Digital Signal 3 or DS3, uses 75-ohm coaxial cables and British Naval Connector (BNC) connectors.

A is incorrect. An RJ-11 connector connects to a plain old telephone service (POTS) line or an analog modem.
B and C are incorrect. An RS-232 connection uses a DE-9 connector and has 9 pins. The DE-9 connector is often referred to as a DB-9 connector.

24. Which of the following protocols uses labels instead of addresses to direct traffic?

    A. Token Ring

    B. DWDM

    C. LTE

    D. MPLS

Answer: **D** is correct. Multiprotocol Label Switching (MPLS) is a wide area network (WAN) protocol that uses labels for addressing. The labels identify paths. None of the other answers use labels.

A is incorrect. A Token Ring network is configured as a circle or a ring. Clients can send traffic when they have a logical token.

B is incorrect. Dense wavelength division multiplexing (DWDM) combines data from different sources onto a fiber cable, each with different light wavelengths.

C is incorrect. Long Term Evolution (LTE) is a wireless standard for smartphones and mobile devices. It is the successor to 3G and commonly referred to as 4G, though it doesn't meet the specific requirements of 4G.

25. What type of media is used with SONET?

    A. Twisted-pair

    B. Coaxial

    C. Satellite

    D. Fiber

Answer: **D** is correct. Synchronous Optical Networking (SONET) is a very fast wide area network (WAN) protocol and it uses fiber-optic media.

A is incorrect. Local area networks (LANs) commonly use twisted-pair cable.

B is incorrect. Coaxial cable is used in bus topology networks.

C is incorrect. SONET does not use satellite connections.

26. Of the following choices, what provides the highest bandwidth for a WAN?

    A. SONET

    B. POTS

    C. T-1

    D. E-1

Answer: **A** is correct. Synchronous Optical Networking (SONET) is a very fast wide area network (WAN) protocol using fiber-optic media. It can use various Optical Carrier (OC) levels such as OC-1 with a bandwidth of about 50 Mbps or OC-768 with a bandwidth of 38 Gbps.

B is incorrect. Plain old telephone service (POTS) connections are limited to about 56 Kbps.
C is incorrect. A T-1 connection has a maximum bandwidth of 1.544 Mbps.
D is incorrect. An E-1 connection has a maximum bandwidth of 2.048 Mbps.

27. Which of the following is a valid WAN technology that does not require a physical medium?
    A. WiMAX
    B. SONET
    C. SDH
    D. T-3

Answer: **A** is correct. Worldwide Interoperability for Microwave Access (WiMAX) is a wide area network (WAN) technology using wireless components. It is commonly used for high-speed Internet access.

B is incorrect. Synchronous Optical Networking (SONET) is a very fast wide area network (WAN) protocol that uses fiber as the physical medium.
C is incorrect. Synchronous Digital Hierarchy (SDH) is the same as SONET and it uses fiber as the physical medium. The term SONET is used in the United States and Canada, and the term SDH is used in other countries.
D is incorrect. T-3 is another wired technology used for WANs with speeds up to 44.736 Mbps.

Objective 1.5 questions. Install and properly terminate various cable types and connectors using appropriate tools.

28. You need to purchase cabling for a LAN in a building your organization recently purchased and you're trying to determine if you should purchase plenum-rated cables. Which of the following should you evaluate to determine what cabling to purchase?
    A. Location of servers
    B. Location of access points
    C. Location of airflow from HVAC
    D. Location of lighting

Answer: **C is correct.** Plenum-rated cable is used to comply with fire codes when a cable runs through a plenum space such as a raised ceiling or raised floor. Forced air for heating, ventilation, and air conditioning (HVAC) systems is commonly sent through the plenum. Technicians often run cable through the plenum space too and these cables must be plenum-rated cables.

A is incorrect. Servers would not be placed in a plenum, so location of the servers is not relevant.
B is incorrect. One of the first steps when creating a small office home office (SOHO) network is to create a list of requirements. These requirements might help determine the best location, but the environment limitations are more important when identifying the best location.
D is incorrect. Based on the requirements, you may not need to run much cable. For example, if a wireless network is acceptable, very little cable will be needed.

29. How many pins are on an RS-232 connector?

    A. 4

    B. 6

    C. 8

    D. 9

Answer: **D** is correct. An RS-232 connection uses a DE-9 connector and has 9 pins. The DE-9 connector is often referred to as a DB-9 connector.

A, B, and C are incorrect. An RS-232 DB-9 connector does not have 4, 6, or 8 pins.

30. What would you use to attach a cable to a wiring block?

    A. Crimper

    B. Certifier

    C. Punch down tool

    D. Butt set

Answer: **C** is correct. A punch down tool is a handheld tool used to connect cables to wiring blocks (such as a 66 block or a 110 block) and network jacks.

A is incorrect. Crimpers are used to secure connectors onto cables, not attach wires to wiring blocks.

B is incorrect. A cable certifier verifies that a cable works and meets specifications.

D is incorrect. Telephone technicians use a butt set to verify a telephone line is working.

31. What type of connection is RS-232 used for?

A. Fiber

B. Coaxial

C. Serial

D. Twisted-pair

Answer: **C** is correct. RS-232 is used for serial connections and commonly uses a DE-9 (sometimes called a DB-9) connector with 9 pins.

A is incorrect. Fiber commonly uses a straight tip (ST) connector, a Standard Connector (SC), a Lucent Connector (LC), or a Mechanical Transfer-Registered Jack (MT-RJ) connector.
B is incorrect. Coaxial commonly uses a British Naval Connector (BNC) connector or an F-connector.
D is incorrect. Twisted-pair cable uses Registered Jack-45 (RJ-45) connectors.

32. What type of connector would an RS-232 cable use?

A. F

B. RJ-45

C. DB-9

D. RJ-11

Answer: **C** is correct. RS-232 is used for serial connections and commonly uses a DB-9 (or, more technically, a DE-9) connector.

A is incorrect. An F-connector is used with Radio Guide-6 (RG-6) coaxial cable, but RS-232 does not use RG-6.
B is incorrect. Twisted-pair cable use RJ-45 connectors.
D is incorrect. Twisted-pair cable used with telephones and analog modems use RJ-11 connectors.

33. You are using CAT5e cables in your network and recently added a 1-Gbps switch. However, several of the computers are not running at 1 Gbps. Of the following choices, what is the BEST choice to resolve the problem?
    A. Replace the cables with CAT6.
    B. Verify the cables with a cable certifier.
    C. Replace the NICs on the computers.
    D. Check the cables with a toner probe.

Answer: **B** is correct**.** A cable certifier is the best choice of those given and it will verify the CAT5e cables are performing at the CAT5e specifications. It's possible for a cable that doesn't fully meet the specifications to work at 100 Mbps, but not at 1,000 Mbps (1 Gbps).

A is incorrect. CAT5e cables support 1 Gbps, so it is not necessary to replace all the cables with CAT6.
C is incorrect. You may want to ensure that the network interface cards (NICs) support the higher speed and are configured to support 1 Gbps. If they are using auto sense (or auto negotiate), they will be configured automatically. Replacing the NICs wouldn't be the best choice before testing the cables.
D is incorrect. A toner probe is commonly used to locate the end of a cable in another room, or verify continuity of a cable, but it won't verify that a cable meets specifications.

34. You just helped about 50 users move into a new building using existing equipment from the original location. Users begin complaining that the network is slow. What can you use to check the wiring in the new building?

A. Cable tester

B. Ping

C. Tracert

D. Cable certifier

Answer: **D** is correct. A cable certifier can verify the cabling meets specifications.

A is incorrect. A cable tester will verify a cable is wired correctly, but won't verify specifications.

B and C are incorrect. Ping and tracert and are used to check connectivity and identify hops in a path. They are not used to check wiring.

35. You need to create two small patch cables to connect Ethernet switches in a network. What would you use to create the cables?

    A. RJ-11 connectors

    B. Crimper

    C. TDR

    D. OTDR

Answer: **B** is correct. Ethernet uses twisted-pair cable, and a crimper is used to secure an RJ-45 connector onto a twisted-pair cable.

A is incorrect. RJ-11 connectors are used for phone wires, and Ethernet switches use RJ-45 connectors.

C and D are incorrect. A time-domain reflectometer (TDR) can identify the location of a break in a cable, and an optical TDR (OTDR) can locate a break in a fiber cable.

36. What would you use to connect a twisted-pair cable to a network jack?
    A. Snips
    B. Punch down tool
    C. Crimper
    D. Butt set

Answer: **B** is correct. Punch down tools are used to connect twisted-pair cable to network jacks at wall plates and to wiring blocks.

A is incorrect. Wire snips are used to cut cables. Large wire snips are strong enough to cut through thick cables.
C is incorrect. A crimper is used to crimp a cable onto a connector, such as a twisted-pair cable onto an RJ-45 connector, but would not be used to crimp a cable onto a network jack at a wall plate.
D is incorrect. A butt set is used to check a telephone line.

37. What type of cable would use an F-connector?
    A. Fiber
    B. Twisted-pair
    C. RG-6
    D. RS-232

Answer: **C** is correct. Radio Guide-6 (RG-6) coaxial cable uses an F-connector.

A is incorrect. Fiber cable would use a straight tip (ST), a Standard Connector (SC), a Lucent Connector (LC), or a Mechanical Transfer-Registered Jack (MT-RJ) connector.
B is incorrect. Twisted-pair cable uses RJ-45 connectors.

D is incorrect. RS-232 uses a 9-pin DE-9 (sometimes called DB-9) connector.

Objective 1.6 questions. Differentiate between common network topologies.

38. Computers within a network are only able to transfer data when they have access to a logical token. What type of topology does this describe?
    A. Star
    B. Ring
    C. Bus
    D. MPLS

Answer: **B** is correct. Ring topologies (often called Token Ring) use a logical token and devices can only communicate when they have access to the token. A ring topology is configured in a circle or ring.

A is incorrect. Star topologies use a central device such as an Ethernet switch or a hub, which do not use tokens.
C is incorrect. Bus topologies do not use tokens. They are rarely used on networks because a failure in one connection results in a failure for all devices on the bus.
D is incorrect. Multiprotocol Label Switching (MPLS) does not use tokens. MPLS is a wide area network (WAN) protocol that uses labels to identify addressing paths.

39. You manage a network that has multiple computers connected via a single Ethernet switch. What topology does this network use?

    A. Ring

    B. Mesh

    C. Bus

    D. Star

Answer: **D** is correct. A network that connects devices via a central switch is using a star topology. The centralized switch has point-to-point connections to each of the devices connected to the switch.

A is incorrect. In a ring topology, computers are connected in a circle. They may connect to a central device known as a multistation access unit (MAU), but not an Ethernet switch.
B is incorrect. In a mesh network, computers will have multiple connections to each other, rather than to a single switch.
C is incorrect. A bus configuration has devices connected directly to each other.

40. A network is configured with a topology that forces devices to wait before communicating on the network. What type of network topology is this?

    A. Ring

    B. Mesh

    C. Bus

    D. Star

Answer: **A** is correct. A Token Ring network is configured as a circle or a ring and clients can only send traffic when they have a logical token.

B is incorrect. In a mesh network, computers will have multiple connections to each other, but the topology doesn't use a token or force devices to wait before communicating.
C is incorrect. A bus configuration has devices connected directly to each other. It does use collision detection, forcing devices to wait after detecting a collision, but not before communicating the first time.
D is incorrect. A network that connects devices via a central switch is using a star topology, and it doesn't use a token or force devices to wait.

41. Which of the following network topologies has a central device that is a potential single point of failure?
    A. FDDI
    B. Mesh
    C. Bus
    D. Star

Answer: **D** is correct. A network that connects devices via a central switch is using a star topology, and the switch is a potential single point of failure. If the switch fails, all devices connected to the switch lose network connectivity.

A is incorrect. A Fiber Distributed Data Interface (FDDI) network uses two rings, with each ring transmitting data in the opposite direction, providing redundancy for the network.
B is incorrect. A mesh network will have multiple connections to each other, providing several layers of redundancy.
C is incorrect. A bus configuration has devices connected directly to each other, not to a central device.

42. Computers within a network are connected in a logical circle. What type of topology is being used?
    A. Ring
    B. Mesh
    C. Star
    D. Bus

Answer: **A** is correct. Devices are connected in a circle when using a ring topology (sometimes called Token Ring). Devices can transmit when they have the logical token. Token Ring networks sometimes use a multistation access unit (MSAU) as a central device.

B is incorrect. A mesh topology has multiple connections (not a single circle) for fault tolerance in case a connection fails.
C is incorrect. A star topology uses a central device such as an Ethernet switch or hub to connect devices.
D is incorrect. Computers in a bus topology are connected in a single line.

43. You are able to transfer files between Bluetooth devices. What type of network are you using?
    A. LAN
    B. PAN
    C. VPN
    D. WAN

Answer: **B** is correct. A personal area network (PAN) is used to transfer files with Bluetooth. In general, the PAN is centered on a person.

A is incorrect. A local area network (LAN) connects computers in a limited area, such as within a home or a single building.

C is incorrect. A virtual private network (VPN) provides access to a private network over a public network (such as the Internet).

D is incorrect. A wide area network (WAN) is a group of two or more networks spread across a large geographical area. There isn't a specific distance that identifies a network as a WAN, but generally, it indicates that two or more networks are in separate cities.

Objective: 1.7 Differentiate between network infrastructure implementations.

44. A company in Silicon Valley owns three buildings within walking distance of each other, and each of these buildings are connected via a single network. What is the BEST name for this network?

    A. CAN

    B. LAN

    C. MAN

    D. PAN

Answer: **A** is correct. A campus area network (CAN) is a network of multiple buildings, but in a limited area.

B is incorrect. A local area network (LAN) connects computers in a limited area, such as within a home or a single building.

C is incorrect. A metropolitan area network (MAN) spans a large area, such as a city or a very large campus. Although three buildings might be described as a MAN, it is more accurate to call it a CAN because it is only a few buildings and the same company owns the buildings.

D is incorrect. A personal area network (PAN) is centered around a person.

45. What is the BEST label for the IP address of ::1?

    A. EUI-64 address

    B. Link-local address

    C. APIPA address

    D. Loopback address

Answer: **D** is correct. The Internet Protocol version 6 (IPv6) address of ::1 is a loopback address.

A is incorrect. The Extended Unique Identifier-64 (EUI-64) address identifies the network interface card for IPv6, similar to how the media access control (MAC) address identifies the network interface card for IPv4.

B is incorrect. A link-local address is an IPv6 address that allows a system to access other devices on the same network. A link-local address cannot pass a router.

C is incorrect. An Automatic Private IP Addressing (APIPA) address is assigned if a Dynamic Host Configuration Protocol (DHCP) client does not receive an IPv6 from a DHCP server. APIPA addresses start with 169.254.

Objective: 1.8 Given a scenario, implement and configure the appropriate addressing schema.

46. Which of the following is a valid IPv4 loopback address?

    A. ::1

    B. 127.0.0.1

    C. 1a-2b-3c-4d-5e-6f

    D. 169.254.75.91

Answer: **B** is correct. The Internet Protocol version 4 (IPv4) loopback address is 127.0.0.1.

A is incorrect. The Internet Protocol version 6 (IPv6) IP address of ::1 is an IPv6 loopback address.

C is incorrect. A media access control (MAC) address is a 48-bit address assigned to a client's network interface card (NIC) and it is typically displayed as six pairs of hexadecimal characters separated with dashes.

D is incorrect. IPv4 addresses that start with 169.254 are Dynamic Host Configuration Protocol (DHCP) addresses. A DHCP client will assign itself an Automatic Private Internet Protocol Addressing (APIPA) address if it cannot reach a DHCP server.

47. Which of the following IPv6-related standards takes place on Layer 2 of the OSI model?

    A. MAC

    B. IP address

    C. EUI-64

    D. Zero compression

Answer: **C** is correct. The Extended Unique Identifier-64 (EUI-64) address identifies the network interface card for IPv6 and it operates on the Data Link layer (Layer 2) of the Open Systems Interconnection (OSI) model.

A is incorrect. The EUI-64 is often derived from the 48-bit media access control (MAC) address, but the MAC address is directly related to IPv4, not IPv6.

B is incorrect. IP addresses (both IPv4 and IPv6) are identified on Layer 3 (the Network layer).

D is incorrect. Zero compression is a rule related to IPv6 addresses (on the Network layer), allowing you to replace a string of zeroes with a double colon (::).

48. You are designing a network segment that only needs 2 IP addresses assigned. You need to conserve the IP address space. What CIDR notation is the BEST choice for this network?

   A. /26

   B. /28

   C. /30

   D. /32

Answer: **C** is correct. The /30 Classless Inter-Domain Routing (CIDR) notation is the best choice. It indicates a subnet mask of 255.255.255.252, which supports two IP addresses and no more.

The formula to determine how many hosts can operate on a network is $2^n - 2$, where *n* is the number of 0 bits in the subnet mask. A subnet mask has 32 bits. If the CIDR notation is /30, it indicates that there are 2 bits left to create subnets. Using the $2^n - 2$ formula, or $2^2 - 2$, or $4 - 2$, you see the answer is 2. This is how many hosts you can have on the network.

A is incorrect. A /26 CIDR notation indicates 6 bits are left for hosts (32 – 26 = 6). Using the $2^n - 2$ formula, or $2^6 - 2$, or $64 - 2$, you see the answer is 62. In other words, /26 supports 62 hosts. However, you only need two IP addresses and you need to conserve IP addresses. This wastes 60 IP addresses, so it is incorrect.

B is incorrect. A /28 CIDR notation indicates 4 bits are left for hosts (32 – 28 = 4). Using the $2^n - 2$ formula, or $2^4 - 2$, or $16 - 2$, you see the answer is 14. In other words, /26 supports 14 hosts. However, you only need two IP addresses and you need to conserve IP addresses. This wastes 12 IP addresses, so it is incorrect.

D is incorrect. A /32 CIDR notation indicates 0 bits are left for hosts (32 – 32 = 0).

49. You are designing a network segment that only needs 58 IP addresses assigned. You need to conserve the IP address space. What CIDR notation is the BEST choice for this network?

    A. /26

    B. /28

    C. /30

    D. /32

Answer: **A** is correct. The /26 Classless Inter-Domain Routing (CIDR) notation is the best choice. It indicates a subnet mask of 255.255.255.192, which supports 62 IP addresses and is the best choice to conserve IP address space.

The formula to determine how many hosts can operate on a network is $2^n - 2$, where *n* is the number of 0 bits in the subnet mask. A subnet mask has 32 bits. If the CIDR notation is /26, it indicates that there are 6 bits left to create subnets. Using the $2^n - 2$ formula, or $2^6 - 2$, or 64 – 2, you see the answer is 62. This is how many hosts you can have on the network.

B is incorrect. A /28 CIDR notation indicates 4 bits are left for hosts (32 – 28 = 4). Using the $2^n - 2$ formula, or $2^4 - 2$, or 16 – 2, you see the answer is 14. In other words, /26 supports 14 hosts. This doesn't support 58 IP addresses.

C is incorrect. A /30 CIDR notation indicates 2 bits are left for hosts (32 – 30 = 2). Using the $2^n - 2$ formula, or $2^2 - 2$, or 4 – 2, you see the answer is 2. In other words, /30 supports 2 hosts. This doesn't support 58 IP addresses.

D is incorrect. A /32 CIDR notation indicates 0 bits are left for hosts (32 – 32 = 0).

50. You are designing a network segment that only needs 24 IP addresses assigned. You need to conserve the IP address space. What CIDR notation is the BEST choice for this network?

A. /25

B. /26

C. /27

D. /28

Answer: **C** is correct. The /27 Classless Inter-Domain Routing (CIDR) notation is the best choice. It indicates a subnet mask of 255.255.255.224, which supports 30 IP addresses and is the best choice to conserve IP address space.

The formula to determine how many hosts can operate on a network is $2^n - 2$, where *n* is the number of 0 bits in the subnet mask. A subnet mask has 32 bits. If the CIDR notation is /27, it indicates that there are 5 bits left to create subnets. Using the $2^n - 2$ formula, or $2^5 - 2$, or $32 - 2$, you see the answer is 30. This is how many hosts you can have on the network.

A is incorrect. A /25 CIDR notation indicates 7 bits are left for hosts ($32 - 25 = 7$). Using the $2^n - 2$ formula, or $2^7 - 2$, or $128 - 2$, you see the answer is 126. In other words, /25 supports 126 hosts. This is much more than the 24 needed and wastes IP addresses.

B is incorrect. A /26 CIDR notation indicates 6 bits are left for hosts ($32 - 26 = 6$). Using the $2^n - 2$ formula, or $2^6 - 2$, or $64 - 2$, you see the answer is 62. In other words, /26 supports 62 hosts. This is much more than the 24 needed and wastes IP addresses.

D is incorrect. A /28 CIDR notation indicates 4 bits are left for hosts ($32 - 28 = 4$). Using the $2^n - 2$ formula, or $2^4 - 2$, or $16 - 2$, you see the answer is

14. In other words, /28 supports 14 hosts, which isn't enough to meet the 24 addresses needed in the question.

51. You are designing a network segment that only needs 32 IP addresses assigned. You need to conserve the IP address space. What CIDR notation is the BEST choice for this network?

    A. /25

    B. /26

    C. /27

    D. /28

Answer: **B** is correct. The /26 Classless Inter-Domain Routing (CIDR) notation is the best choice. It indicates a subnet mask of 255.255.255.192, which supports 62 IP addresses and is the best choice to conserve IP address space.

The formula to determine how many hosts can operate on a network is $2^n - 2$, where n is the number of 0 bits in the subnet mask. A subnet mask has 32 bits. If the CIDR notation is /26, it indicates that there are 6 bits left to create subnets. Using the $2^n - 2$ formula, or $2^6 - 2$, or $64 - 2$, you see the answer is 62. This is how many hosts you can have on the network.

A is incorrect. A /25 CIDR notation indicates 7 bits are left for hosts ($32 - 25 = 7$). Using the $2^n - 2$ formula, or $2^7 - 2$, or $128 - 2$, you see the answer is 126. In other words, /25 supports 126 hosts. This is much more than the 32 needed and wastes IP addresses.

C is incorrect. A /27 CIDR notation indicates 5 bits are left for hosts ($32 - 27 = 5$). Using the $2^n - 2$ formula, or $2^5 - 2$, or $32 - 2$, you see the answer is 30. In other words, /27 supports 30 hosts, which isn't enough to meet the 32 addresses needed in the question.

D is incorrect. A /28 CIDR notation indicates 4 bits are left for hosts (32 – 28 = 4). Using the $2^n - 2$ formula, or $2^4 - 2$, or 16 – 2, you see the answer is 14. In other words, /28 supports 14 hosts, which isn't enough to meet the 32 addresses needed in the question.

52. You are designing a network segment that only needs 12 IP addresses assigned. You need to conserve the IP address space. What CIDR notation is the BEST choice for this network?

  A. /26

  B. /27

  C. /28

  D. /29

Answer: **C** is correct. The /28 Classless Inter-Domain Routing (CIDR) notation is the best choice. It indicates a subnet mask of 255.255.255.240, which supports 14 IP addresses and is the best choice to conserve IP address space.

The formula to determine how many hosts can operate on a network is $2^n - 2$, where *n* is the number of 0 bits in the subnet mask. A subnet mask has 32 bits. If the CIDR notation is /28, it indicates that there are 4 bits left to create subnets. Using the $2^n - 2$ formula, or $2^4 - 2$, or 16 – 2, you see the answer is 14. This is how many hosts you can have on the network.

A is incorrect. A /26 CIDR notation indicates 6 bits are left for hosts (32 – 26 = 6). Using the $2^n - 2$ formula, or $2^6 - 2$, or 64 – 2, you see the answer is 62. In other words, /26 supports 62 hosts. This is much more than the 12 needed and wastes IP addresses.

B is incorrect. A /27 CIDR notation indicates 5 bits are left for hosts (32 – 27 = 5). Using the $2^n - 2$ formula, or $2^5 - 2$, or 32 – 2, you see the answer is 30. In other words, /27 supports 30 hosts.
D is incorrect. A /29 CIDR notation indicates 4 bits are left for hosts (32 – 29 = 3). Using the $2^n - 2$ formula, or $2^3 - 2$, or 8 – 2, you see the answer is 6. In other words, /29 supports 6 hosts, which isn't enough to meet the 12 addresses needed in the question.

53. Using ipconfig, you see a computer has an IP address of 169.254.4.23 with a subnet mask of 255.255.0.0. What type of address is this?

    A. IPv6

    B. APIPA

    C. DHCP assigned

    D. DNS assigned

Answer: **B** is correct. An address starting with 169.254.x.x is an Automatic Private Internet Protocol Addressing (APIPA) address.

A is incorrect. Internet Protocol version 6 (IPv6) addresses use hexadecimal characters, not decimal characters.
C is incorrect. APIPA addresses are assigned when a Dynamic Host Configuration Protocol (DHCP) client requests a DHCP lease, but a DHCP server doesn't offer a DHCP lease. In other words, a DHCP server never assigns an APIPA address.
D is incorrect. Domain Name System (DNS) servers resolve host names to IP addresses with A or AAAA records, IP addresses to host names with Pointer (PTR) records, locate mail servers with MX (Mail Exchanger) records, and allow systems to have an alias with CNAME (Canonical Name) records. DNS servers do not assign any type of IP addresses.

54. You are troubleshooting a computer system and you determine it has been assigned an IP address of 169.254.45.83. What does this indicate?

    A. DNS could not be reached.

    B. DHCP could not be reached.

    C. The default gateway could not be reached.

    D. The computer's firewall is enabled.

Answer: **B** is correct. An address starting with 169.254 is an Automatic Private Internet Protocol Addressing (APIPA) address and is assigned to a Dynamic Host Configuration Protocol (DHCP) client when a DHCP server cannot be reached. Any time you see an APIPA address, you know the computer is a DHCP client and it didn't receive a DHCP lease.

A is incorrect. Domain Name System (DNS) is used for name resolution and would not cause a system to have an APIPA address.
C is incorrect. The default gateway is assigned by DHCP to a DHCP client and an APIPA address indicates that the client was unable to reach a DHCP server. Also, APIPA addresses do not assign a default gateway.
D is incorrect. Enabling the computer's firewall would not block DHCP traffic and would not prevent the client from receiving a DHCP address.

55. Which of the following provides fault tolerance for DHCP?

    A. Dynamic IP address assignments

    B. Exclusions

    C. APIPA

    D. DNS

Answer: **C** is correct. Automatic Private IP Addressing (APIPA) address acts as a failover mechanism for Dynamic Host Configuration Protocol

(DHCP). If DHCP fails to assign a lease to a DHCP client, APIPA will assign an address in the range of 169.254.0.1/16 to 169.254.255.254/16.

A is incorrect. DHCP provides dynamic IP address assignments along with assigning other Transmission Control Protocol/Internet Protocol (TCP/IP) configuration information, but it can't provide fault tolerance for itself.
B is incorrect. An exclusion in DHCP ensures that a specific IP address is not assigned by DHCP, but is instead excluded from the DHCP scope. This is used if another device has been manually assigned an IP address, and it prevents an IP address conflict.
D is incorrect. Domain Name System (DNS) is used to resolve host names to IP addresses, but it does not provide fault tolerance for DHCP.

56. What can you use to dynamically assign the same IP address to a printer configured as a network device?
    A. DNS
    B. DHCP reservation
    C. SNMP
    D. DHCP exclusion

Answer: **B** is correct. Dynamic Host Configuration Protocol (DHCP) is used to dynamically assign IP addresses to network devices, including network printers that can be configured as DHCP clients. A DHCP reservation maps the IP address to the printer's media access control (MAC) address. Once a DHCP reservation is configured, DHCP will always issue the same IP address to this printer.

A is incorrect. Domain Name System (DNS) is used to resolve host names to IP addresses with A records (also called host records). DNS can also resolve IP addresses to host names with Pointer (PTR) records, but it does not assign IP addresses.

C is incorrect. The Simple Network Management Protocol (SNMP) is used to administer and monitor network devices.

D is incorrect. A DHCP exclusion would be used if the printer is manually assigned an IP address within a DHCP scope and you want to ensure that the address is not issued to any other DHCP clients.

57. Of the following choices, what is an address that would be assigned if a DHCP client cannot reach a DHCP server?
    - A. 10.8.34.2
    - B. 169.254.45.98
    - C. 172.16.4.34
    - D. 192.168.1.45

Answer: **B** is correct. A Dynamic Host Configuration Protocol (DHCP) client will assign itself an Automatic Private Internet Protocol Addressing (APIPA) address if it cannot reach a DHCP server. APIPA addresses start with 169.254.

A is incorrect. This is a Class A address. Class A addresses are in this range: 1.0.0.0 to 126.255.255.254.

C is incorrect. This is a Class B address. Class B addresses are in this range: 128.0.0.0 to 191.255.255.254.

D is incorrect. This is a Class C address. Class C addresses are in this range: 192.0.0.0 to 223.255.255.254.

58. Which of the following is a valid IPv4 address?

A. 192.168.1.200

B. 192:168:1:200

C. ::1

D. 1a-2b-3c-4d-5e-6f

Answer: **A** is correct. 192.158.1.200 is a valid Internet Protocol version 4 (IPv4) address.

B is incorrect. IPv4 uses a dotted decimal format. It does not separate the decimals with colons, but Internet Protocol version 6 (IPv6) does.
C is incorrect. The loopback address for IPv6 is ::1. The loopback address for IPv4 is 127.0.0.1.
D is incorrect. A media access control (MAC) address is a 48-bit address assigned to a client's NIC and it is typically displayed as six pairs of hexadecimal characters separated with dashes.

59. What class of IP address is 224.100.200.3?

A. Class A

B. Class B

C. Class C

D. Class D

Answer: **D** is correct. Class D addresses are used for multicasting and they start with 224.

A is incorrect. Class A addresses are in the range of 1.0.0.0 to 126.255.255.254. In other words, the first number is any number from 1 to 126. 127 is reserved for testing and 127.0.0.1 is the loopback address.

B is incorrect. Class B addresses are in the range of 128.0.0.0 to 191.255.255.254. In other words, the first number is any number from 128 to 191. 127 is reserved for testing and 127.0.0.1 is the loopback address.

C is incorrect. Class C addresses are in the range of 192.0.0.0 to 223.255.255.254. In other words, the first number is any number from 192 to 223.

60. Which of the following is a Class B address?

A. 10.71.12.73

B. 172.16.34.67

C. 192.168.100.5

D. 224.54.23.12

Answer: **B** is correct. Class B addresses are in the range of 128.0.0.0 to 191.255.255.254. In other words, the first number is any number from 128 to 191, and 172 is in this range.

A is incorrect. Class A addresses are in the range of 1.0.0.0 to 126.255.255.254. In other words, the first number is any number from 1 to 126. 127 is reserved for testing and 127.0.0.1 is the loopback address.

C is incorrect. Class C addresses are in the range of 192.0.0.0 to 223.255.255.254. In other words, the first number is any number from 192 to 223.

D is incorrect. Class D addresses (used for multicasting) are in the range of 224.0.0.0 to 239.255.255.255.

61. Which of the following is an example of an IPv4 address using CIDR notation?

A. 127.0.0.1

B. 192.168.1.1

C. 192.168.5.1/30

D. 169.254.17.4/36

Answer: **C** is correct. Classless Inter-Domain Routing (CIDR) uses a slash (/) and a decimal number to indicate how many bits are one (1) in the subnet mask. The /30 indicates that the subnet mask is 255.255.255.252.

A is incorrect. 127.0.0.1 is the loopback address, but it doesn't use CIDR notation.
B is incorrect. An address without a slash is not using CIDR notation.
D is incorrect. An address starting with 169.254 is an Automatic Private Internet Protocol Addressing (APIPA) address and it always has a subnet mask of 255.255.0.0. If CIDR notation was used, it would be /16. IP addresses and subnet masks have only 32 bits, so a CIDR notation of /36 is not valid.

Objective: 1.9 Explain the basics of routing concepts and protocols.

62. All routers in your network have learned the same routing information. What is the BEST name for this state?

A. Split-horizon

B. Convergence

C. High availability

D. Balanced load

Answer: **B** is correct. Convergence is the state of routers when they have learned the same routing information. At convergence, they have learned all there is to learn within the network using a routing protocol.

A is incorrect. Split-horizon route advertisements is a method used to prevent routing loops with Routing Information Protocol version 2 (RIPv2). It prevents the router from advertising a route on the same interface where the router learned the route.

C is incorrect. High availability refers to uptime for a system. Redundancy, fault tolerance, and business continuity practices help ensure systems remain available even if they suffer a fault.

D is incorrect. A load balancer can balance the load among multiple servers, but convergence is unrelated to load balancers.

63. Management wants to ensure that critical systems continue to operate in the event of a disaster. Which of the following is management trying to ensure?

    A. Convergence

    B. HSRP

    C. VRRP

    D. High availability

Answer: **D** is correct. Redundancy, fault tolerance, and business continuity practices help ensure high availability of systems, even in the event of a disaster.

A is incorrect. Convergence is the state of routers when they have learned the same routing information. It is not related to high availability.

B is incorrect. Hot Standby Router Protocol (HSRP) provides fault tolerance for a default gateway. It is one of many methods that can contribute to high availability.

C is incorrect. Virtual Router Redundancy Protocol (VRRP) uses virtual routers to increase the availability of routing paths. It is one of many methods that can contribute to high availability.

64. A network administrator has been creating a baseline of network performance. During this process, he realizes that one router is operating significantly slower than the other routers on the network, but it is handling about the same amount of traffic as other routers. What is the MOST likely cause for this issue?
    A. Processor issues
    B. Hop counts
    C. Split-horizon problem
    D. Expired hop count

Answer: **A** is correct. The most likely cause of those given is that the router's processor is not making routing decisions as quick as other routers' processors. The reason may be that it is an older, slower processor, or that it has developed a fault.

B is incorrect. Hop counts refers to how many routers a packet goes through and is unrelated to how fast a router operates.
C is incorrect. Split-horizon is a preventive solution for routing loops with Routing Information Protocol version 2 (RIPv2). It is not a problem.
D is incorrect. A hop is simply a router in the path to the destination, and if the hop count expires, the traffic is dropped. This wouldn't slow down a router because the router doesn't do anything with the traffic.

65. Which of the following BEST describes the next hop within networking?
    - A. The routing table
    - B. The address of the next hub in a path
    - C. The address of the next router in a path
    - D. The broadcast domain

Answer: **C** is correct. Data packets are sent to a network through routers and the next router in the path is referred to as the next hop. Additionally, the next router in the path is sometimes known as the gateway to the next network.

A is incorrect. A routing table identifies different paths to remote networks, but the table isn't called the next hop.
B is incorrect. Hubs do not have addresses and are not referred to as hops.
D is incorrect. A broadcast domain is a group of network devices that can send and receive broadcast addresses to each other. Routers do not pass broadcast traffic but instead create separate broadcast domains.

66. Which of the following choices can a router use to share information with neighboring routers?
    - A. RDP
    - B. RIPv2
    - C. IMAP
    - D. TFTP

Answer: **B** is correct. Routers in small networks can use Routing Information Protocol version 2 (RIPv2) to share information with neighboring routers.

A is incorrect. Remote Desktop Protocol (RDP) is used to connect to other systems in Microsoft networks using port 3389.
C is incorrect. Internet Message Access Protocol (IMAP) is a mail-based protocol using port 143.
D is incorrect. Trivial File Transfer Protocol (TFTP) is a form of FTP that uses User Datagram Protocol (UDP) instead of Transmission Control Protocol (TCP) over port 69.

67. An organization maintains a private cloud, which connects data from three different data centers. Each data center is located at a separate geographical location to maintain high availability even if a disaster eliminates network connectivity for any one of the data centers. Which of the following provides the BEST solution to meet this need?

    A. APIPA
    B. Hop counts
    C. BGP
    D. Codec

Answer: **C** is correct. The Border Gateway Protocol (BGP) is the best choice. Although most organizations don't need BGP, it is useful if an organization maintains multiple links to the Internet and can help ensure that a network can use alternate links if necessary.

A is incorrect. Automatic Private IP Addressing (APIPA) address provides fault tolerance for Dynamic Host Configuration Protocol (DHCP) clients that cannot obtain an IP address from a DHCP server. It does not provide fault tolerance for network connections.
B is incorrect. Hop counts refers to how many routers a packet goes through and is unrelated to how fast a router operates.

D is incorrect. A coder-decoder (codec) converts audio signals into a compressed digital form. It does not provide fault tolerance for network connections.

68. Which of the following is a routing protocol that uses the first open shortest path it can identify?
    A. RIPv2
    B. APIPA
    C. OSPF
    D. CIDR

Answer: **C** is correct. Open Shortest Path First (OSPF) is a link-state routing protocol that identifies the shortest path based on the current status (or current state of the link). The current status verifies the path is open.

A is incorrect. Routing Information Protocol version 2 (RIPv2) is a distance-vector routing protocol that uses a hop count as a metric.
B is incorrect. Automatic Private IP Addressing (APIPA) address is not a routing protocol. It assigns IP addresses starting with 169.254.x.x for Dynamic Host Configuration Protocol (DHCP) clients that cannot obtain an IP address from a DHCP server.
D is incorrect. Classless Inter-Domain Routing (CIDR) is not a routing protocol. It is a way of using IP addresses without following the original Classful standards of Class A, Class B, and Class C.

69. A database server takes approximately 2 seconds to respond to database queries when going through a legacy router. What is another name for this?
    A. Uptime
    B. Redundancy

C. Interference

D. Latency

Answer: **D** is correct. Latency refers to the amount of time it takes for traffic to travel over a network. Ideally, latency should be low.

A is incorrect. Uptime refers to how long a system has been operational.
B is incorrect. Redundancy refers to the addition of identical components to add fault tolerance.
C is incorrect. Interference can disrupt a signal and contribute to latency. For example, electromagnetic interference (EMI) from power sources or fluorescent fixtures can interfere with the signal, requiring it to be retransmitted multiple times before a system has a usable signal.

70. Which of the following are the most sensitive to latency?

A. Video teleconferencing

B. SSL VPN

C. HTTPS

D. Traffic shaping

Answer: **A** is correct. Video teleconferencing (sometimes called video conferencing) is the most sensitive to latency of those listed. Latency refers to a delay. Video conferences are held in real time so delays result in long gaps while participants are waiting for a response. Similarly, Voice over IP (VoIP) sessions are commonly in real time, so delays are disruptive to the conversation. Satellite connections are the most susceptible to latency.

B is incorrect. A Secure Sockets Layer (SSL) virtual private network (VPN) allows users to connect to a company network from a remote location using a web browser. However, delays are acceptable.

C is incorrect. Hypertext Transfer Protocol Secure (HTTPS) provides secure sessions over the web and some delay is acceptable while a secure session is established.

D is incorrect. Traffic shaping is used to control bandwidth for specific types of bandwidth, such as reducing the amount of bandwidth available for audio or video streaming. Traffic shaping may result in higher latency for audio and video if it limits the amount of bandwidth for this traffic. However, traffic shaping is not sensitive to latency itself.

71. What is the MOST likely result of misconfiguring the AS number on a network device?

    A. BGP routing issues

    B. Internal DNS issues

    C. DHCP issues

    D. OSPF issues

Answer: **A** is correct. Border Gateway Protocol (BGP) uses autonomous system (AS) numbers for routing on the Internet. If the AS numbers are used incorrectly, they will cause problems for BGP.

B is incorrect. An internal Domain Name System (DNS) server will not be affected because the internal DNS server wouldn't access the Internet.

C is incorrect. Dynamic Host Configuration Protocol (DHCP) is used internally, so it wouldn't be affected.

D is incorrect. Open Shortest Path First (OSPF) is an internal routing protocol, so it wouldn't be affected.

Objective: 1.10 Identify the basics elements of unified communication technologies.

72. An organization is setting up video conferencing equipment to support better communication between separate offices. It will use VoIP. Which of the following will the organization MOST likely include with this deployment?
    A. VRRP
    B. BGP
    C. SIP
    D. HSRP

Answer: **C** is correct. It is common to use Session Initiation Protocol (SIP) and the H.323 standard with video conferencing. A coder-decoder (codec) converts audio signals into a compressed digital form, which can be transmitted using Voice over IP (VoIP).

A is incorrect. Virtual Router Redundancy Protocol uses virtual routers to increase the availability of routing paths. It is not directly related to VoIP.
B is incorrect. The Border Gateway Protocol (BGP) is useful if an organization maintains multiple links to the Internet. It can help ensure that a network can use alternate links if necessary. However, the scenario didn't indicate this type of high availability was necessary.
D is incorrect. Hot Standby Router Protocol (HSRP) provides fault tolerance for a default gateway. It is not directly related to VoIP.

73. An organization is setting up video conferencing equipment to support better communication between offices in different cities. It will use VoIP. Which of the following will the organization MOST likely include with this deployment?

    A. CAN

    B. Codec

    C. VLAN

    D. MIMO

Answer: **B** is correct. A coder-decoder (codec) converts audio signals into a compressed digital form, which can be transmitted using Voice over IP (VoIP). It's common to use Session Initiation Protocol (SIP) and the H.323 standard with video conferencing.

A is incorrect. A campus area network (CAN) is a network of multiple buildings in a limited area. It would not extend to different cities.
C is incorrect. A virtual local area network (VLAN) provides network segmentation and increased security by isolating a network, but it wouldn't necessarily be needed in a video conferencing setup.
D is incorrect. Multiple-input, multiple-output (MIMO) refers to a multiple antenna configuration with wireless protocols such as 802.11n and 802.11ac. It is not related to video conferencing.

74. IT management is implementing several different QoS features. What benefit will this provide?

    A. Limit the amount of video streaming on a network

    B. Block malicious traffic from reaching a network

    C. Provide redundancy

    D. Ensure predictable network performance

Answer: **D** is correct. Quality of service (QoS) refers to a group of technologies and techniques that result in predictable network performance. QoS methods can improve availability or uptime of a system, reduce latency or delays, and provide overall better performance.

A is incorrect. QoS may limit the amount of audio or video streaming on a network using traffic shaping methods, but this is only one element of QoS.

B is incorrect. Blocking malicious traffic is done with firewalls or intrusion prevention systems and is not directly related to QoS.

C is incorrect. QoS may include redundant components to increase availability, but redundancy is not the benefit and is not required for QoS.

Objective: 1.11 Compare and contrast technologies that support cloud and virtualization.

75. What is a virtual switch?

    A. A switch used for a virtual LAN

    B. A switch used for VPNs

    C. A logical switch that functions like a physical switch

    D. A planned change

Answer: **C** is correct. A virtual switch is a logical switch used within a virtual network. It functions like a physical switch and connects virtual machines.

A is incorrect. A virtual local area network (VLAN) is created with a physical switch.

C is incorrect. Virtual private networks (VPNs) are not created with switches.

D is incorrect. A switch refers to a device (virtual or physical) that connects devices. It is not a change.

76. You want to run multiple operating systems on a server within your network. What would you use?
    A. VLAN
    B. Virtual switch
    C. Virtual machines
    D. NaaS

Answer: **C** is correct. Virtual machines are separate instances of fully running operating systems on a single system. It's possible to run multiple different operating systems using virtual machines. It's also possible to run multiple virtual machines using the same operating system such as multiple virtual servers running Windows Server 2008.

A is incorrect. A virtual local area network (VLAN) is created with a physical switch to logically separate computers on a network.
B is incorrect. Virtual switches are used on virtual servers to create separate virtual networks.
D is incorrect. Network as a Service (NaaS) is a cloud-based service that provides networking services via the cloud or Internet.

77. The Costington Department store hosts an application via the cloud. Authorized employees can access the application to submit sales and marketing data. What type of model does this describe?
    A. Community PaaS
    B. Public SaaS
    C. Hybrid IaaS
    D. Private SaaS

Answer: **D** is correct. This is an example of a private Software as a Service (SaaS) model. The software is the vendor application that is accessible via the cloud. It is private because it is operated exclusively for a single organization.

A is incorrect. It is not a Platform as a Service (PaaS) model. A PaaS model provides customers with preconfigured systems via the cloud. It includes an easy-to-configure operating system, combined with appropriate applications and on-demand computing. It is not a community cloud model. A community cloud is shared between two or more organizations.
B is incorrect. It is not a public cloud model. A public model is available to the public, not just the employees from a single organization.
C is incorrect. It is not an Infrastructure as a Service (IaaS) model. An IaaS model includes hardware via the cloud in a self-managed platform, but not applications. It is not a hybrid cloud model. A hybrid model includes two or more cloud models (public, private, and community).

78. The Springfield Nuclear Power Plant is a private company and it is sharing resources with the Springfield public school system via the cloud. No other organization can access these resources. What type of cloud deployment model is this?
    A. Community
    B. Hybrid
    C. Public
    D. Private

Answer: **A** is correct. A community cloud is shared by two or more organizations. The fact that a company is a private company or that a school system is public is not relevant to the type of cloud deployment model.

B is incorrect. A hybrid cloud is a combination of any two or more clouds. It can be two clouds of the same type or different types. For example, an organization can have two separate private clouds from two different business entities, and then combine them as a hybrid cloud.

C is incorrect. A public cloud is not exclusive to any single or group of organizations. Instead, it can be used by any organization.

D is incorrect. A private cloud is used by a single organization.

79. The Springfield Nuclear Power Plant has created an online application teaching nuclear physics. Students in the Springfield Elementary School access this application via the cloud, and teachers can monitor the students' progress. What type of cloud service model is this?
    A. IaaS
    B. PaaS
    C. SaaS
    D. Public

Answer: **C** is correct. This is a Software as a Service (SaaS) model. The software is the online application and the cloud provider (the Springfield Nuclear Power Plant in this example) maintains it.

A is incorrect. Infrastructure as a Service (IaaS) provides customers with the hardware via the cloud. Customers are responsible for installing the operating system and any applications.

B is incorrect. Platform as a Service (PaaS) is a computing platform. For example, a cloud provider can provide a server with a preconfigured operating system.
D is incorrect. Public is a type of cloud deployment model, not a type of cloud service model. Although the question didn't specify, if any organization can access the application, it would be public.

80. The database stored on a SQL server has grown to several terabytes in size. Backups to tape take too long and the organization wants to reduce the time it takes to do a backup of the database. Which of the following would meet this need at the LOWEST cost?
    A. iSCSI SAN
    B. FCoE SAN
    C. PaaS
    D. NAS

Answer: **D** is correct. Network attached storage (NAS) is the best choice because it is significantly less expensive than a storage area network (SAN).

A and B are incorrect. A SAN is significantly more expensive to implement than a NAS solution. This includes both an Internet Small Computer System Interface (iSCSI) SAN and a Fibre Channel over Ethernet (FCoE) SAN.
C is incorrect. Platform as a Service (PaaS) is a cloud-based computing platform, but it isn't appropriate to back up a huge database directly to a cloud solution.

Objective: 1.12 Given a set of requirements, implement a basic network.

81. You are planning a SOHO network for a business owner. Which of the following is a logical first step?

    A. Purchase the equipment.

    B. Create the website.

    C. List the requirements.

    D. Run the cable.

Answer: **C** is correct. One of the first steps when creating a small office home office (SOHO) network is to identify the requirements and the limitations or constraints.

A is incorrect. You shouldn't purchase the equipment until you've identified what is needed. A wireless router might be needed or desirable, but if you purchase one and then talk to the owner, you might learn that a wireless network is unacceptable to the owner.

B is incorrect. A SOHO network won't necessarily require a web server or a website.

D is incorrect. Based on the requirements, you might not need to run much cable. For example, if a wireless network is acceptable, very little cable will be needed.

82. You are planning a SOHO network for a business owner and need to identify the best location for a server. Which of the following should you consider first?

    A. Equipment limitations

    B. List of requirements

    C. Environment limitations

    D. Compatibility requirements

Answer: **C** is correct. The environment limitations are a primary consideration when identifying the location of equipment in a small office home office (SOHO) network.

A is incorrect. The equipment limitations affect the operation of the network, but won't affect where they are located.

B is incorrect. One of the first steps when creating a SOHO network is to create a list of requirements. These requirements might help determine the best location, but the environment limitations are more important when identifying the best location.

D is incorrect. Based on the requirements, you might not need to run much cable. For example, if a wireless network is acceptable, very little cable will be needed.

»Get Certified »Get Ahead

Chapter 2 Network Operations

Network Operations topics are 20 percent of the CompTIA Network + exam. The objectives in this domain are:

2.1 Given a scenario, use appropriate monitoring tools.

- Packet/network analyzer
- Interface monitoring tools
- Port scanner
- Top talkers/listeners
- SNMP management software
    - Trap
    - Get
    - Walk
    - MIBS
- Alerts
    - Email
    - SMS
- Packet flow monitoring
- SYSLOG
- SIEM
- Environmental monitoring tools
    - Temperature
    - Humidity
- Power monitoring tools
- Wireless survey tools
- Wireless analyzers

2.2 Given a scenario, analyze metrics and reports from monitoring and tracking performance tools.

- Baseline
- Bottleneck
- Log management
- Graphing
- Utilization
    - Bandwidth
    - Storage
    - Network device CPU
    - Network device memory
    - Wireless channel utilization
- Link status
- Interface monitoring
    - Errors
    - Utilization

  - Discards
  - Packet drops
  - Interface resets
  - Speed and duplex

2.3 Given a scenario, use appropriate resources to support configuration management.

- Archives/backups
- Baselines
- On-boarding and off-boarding of mobile devices
- NAC
- Documentation
  - Network diagrams (logical/physical)
  - Asset management
  - IP address utilization
  - Vendor documentation
  - Internal operating procedures/policies/standards2.4 Given a scenario, troubleshoot common wireless problems.

2.4 Explain the importance of implementing network segmentation.

- SCADA systems/Industrial control systems
- Legacy systems
- Separate private/public networks
- Honeypot/honeynet
- Testing lab
- Load balancing
- Performance optimization
- Security
- Compliance

2.5 Given a scenario, install and apply patches and updates.

- OS updates
- Firmware updates
- Driver updates
- Feature changes/updates
- Major vs minor updates
- Vulnerability patches
- Upgrading vs downgrading
  - Configuration backup

2.6 Given a scenario, configure a switch using proper features.

- VLAN
  - Native VLAN/Default VLAN
  - VTP
- Spanning tree (802.1d)/rapid spanning tree (802.1w)
  - Flooding
  - Forwarding/blocking
  - Filtering
- Interface configuration

  - Trunking/802.1q
  - Tag vs untag VLANs
  - Port bonding (LACP)
  - Port mirroring (local vs remote)
  - Speed and duplexing
  - IP address assignment
  - VLAN assignment
- Default gateway
- PoE and PoE+ (802.3af, 802.3at)
- Switch management
  - User/passwords
  - AAA configuration
  - Console
  - Virtual terminals
  - In-band/Out-of-band management
- Managed vs unmanaged

2.7 Install and configure wireless LAN infrastructure and implement the appropriate technologies in support of wireless capable devices.

- Small office/home office wireless router
- Wireless access points
  - Device density
  - Roaming
  - Wireless controllers
    - VLAN pooling
    - LWAPP
- Wireless bridge
- Site surveys
  - Heat maps
- Frequencies
  - 2.4 Ghz
  - 5.0 Ghz
- Channels
- Goodput
- Connection types
  - 802.11a-ht
  - 802.11g-ht
- Antenna placement
- Antenna types
  - Omnidirectional
  - Unidirectional
- MIMO/MUMIMO
- Signal strength
  - Coverage
  - Differences between device antennas
- SSID broadcast

- Topologies
    - Adhoc
    - Mesh
    - Infrastructure
- Mobile devices
    - Cell phones
    - Laptops
    - Tablets
    - Gaming devices
    - Media devices

**

Practice Test Mode Section — Practice Test Questions without Answers for Network Operations

1. Your organization has contracted with a cloud-based company to provide access to an application via the cloud. However, application performance is extremely slow. Which of the following tools would you use to identify outages?

   A. Protocol analyzer

   B. Sniffer

   C. Environmental monitor

   D. Network analyzer

2. Which of the following will identify running services on a host?

   A. IDS

   B. IPS

   C. Port scanner

   D. Protocol analyzer

3. You are configuring an application that will automate monitoring of network devices. You need to ensure the application and the network devices use a secure protocol. Which of the following is the BEST choice?

   A. SNMPv3

   B. SMTP

   C. Syslog

   D. SIEM

4. You manage several Linux servers and a Windows server. What can you use to centrally manage the logs for these servers?
   A. Syslog
   B. Network sniffer
   C. SNMPv3
   D. Baselines

5. Attackers recently attacked your organization, resulting in a serious data breach. Security personnel want to consolidate and analyze security logs from multiple systems. Additionally, they want to add real-time monitoring capabilities so that they are alerted to problems sooner. Which of the following is the BEST choice to do so?
   A. SIEM
   B. SMTP
   C. SNMP
   D. SCADA

6. Management recently updated the security policy and added the following requirement: "All network infrastructure devices (such as routers, firewalls, and security appliances) must send system-level information to a single server." What should administrators implement to ensure they can review this information?
   A. An SSO server
   B. A RADIUS server
   C. An 802.1x server
   D. A syslog server

7. Several systems have rebooted themselves at about 1:00 p.m. several times in the past week. Which of the following tools would provide the BEST information to identify the problem?
   A. Syslog
   B. Environmental monitor
   C. Toner analyzer
   D. Certifier

8. Which of the following protocols would a network technician use to securely manage network devices such as routers and switches?
   A. SMTP
   B. SIEM
   C. NAC
   D. SNMPv3

9. What information would a port scanner help an attacker determine?
   A. Services or protocols on a system
   B. MAC filters on switch ports
   C. MAC filters on router ports
   D. Existence of a honeypot

10. Your organization is preparing to upgrade the network infrastructure to improve performance. Management wants to verify the upgrade has actually improved performance. What should you complete before the start of the upgrade to meet this need?
   A. Graphing
   B. Baseline
   C. Network diagram
   D. Change management paperwork

11. An 802.11 wireless device is configured to use channel 149. What frequency range is it MOST likely using?
    A. 2.4 GHz
    B. 5.0 GHz
    C. 2.0 GHz
    D. 5.4 GHz

12. After plugging in a twisted-pair patch cable, you notice the link light is not lit. After examining the cable, you see a space between the end of the wires and the edge of the RJ-45 connector. What is the likely problem?
    A. Split cable
    B. Bad connectors
    C. Cable placement
    D. Cross-talk

13. The auto sense feature of a switch has failed. What should be configured to bypass this feature?
    A. IP address, subnet mask, and default gateway
    B. Port speed and port duplex
    C. Port mirroring and a SPAN port
    D. RIP password

14. After turning off auto sense on a switch and manually configuring the ports to use 1 Gbps, two computers stop communicating through the switch. What is the MOST likely reason?
    A. One of the two devices is using autonegotiation.
    B. One of the two devices does not support 1,000 Mbps.

C. The two devices are using half-duplex modes.

D. One of the two devices has the wrong default gateway.

15. A helpdesk technician regularly issues laptops to employees when necessary. When doing so, the technician updates an online database that documents details about the laptop, such as the model and serial number. The technician also documents the name of the user receiving the laptop. What is the purpose of these steps?

    A. Asset management

    B. Baselines

    C. Onboarding

    D. Change management

16. You are responsible for ensuring that network diagrams are kept up to date. Of the following choices, what would you do?

    A. Update after NESSUS or NMAP scans.

    B. Update after IDS alerts.

    C. Update before new technicians are hired.

    D. Ensure the diagrams are updated when connections are modified.

17. You're trying to determine how many broadcast domains you have on the network. What type of diagram would be the easiest to use to identify the broadcast domains?

    A. Logical network diagram

    B. Physical network diagram

    C. Wiring schematic diagram

    D. Baseline diagram

18. A NAC solution examines system characteristics, such as the status of antivirus software, installed patches, the status of the firewall, and certain Windows Registry settings. Based on the results of this examination, the NAC solution either grants or denies access. Which of the following BEST identifies this process?

    A. Quarantine assessment

    B. Vulnerability scanning

    C. Asset management

    D. Posture assessment

19. Which of the following identifies a security benefit of network segmentation using VLANs?

    A. Fault tolerance

    B. Port mirroring

    C. Supports SCADA

    D. Security through isolation

20. Which of the following may contain a database without any real data to lure an attacker away from the live network?

    A. Port scanner

    B. Honeypot

    C. IDS

    D. IPS

21. Your network has recently been attacked. If the attacker returns, you want to tempt him with false data. What would you use?

    A. Honeypot

    B. IDS

C. IPS

D. Port scanner

22. After recently updating a server with a new service pack, a server-based application no longer operates properly. Which of the following can prevent a similar incident in the future?

    A. Use virtualization and take snapshots before deploying updates.

    B. Roll back the drivers installed with the service pack.

    C. Implement automatic updates.

    D. Test updates on a test server.

23. Administrators are connecting to a remote server using an encrypted tunnel. However, a recent exploit allows attackers to view data within the encrypted tunnel. Which of the following is the MOST likely fix for this problem?

    A. Connect using Telnet.

    B. Install new drivers.

    C. Block port 80.

    D. Install recommended updates.

24. You are tasked with implementing an approved change to a server. Users have been notified that there will be an outage of approximately 1 hour long, which is the approved maintenance window. What should you do if you are unable to complete the change within the allotted time?

    A. Roll back the drivers.

    B. Test the change on a test server.

    C. Roll back the changes.

    D. Extend the maintenance window.

25. After a recent software update, a user is no longer able to access a 3D printer through a company-created application. After investigation, you discover that the update installed incompatible drivers on the user's system. Of the following choices, what will MOST likely restore the user's system capabilities?

    A. Install a new operating system on the user's system.

    B. Roll back the drivers.

    C. Test the drivers on a test system.

    D. Replace the printer.

26. Software developers are working on a major update to an e-commerce web application. They need to complete these changes as quickly as possible. However, management wants to ensure the changes do not cause outages on the production server. Which of the following provides the BEST solution?

    A. Ensure the developers only update the server in the DMZ.

    B. Create a test environment and test the updates on the test environment.

    C. Test the update on the production server.

    D. Request a maintenance window to install the update.

27. You discover that a web-based application used by employees is not up to date and has a potential security flaw. You want to update this to the current version. What should you do first?

    A. Create a test environment and test the updates on the test environment.

    B. Deploy the update as soon as possible.

    C. Test the update on the web-based application.

    D. Verify the update has been deployed.

28. Your organization hired external security professionals to test the security of an e-commerce web application hosted on a web server. After performing a penetration test, they discover that they can access sensitive data via the server. Which of the following is the MOST likely solution to resolve this issue?

    A. Install VTP on the web server.

    B. Block access to the web server via port 80.

    C. Block access to the web server via port 443.

    D. Install current patches onto the web server.

29. Many computers in your organization have recently been infected by malware. A security team discovered these systems were using older application versions that were vulnerable to known attacks. Which of the following would the security team MOST likely recommend to mitigate this problem?

    A. Enable host-based firewalls.

    B. Provide training to users.

    C. Implement a patch management program.

    D. Perform periodic vulnerability scans.

30. A large network has VLANs configured on several switches. You want to reduce the administration related to these switches. What can you use?

    A. VTP

    B. NAT

    C. PAT

    D. Virtual PBX

31. What does 802.3af define?

    A. LACP

    B. PoE

    C. VPN

    D. Spanning tree

32. Which of the following protocols supports the use of two or more links as a single link?

    A. LACP

    B. RSTP

    C. VTP

    D. PoE+

33. Which of the following concepts supports the use of two or more links as a single link?

    A. Port mirroring

    B. Port scanning

    C. Port security

    D. Port bonding

34. Network administrators connect to switches remotely. Occasionally, two administrators attempt to connect to the same switch remotely, but the switch blocks the second connection until the first connection is terminated. What change will allow both administrators to connect simultaneously?

    A. Implement port mirroring on the switch.

    B. Increase the number of virtual terminals available on the switch.

    C. Add an additional VLAN on the switch.

    D. Implement VTP.

35. You need to install an access point in a location that doesn't have a power source. What can you use?
    A. QoS
    B. PoE
    C. Half-duplex
    D. Full-duplex

36. What standard describes PoE?
    A. 802.3af
    B. 802.11i
    C. 802.1q
    D. 802.1x

37. A technician plugged a cable into two ports on a switch and it didn't cause any problems. The technician then plugged the same cable into a second switch and all users connected to the switch lost connectivity. What explains this behavior?
    A. The first switch had STP installed.
    B. The second switch had STP installed.
    C. The first switch is using PoE.
    D. The second switch is using PoE.

38. Network administrators have configured VLANs within your network. They want switches to share VLAN information with other switches in the network automatically. Which of the following is the BEST choice?
    A. VTP
    B. PoE
    C. VPN
    D. LACP

39. You need to extend your network to a neighboring building. You decide to connect them using a wireless solution supporting 802.11ac. What type of antenna will provide the BEST performance?

    A. Omnidirectional

    B. Isotropic

    C. Dipole

    D. Yagi

40. You are configuring a wireless router for a business owner. The owner wants to secure access to his wireless network. Which of the following may help?

    A. Enable the SSID broadcast.

    B. Disable the SSID broadcast.

    C. Ensure the footprint is as large as possible.

    D. Increase the power output of the antenna.

41. You are designing a wireless network for a small business. You recommend 802.11n due to its high speed. Which of the following allows 802.11n to have significantly higher speeds than its predecessors?

    A. Yagi antenna

    B. Dipole antenna

    C. MIMO antenna type

    D. Isotropic antenna

42. A business owner is configuring a wireless network at his business location. He wants to make it more difficult to discover the wireless network. What can he do?

    A. Enable WPA2.

    B. Disable SSID broadcasting.

    C. Use 802.11n.

    D. Use channel 11.

Review Mode Section — Practice Test Questions with Answers for Network Operations

Objective: 2.1 Given a scenario, use appropriate monitoring tools.

1. Your organization has contracted with a cloud-based company to provide access to an application via the cloud. However, application performance is extremely slow. Which of the following tools would you use to identify outages?
   A. Protocol analyzer
   B. Sniffer
   C. Environmental monitor
   D. Network analyzer

Answer: **D** is correct. A network analyzer can measure the performance of a network, including identifying outages and top talkers (users generating the most traffic) and protocols using the most bandwidth.

A and B are incorrect. A protocol analyzer (also called a sniffer) can capture and analyze traffic, but isn't as well suited for identifying outages as a protocol analyzer is for measuring the application performance.
C is incorrect. An environmental monitor records environmental conditions such as temperature and humidity. It does not measure network application performance.

2. Which of the following will identify running services on a host?
   A. IDS
   B. IPS

C. Port scanner

D. Protocol analyzer

Answer: **C** is correct. A port scanner detects open ports, and, based on the open ports, it can identify services running on a host system. For example, if port 80 is open, it indicates that the service listening for Hypertext Transfer Protocol (HTTP) requests is running.

A is incorrect. An intrusion detection system (IDS) will detect attacks.
B is incorrect. An intrusion prevention system (IPS) will detect and block attacks.
D is incorrect. A protocol analyzer (also called a sniffer) can capture and analyze packets sent over a network.

3. You are configuring an application that will automate monitoring of network devices. You need to ensure the application and the network devices use a secure protocol. Which of the following is the BEST choice?

    A. SNMPv3

    B. SMTP

    C. Syslog

    D. SIEM

Answer: **A** is correct. Simple Network Management Protocol version 3 (SNMPv3) is a secure protocol used to monitor and remotely monitor network devices and is the best choice.

B is incorrect. Simple Mail Transfer Protocol (SMTP) is used for sending email, not monitoring network devices.

C is incorrect. Syslog can be used to centrally manage logging from multiple devices, including multiple servers, but SNMPv3 is a better choice when monitoring network devices.
D is incorrect. A Security Information and Event Management (SIEM) system collects events in real time and raises alerts. It is not a protocol used to manage network devices.

4. You manage several Linux servers and a Windows server. What can you use to centrally manage the logs for these servers?
   A. Syslog
   B. Network sniffer
   C. SNMPv3
   D. Baselines

Answer: **A** is correct. Syslog can be used to centrally manage logging from multiple devices, including multiple servers. It originated on Unix systems and is currently standardized as a generic logging protocol in RFC 5424.

B is incorrect. A network sniffer (also known as a protocol analyzer) can be used to capture and analyze traffic sent over a network, but it is not used to centrally manage logs.
C is incorrect. Simple Network Management Protocol version 3 (SNMPv3) is a protocol used for managing devices. It is the most secure compared with SNMP and SNMPv2, but it is not used to manage server logs.
D is incorrect. Baselines are starting points and are often used as a part of configuration management, but they are not used to centrally manage logs.

5. Attackers recently attacked your organization, resulting in a serious data breach. Security personnel want to consolidate and analyze security logs from multiple systems. Additionally, they want to add real-time monitoring capabilities so that they are alerted to problems sooner. Which of the following is the BEST choice to do so?
    A. SIEM
    B. SMTP
    C. SNMP
    D. SCADA

Answer: **A** is correct. A Security Information and Event Management (SIEM) system can aggregate logs collected from multiple systems. Additionally, it focuses on real-time events and can provide alerts when events of interest occur.

B is incorrect. Simple Mail Transfer Protocol (SMTP) is used to send email and would not be useful in this scenario.
C is incorrect. Simple Network Management Protocol (SNMP) is used to manage and monitor network devices, such as routers or switches.
D is incorrect. A Supervisory Control and Data Acquisition (SCADA) system is used for industrial control systems. SCADA systems are typically isolated or segmented away from the network and wouldn't be used to provide real-time monitoring of the network.

6. Management recently updated the security policy and added the following requirement: "All network infrastructure devices (such as routers, firewalls, and security appliances) must send system-level information to a single server." What should administrators implement to ensure they can review this information?

A. An SSO server

B. A RADIUS server

C. An 802.1x server

D. A syslog server

Answer: **D** is correct. Syslog is a message-logging standard. A syslog server is a centralized server that can collect logs from multiple devices, and it includes the ability to filter and analyze the entries.

A is incorrect. Single sign-on (SSO) allows users to log on once and be able to access multiple resources without logging on again. It is unrelated to logging.

B is incorrect. A Remote Authentication Dial-In User Service (RADIUS) provides a centralized authentication service, and it isn't used to collect logs from network devices.

C is incorrect. RADIUS is often used as an 802.1x server, and it can prevent users from accessing a network until they log on. 802.1x does not collect logs from network devices.

7. Several systems have rebooted themselves at about 1:00 p.m. several times in the past week. Which of the following tools would provide the BEST information to identify the problem?

   A. Syslog

   B. Environmental monitor

   C. Toner analyzer

   D. Certifier

Answer: **B** is correct. An environmental monitor logs environmental conditions such as temperature and humidity regularly. These logs can be reviewed to identify the conditions that may have resulted in the reboots. In this case, it could be that the AC was overworked at midday and systems rebooted due to high temperatures. Although not given as a possible answer, power monitoring tools would be the best choice.

A is incorrect. A syslog would record reboots, but it isn't the best choice for monitoring the environment.
C is incorrect. A protocol analyzer (also called a sniffer) can capture packets, analyze packets, and can help detect a potential attack, but there's no such thing as a toner analyzer.
D is incorrect. A certifier is used to test and verify cables.

8. Which of the following protocols would a network technician use to securely manage network devices such as routers and switches?
   A. SMTP
   B. SIEM
   C. NAC
   D. SNMPv3

Answer: **D** is correct. Network technicians commonly use Simple Network Management Protocol version 3 (SNMPv3) for managing network devices. SNMPv3 is more secure than SNMP and SNMPv2.

A is incorrect. Simple Mail Transfer Protocol (SMTP) is used to send email, not manage devices.
B is incorrect. A Security Information and Event Management (SIEM) system collects events in real time and raises alerts, but it is not used to manage network devices.

C is incorrect. A network access control (NAC) system monitors systems for predefined health status and prevents unhealthy systems from accessing the network.

9. What information would a port scanner help an attacker determine?
   A. Services or protocols on a system
   B. MAC filters on switch ports
   C. MAC filters on router ports
   D. Existence of a honeypot

Answer: **A** is correct. A port scanner identifies open ports and, if a well-known port is open, it indicates the related service or protocol is likely running or enabled. For example, if port 25 is open, it indicates Simple Mail Transfer Protocol (SMTP) is being used and related email services will likely be running on a system.

B and C are incorrect. Media access control (MAC) address filters can restrict access to routers and switches based on a client's MAC address, but a port scanner cannot detect MAC filters.
D is incorrect. A honeypot is a system configured to look like an attractive target to lure attackers away from a live network.

Objective: 2.2 Given a scenario, analyze metrics and reports from monitoring and tracking performance tools.

10. Your organization is preparing to upgrade the network infrastructure to improve performance. Management wants to verify the upgrade has actually improved performance. What should you complete before the start of the upgrade to meet this need?

A. Graphing

B. Baseline

C. Network diagram

D. Change management paperwork

Answer: **B** is correct. By capturing a baseline of performance metrics before the upgrade, you can use it for comparisons after the test.

A is incorrect. Although you might be able to graph your baseline data, graphing by itself doesn't indicate what data you are graphing.
C is incorrect. A network diagram would show the layout of the network and it should already exist for the current layout. Additionally, it will not allow you to determine if the upgrade improved performance.
D is incorrect. Although change management paperwork may be required (based on the organization's change management process), this paperwork is not likely to capture metrics for performance comparisons.

11. An 802.11 wireless device is configured to use channel 149. What frequency range is it MOST likely using?

    A. 2.4 GHz

    B. 5.0 GHz

    C. 2.0 GHz

    D. 5.4 GHz

Answer: **B** is correct. It is most likely using the 5.0-GHz frequency range. The 5.0-GHz frequency range includes channels 7 to 196. These channels are not available in all countries.

A is incorrect. The 2.4-GHz range includes a maximum of 14 channels.

C and D are incorrect. 2.0 GHz and 5.4 GHz are not valid frequency ranges for 802.11 wireless devices.

12. After plugging in a twisted-pair patch cable, you notice the link light is not lit. After examining the cable, you see a space between the end of the wires and the edge of the RJ-45 connector. What is the likely problem?
    A. Split cable
    B. Bad connectors
    C. Cable placement
    D. Cross-talk

Answer: **B** is correct. The link light is likely not lit due to a bad connector. There should not be a visible space between the end of the copper wire and the edge of the RJ-45 connector.

A is incorrect. A split cable has a break in it within the cable, not at the connector. For example, if a cable is on the floor and has been stepped on or run over by a chair, it can result in a split cable.
C is incorrect. Cable placement refers to where the cable is placed, which can cause problems. For example, running cables through a power junction box or over a fluorescent light fixture can result in electromagnetic interference (EMI) problems. Running cable along a floor where it can be a trip hazard or stepped on is another example of incorrect cable placement.
D is incorrect. Cross-talk refers to signals crossing from one cable to another. Removing the twists in a cable can result in cross-talk.

13. The auto sense feature of a switch has failed. What should be configured to bypass this feature?

A. IP address, subnet mask, and default gateway

B. Port speed and port duplex

C. Port mirroring and a SPAN port

D. RIP password

Answer: **B** is correct. When auto sense (also called autonegotiation) is working, the port speed and port duplex settings are automatically configured to the fastest configuration supported by both devices in the connection. If auto sense fails, these settings should be configured manually.

A is incorrect. The IP address, subnet mask, and default gateway settings can be automatically configured by Dynamic Host Configuration Protocol (DHCP), and are not assigned to ports on a switch.
C is incorrect. Port mirroring is used to direct a copy of all traffic into a switch out a specific port used for mirroring. This is also called the Switched Port Analyzer (SPAN) port on Cisco switches.
D is incorrect. Routing Information Protocol (RIP) is used by routers to share information with other routers. It is not used by switches.

14. After turning off auto sense on a switch and manually configuring the ports to use 1 Gbps, two computers stop communicating through the switch. What is the MOST likely reason?

A. One of the two devices is using autonegotiation.

B. One of the two devices does not support 1,000 Mbps.

C. The two devices are using half-duplex modes.

D. One of the two devices has the wrong default gateway.

Answer: **B** is correct. The most likely reason is that the network interface cards (NICs) on these two computers do not support 1 Gbps (1,000 Mbps), or that they are manually set to a different speed.

A is incorrect. Autonegotiation is the same as auto sense and it allows the computers to automatically sense the speed and mode of the other device and automatically configure the NIC to match the other device. Using autonegotiation will not cause the devices to stop working.
C is incorrect. If both devices are using half-duplex (not common for 1 Gbps), they will operate using the slower half-duplex mode, but they will not stop communicating. In half-duplex mode, data can be sent or received over a cable but not at the same time, whereas in full-duplex mode, data can be sent and received at the same time.
D is incorrect. The default gateway is the address of an interface on the near side of a router, which would be after the switch. The wrong default gateway would prevent the computers from communicating outside the network through a router, but wouldn't affect communication through the switch.

Objective: 2.3 Given a scenario, use appropriate resources to support configuration management.

15. A helpdesk technician regularly issues laptops to employees when necessary. When doing so, the technician updates an online database that documents details about the laptop, such as the model and serial number. The technician also documents the name of the user receiving the laptop. What is the purpose of these steps?
    A. Asset management
    B. Baselines

C. Onboarding

D. Change management

Answer: **A** is correct. Asset management steps include documenting the location of valuable assets. This is especially useful when issuing laptops and other mobile devices to users.

B is incorrect. Baselines are starting points, such as a baseline operating system image, or a baseline of performance metrics, but modifying an online database for equipment is not a baseline.

C is incorrect. Onboarding refers to the procedures used to add users to a network, such as for new employees or authorized third-party vendors.

D is incorrect. Change management ensures that system configuration changes don't result in unintended outages.

16. You are responsible for ensuring that network diagrams are kept up to date. Of the following choices, what would you do?

    A. Update after NESSUS or NMAP scans.

    B. Update after IDS alerts.

    C. Update before new technicians are hired.

    D. Ensure the diagrams are updated when connections are modified.

Answer: **D** is correct. Network diagrams should be updated when the environment changes to keep them up to date. This includes events when connections are modified or any other components on the network diagram are modified.

A is incorrect. NESSUS and NMAP are two vulnerability scanners used to identify vulnerabilities in a network. However, just doing a scan doesn't require updating documentation unless the environment has changed.
B is incorrect. An intrusion detection system (IDS) alert indicates a possible intrusion, but this does not require updating documentation.
C is incorrect. Up-to-date documentation is useful for new technicians, but it also helps anyone troubleshooting a network, so it should be done whenever the environment changes.

17. You're trying to determine how many broadcast domains you have on the network. What type of diagram would be the easiest to use to identify the broadcast domains?
    A. Logical network diagram
    B. Physical network diagram
    C. Wiring schematic diagram
    D. Baseline diagram

Answer: **A** is correct. A logical network diagram would identify broadcast domains typically by identifying subnets or network addresses. For example, a logical network diagram could show two networks using 192.168.1.0/24 and 192.168.2.0/24 and each of these networks would be a broadcast domain. A logical network diagram shows some devices, but not necessarily all the devices. For example, two subnets could be separated by a router and the router would be shown. On the other hand, devices in each subnet would connect to a switch; however, the switch might not be shown on the logical network diagram, but instead only implied. The term *network map* is used interchangeably with both *logical network diagram* and *physical network diagram*.

B is incorrect. A physical network diagram would show devices in a network and cables used to connect them. Although you might be able to identify the number of broadcast domains by looking at the routers and switches, this might give an incorrect result if any of the switches are used for virtual local area networks (VLANs).
C is incorrect. A wiring schematic diagram (sometimes called a wire scheme) shows the pinouts for cables.
D is incorrect. A baseline is a starting point and isn't a type of diagram. It can be a configuration baseline, a security baseline for a computer, or a performance baseline for a system or a network.

18. A NAC solution examines system characteristics, such as the status of antivirus software, installed patches, the status of the firewall, and certain Windows Registry settings. Based on the results of this examination, the NAC solution either grants or denies access. Which of the following BEST identifies this process?
    - A. Quarantine assessment
    - B. Vulnerability scanning
    - C. Asset management
    - D. Posture assessment

Answer: **D**. A network access control (NAC) posture assessment assesses the security posture of a system. This includes the status of antivirus software, installed patches, the status of the firewall, certain Windows Registry settings, and more.

A is incorrect. Clients that don't pass the posture assessment are typically placed in a quarantine network until they meet the NAC requirements. However, NAC doesn't use the term quarantine assessment.

B is incorrect. Vulnerability scanning can identify vulnerabilities in systems, but it only provides a report. A vulnerability scan cannot grant or deny access to a network.
C is incorrect. Assess management attempts to document the location of valuable assets, but it does not grant or deny access to a network.

Objective: 2.4 Explain the importance of implementing network segmentation.

19. Which of the following identifies a security benefit of network segmentation using VLANs?
    A. Fault tolerance
    B. Port mirroring
    C. Supports SCADA
    D. Security through isolation

Answer: **D** is correct. Virtual local area networks (VLANs) provide network segmentation and increase security by isolating the network. Routers also provide security through isolation because they segment networks.

A is incorrect. VLANs do not provide fault tolerance or redundancy.
B is incorrect. Switches support port mirroring (redirecting a copy of all traffic to a monitoring port), but this is not a security benefit of VLANs.
C is incorrect. A Supervisory Control and Data Acquisition (SCADA) system is used for industrial control systems and SCADA systems benefit from network segmentation. However, supporting SCADA is not a security benefit of network segmentation using VLANs.

20. Which of the following may contain a database without any real data to lure an attacker away from the live network?

    A. Port scanner

    B. Honeypot

    C. IDS

    D. IPS

Answer: **B** is correct. A honeypot is a single computer that includes data that may look valuable to an attacker but does not have anything of value. The goal of a honeypot is to lure an attacker away from a live network. Security administrators use it to observe an attacker's methods.

A is incorrect. A port scanner can scan a system for open ports to determine protocols or services in use.

C is incorrect. An intrusion detection system (IDS) attempts to detect and respond to attacks.

D is incorrect. An intrusion prevention system (IPS) is similar to an IDS, but it can block malicious activity and prevent it from reaching the network, whereas an IDS detects the activity after it occurs.

21. Your network has recently been attacked. If the attacker returns, you want to tempt him with false data. What would you use?

    A. Honeypot

    B. IDS

    C. IPS

    D. Port scanner

Answer: **A** is correct. A honeypot is a server that includes false data (such as a database with bogus data) and is used to tempt an attacker. While attackers are in the honeypot, they are not in the live network and administrators can safely observe their activity.

B is incorrect. An intrusion detection system (IDS) can detect an attack, but it does not include false data.
C is incorrect. An intrusion prevention system (IPS) can detect and prevent an attack, but it does not include false data.
D is incorrect. A port scanner scans a system for open ports to identify services or protocols that are likely running based on open ports, but it does not include false data.

Objective: 2.5 Given a scenario, install and apply patches and updates.

22. After recently updating a server with a new service pack, a server-based application no longer operates properly. Which of the following can prevent a similar incident in the future?
    A. Use virtualization and take snapshots before deploying updates.
    B. Roll back the drivers installed with the service pack.
    C. Implement automatic updates.
    D. Test updates on a test server.

Answer: **D** is correct. Testing updates on a test server before deploying them to live production servers will prevent incidents such as this. A test server will prevent similar incidents in the future.

A is incorrect. Virtualization and snapshots will limit the outage, but won't prevent the outage. By taking a snapshot before the update, administrators can revert the virtual machine to the state it was in before the update.

B is incorrect. Rolling back drivers might restore the system, but it will not prevent similar incidents in the future.
C is incorrect. Automatic updates will deploy the updates without testing them, so they will not prevent the problem described in the scenario.

23. Administrators are connecting to a remote server using an encrypted tunnel. However, a recent exploit allows attackers to view data within the encrypted tunnel. Which of the following is the MOST likely fix for this problem?
    A. Connect using Telnet.
    B. Install new drivers.
    C. Block port 80.
    D. Install recommended updates.

Answer: **D** is correct. The most likely fix of the answers given is to install recommended updates. Vendors release updates to resolve problems with exploits.

A is incorrect. Telnet is not a suitable alternative because it sends data across a network in cleartext.
B is incorrect. Drivers are used for hardware issues, such as accessing external peripherals. It's unlikely that installing new drivers will resolve problems with an exploit related to a software encrypted tunnel.
C is incorrect. Hypertext Transfer Protocol (HTTP) uses port 80, but it doesn't use an encrypted tunnel, so it wouldn't apply in this example.

24. You are tasked with implementing an approved change to a server. Users have been notified that there will be an outage of approximately 1 hour long, which is the approved maintenance window. What should you do if you are unable to complete the change within the allotted time?
    A. Roll back the drivers.
    B. Test the change on a test server.
    C. Roll back the changes.
    D. Extend the maintenance window.

Answer: **C** is correct. Approved changes should include a rollback procedure to implement if it isn't possible to implement the changes within the allotted time.

A is incorrect. If the change updated drivers, then you would roll back the drivers. However, the scenario didn't indicate what would be changed.
B is incorrect. Testing the change on a test server is appropriate. However, that would be done before approving the change.
D is incorrect. It is not appropriate to extend an approved maintenance window beyond the allotted time.

25. After a recent software update, a user is no longer able to access a 3D printer through a company-created application. After investigation, you discover that the update installed incompatible drivers on the user's system. Of the following choices, what will MOST likely restore the user's system capabilities?
    A. Install a new operating system on the user's system.
    B. Roll back the drivers.
    C. Test the drivers on a test system.
    D. Replace the printer.

Answer: **B** is correct. Because the update installed incompatible drivers on the user's system, the solution is to roll back the drivers to the previous version.

A is incorrect. It is not necessary to install a new operating system.
C is incorrect. Testing the drivers on a test system will prevent a similar incident, but won't restore the system affected in this scenario.
D is incorrect. If the printer worked before an update, the update should be rolled back rather than purchasing a new printer.

26. Software developers are working on a major update to an e-commerce web application. They need to complete these changes as quickly as possible. However, management wants to ensure the changes do not cause outages on the production server. Which of the following provides the BEST solution?
    A. Ensure the developers only update the server in the DMZ.
    B. Create a test environment and test the updates on the test environment.
    C. Test the update on the production server.
    D. Request a maintenance window to install the update.

Answer: **B** is correct. Testing modifications on a test server before deploying them to a live production server will prevent outages on the production server. This includes when changes must be completed as quickly as possible.

A is incorrect. The live production server is very likely in the demilitarized zone (DMZ), so updating that server will not mitigate potential outages.
C is incorrect. Testing the update on the production system might cause an outage.

D is incorrect. It's appropriate to request a maintenance window, but only after testing the update.

27. You discover that a web-based application used by employees is not up to date and has a potential security flaw. You want to update this to the current version. What should you do first?
    A. Create a test environment and test the updates on the test environment.
    B. Deploy the update as soon as possible.
    C. Test the update on the web-based application.
    D. Verify the update has been deployed.

Answer: **A** is correct. You should test updates in a test environment to prevent potential outages on the live production server.

B is incorrect. You should test the update before deploying it.
C is incorrect. You should not test the update on the web-based application because it is the production system.
D is incorrect. You would verify the update has been deployed, after you've tested it and deployed it.

28. Your organization hired external security professionals to test the security of an e-commerce web application hosted on a web server. After performing a penetration test, they discover that they can access sensitive data via the server. Which of the following is the MOST likely solution to resolve this issue?
    A. Install VTP on the web server.
    B. Block access to the web server via port 80.
    C. Block access to the web server via port 443.
    D. Install current patches onto the web server.

Answer: **D** is correct. The most likely solution of those given is to install current patches on the web server. If testers can access sensitive data via the server, it indicates a vulnerability and most vulnerabilities can be mitigated with an update or patch.

A is incorrect. VLAN Trunk Protocol (VTP) allows switches to share virtual local area network (VLAN) information.
B and C are incorrect. An e-commerce web application most likely uses Hypertext Transfer Protocol (HTTP) and HTTP Secure (HTTPS) over ports 80 and 443, respectively, so these ports shouldn't be blocked.

29. Many computers in your organization have recently been infected by malware. A security team discovered these systems were using older application versions that were vulnerable to known attacks. Which of the following would the security team MOST likely recommend to mitigate this problem?
    A. Enable host-based firewalls.
    B. Provide training to users.
    C. Implement a patch management program.
    D. Perform periodic vulnerability scans.

Answer: **C** is correct. A patch management program can help ensure systems are up to date with current versions of applications.

A is incorrect. A host-based firewall will not protect against unpatched applications.
B is incorrect. Training is useful, but it will not protect against out-of-date applications.
D is incorrect. Vulnerability scans can help discover unpatched systems, but a patch management program will ensure they are patched.

Objective: 2.6 Given a scenario, configure a switch using proper features.

30. A large network has VLANs configured on several switches. You want to reduce the administration related to these switches. What can you use?

    A. VTP

    B. NAT

    C. PAT

    D. Virtual PBX

Answer: **A** is correct. VLAN Trunk Protocol (VTP) will send virtual local area network (VLAN) definitions to all switches in a VTP domain, reducing the administration required to manage these switches. VTP is proprietary to Cisco.

B and C are incorrect. Network Address Translation (NAT) and Port Address Translation (PAT) translate public and private IP addresses and allow internal computers to share a common public IP address.
D is incorrect. A virtual private branch exchange (PBX) allows customers to lease access to a PBX service for professional telephone services without purchasing and managing the hardware for a traditional PBX.

31. What does 802.3af define?

    A. LACP

    B. PoE

    C. VPN

    D. Spanning tree

Answer: **B** is correct. The 802.3af protocol describes Power over Ethernet (PoE). PoE provides power to devices over Ethernet cable. 802.3at is an upgrade to PoE known as Power over Ethernet Plus (PoE plus).

A is incorrect. 802.3ad defines the Link Aggregation Control Protocol (LACP), which supports bundling multiple links together (also called port bonding).
C is incorrect. A virtual private network (VPN) provides private access to a public network, but it is not defined by a single 802.3 standard.
D is incorrect. 802.1d defines Spanning Tree Protocol (STP) and 802.1w defines Rapid Spanning Tree Protocol (RSTP).

32. Which of the following protocols supports the use of two or more links as a single link?
    A. LACP
    B. RSTP
    C. VTP
    D. PoE+

Answer: **A** is correct. Link Aggregation Control Protocol (LACP) supports port bonding. Port bonding bundles multiple ports together as a single link. 802.3ad defines LACP.

B is incorrect. Rapid Spanning Tree Protocol (RSTP) is an improvement over Spanning Tree Protocol (STP), and both help prevent bridge loops.
C is incorrect. The VLAN Trunk Protocol (VTP) allows switches to share virtual local area network (VLAN) information.

D is incorrect. Power over Ethernet Plus (PoE plus) is an improvement over Power over Ethernet (PoE), and it provides power to devices over Ethernet cable.

33. Which of the following concepts supports the use of two or more links as a single link?
    A. Port mirroring
    B. Port scanning
    C. Port security
    D. Port bonding

Answer: **D** is correct. Port bonding bundles multiple ports together as a single link. 802.3ad defines Link Aggregation Control Protocol (LACP), which supports port bonding.

A is incorrect. Port mirroring redirects a copy of all traffic to a monitoring port, but it doesn't bundle links together.
B is incorrect. Port scanning refers to scanning a system to identify open ports and services running on a system.
C is incorrect. Port security refers to steps you'd take to prevent unauthorized devices from connecting to a switch.

34. Network administrators connect to switches remotely. Occasionally, two administrators attempt to connect to the same switch remotely, but the switch blocks the second connection until the first connection is terminated. What change will allow both administrators to connect simultaneously?
    A. Implement port mirroring on the switch.
    B. Increase the number of virtual terminals available on the switch.

C. Add an additional VLAN on the switch.

D. Implement VTP.

Answer: **B** is correct. Adding additional virtual terminals to the switch will allow additional connections.

A is incorrect. Port mirroring redirects a copy of all traffic to a monitoring port, but it doesn't increase the number of virtual terminals.
C is incorrect. A virtual local area network (VLAN) is unrelated to virtual terminals.
D is incorrect. The VLAN Trunk Protocol (VTP) allows switches to share VLAN information, but it doesn't provide additional virtual terminals.

35. You need to install an access point in a location that doesn't have a power source. What can you use?

    A. QoS

    B. PoE

    C. Half-duplex

    D. Full-duplex

Answer: **B** is correct. Power over Ethernet (PoE) is a standard that provides power over an Ethernet cable (such as CAT5 or CAT6 cable) in addition to the data. It is defined in 802.3af.

A is incorrect. Quality of service (QoS) often refers to managing the problems related to Voice over IP (VoIP) traffic, but is not related to power.
C is incorrect. Half-duplex indicates that data can be sent or received on the same cable, but not at the same time. It is not related to a power source for a wireless access point (WAP).

D is incorrect. Full-duplex indicates the data can be sent and received on the same cable at the same time. It is not related to a power source for a WAP.

36. What standard describes PoE?

    A. 802.3af

    B. 802.11i

    C. 802.1q

    D. 802.1x

Answer: **A** is correct. 802.3af describes Power over Ethernet, which provides power over an Ethernet cable (such as Category 6 cable) to a device.

B is incorrect. 802.11i describes Wi-Fi Protected Access II (WPA2), which supersedes Wired Equivalent Privacy (WEP).
C is incorrect. 802.1q defines virtual local area networks (VLANs).
D is incorrect. 802.1x is used for port authentication. As an example, WPA2-Enterprise can use Remote Authentication Dial-In User Service (RADIUS) as an 802.1x authentication server.

37. A technician plugged a cable into two ports on a switch and it didn't cause any problems. The technician then plugged the same cable into a second switch and all users connected to the switch lost connectivity. What explains this behavior?

    A. The first switch had STP installed.

    B. The second switch had STP installed.

    C. The first switch is using PoE.

    D. The second switch is using PoE.

Answer: **A** is correct. Spanning Tree Protocol (STP) or Rapid STP (RSTP) will stop a switching loop from causing a broadcast storm when two ports are connected with a cable. If STP was installed on the first switch, the cable doesn't cause problems. The second switch isn't protected with STP, so the cable caused a broadcast storm, blocking user connectivity.

B is incorrect. Without STP or RSTP installed on the switch, the broadcast storm can block all connectivity for users.
C and D are incorrect. Power over Ethernet (PoE) allows network devices to receive power over Ethernet cables, but it is unrelated to a switching loop.

38. Network administrators have configured VLANs within your network. They want switches to share VLAN information with other switches in the network automatically. Which of the following is the BEST choice?

    A. VTP
    B. PoE
    C. VPN
    D. LACP

Answer: **A** is correct. The VLAN Trunk Protocol (VTP) allows switches to share virtual local area network (VLAN) information.

B is incorrect. The 802.3af protocol describes Power over Ethernet (PoE) and provides power to devices over the Ethernet cable. 802.3at is an upgrade known as Power over Ethernet Plus (PoE plus).
C is incorrect. A virtual private network (VPN) provides private access to a public network. VPNs are unrelated to VLANs.

D is incorrect. Link Aggregation Control Protocol (LACP) bundles multiple ports together as a single link (also called port bonding).

Objective: 2.7 Install and configure wireless LAN infrastructure and implement the appropriate technologies in support of wireless capable devices.

39. You need to extend your network to a neighboring building. You decide to connect them using a wireless solution supporting 802.11ac. What type of antenna will provide the BEST performance?
    A. Omnidirectional
    B. Isotropic
    C. Dipole
    D. Yagi

Answer: **D** is correct. A Yagi antenna is a common type of directional antenna and this solution requires a directional antenna.

A is incorrect. An omnidirectional antenna doesn't provide the same gain between two buildings as a directional antenna.
B is incorrect. An isotropic antenna is a theoretical concept where an antenna has a perfect three-dimensional omnidirectional radiation pattern of 360 degrees vertically and horizontally.
C is incorrect. A dipole antenna is an omnidirectional antenna.

40. You are configuring a wireless router for a business owner. The owner wants to secure access to his wireless network. Which of the following may help?
    A. Enable the SSID broadcast.
    B. Disable the SSID broadcast.

C. Ensure the footprint is as large as possible.

D. Increase the power output of the antenna.

Answer: **B** is correct. The service set identifier (SSID) is the network name, and disabling SSID broadcast limits the view of the wireless network. Although this is thought by some to provide security, it is easily beaten by an attacker with a little bit of knowledge, but it is still the best choice of those given.

A is incorrect. Enabling the SSID doesn't contribute to security, but it does make the wireless network easy to use.
C is incorrect. A large footprint indicates the wireless network will broadcast farther away. This makes it easier for a war driver to capture the signal and does not contribute to security, but a smaller footprint may be beneficial.
D is incorrect. Increasing the power output of the antenna increases the footprint and does not contribute to security. On the other hand, decreasing the power output would create a smaller footprint and may be beneficial.

41. You are designing a wireless network for a small business. You recommend 802.11n due to its high speed. Which of the following allows 802.11n to have significantly higher speeds than its predecessors?

A. Yagi antenna

B. Dipole antenna

C. MIMO antenna type

D. Isotropic antenna

Answer: **C** is correct. 802.11n supports multiple-input, multiple-output (MIMO) antenna. This is a major reason why 802.11n supports higher speeds.

A is incorrect. A Yagi antenna is a common type of directional antenna, but a directional antenna doesn't contribute to higher speeds with 802.11n.
B is incorrect. A dipole antenna is an omnidirectional antenna, but a directional antenna doesn't contribute to higher speeds with 802.11n.
D is incorrect. An isotropic antenna is a theoretical concept where an antenna has a perfect three-dimensional omnidirectional radiation pattern of 360 degrees vertically and horizontally, but this doesn't contribute to higher speeds with 802.11n.

42. A business owner is configuring a wireless network at his business location. He wants to make it more difficult to discover the wireless network. What can he do?
    - A. Enable WPA2.
    - B. Disable SSID broadcasting.
    - C. Use 802.11n.
    - D. Use channel 11.

Answer: **B** is correct. Disabling service set identifier (SSID) broadcasting can make it more difficult to discover a wireless network. The SSID is still included in packets sent over the air, so a dedicated attacker can still discover it, but it makes it more difficult for casual users to discover it.

A is incorrect. Wi-Fi Protected Access II (WPA2) provides the best security protection with encryption methods. It will not hide the network, but instead make it difficult for unauthorized users to connect to it.

C is incorrect. 802.11n is a newer wireless protocol using multiple-input, multiple-output (MIMO) technologies supporting speeds up to 600 Mbps, but it does not hide the network.

D is incorrect. Using a different channel does not hide a wireless network.

»Get Certified »Get Ahead

Chapter 3 Network Security

Network Security topics are 18 percent of the CompTIA Network + exam. The objectives in this domain are:

3.1 Compare and contrast risk related concepts.

- Disaster recovery
- Business continuity
- Battery backups/UPS
- First responders
- Data breach
- End user awareness and training
- Single point of failure
    - Critical nodes
    - Critical assets
    - Redundancy
- Adherence to standards and policies
- Vulnerability scanning
- Penetration testing

3.2 Compare and contrast common network vulnerabilities and threats.

- Attacks/threats
    - Denial of service
        - Distributed DoS
            - Botnet
            - Traffic spike
            - Coordinated attack
        - Reflective/amplified
            - DNS
            - NTP
            - Smurfing
        - Friendly/unintentional DoS
        - Physical attack
            - Permanent DoS
    - ARP cache poisoning
    - Packet/protocol abuse
    - Spoofing
    - Wireless
        - Evil twin
        - Rogue AP
        - War driving
        - War chalking
        - Bluejacking
        - Bluesnarfing

        - WPA/WEP/WPS attacks
    - Brute force
    - Session hijacking
    - Social engineering
    - Man-in-the-middle
    - VLAN hopping
    - Compromised system
    - Effect of malware on the network
    - Insider threat/malicious employee
    - Zero day attacks
- Vulnerabilities
    - Unnecessary running services
    - Open ports
    - Unpatched/legacy systems
    - Unencrypted channels
    - Clear text credentials
    - Unsecure protocols
        - TELNET
        - HTTP
        - SLIP
        - FTP
        - TFTP
        - SNMPv1 and SNMPv2
    - TEMPEST/RF emanation

3.3 Given a scenario, implement network hardening techniques.

- Anti-malware software
    - Host-based
    - Cloud/server-based
    - Network-based
- Switch port security
    - DHCP snooping
    - ARP inspection
    - MAC address filtering
    - VLAN assignments
        - Network segmentation
- Security policies
- Disable unneeded network services
- Use secure protocols
    - SSH
    - SNMPv3
    - TLS/SSL
    - SFTP
    - HTTPS
    - IPsec
- Access lists
    - Web/content filtering

  - Port filtering
  - IP filtering
  - Implicit deny
- Wireless security
  - WEP
  - WPA/WPA2
    - Enterprise
    - Personal
  - TKIP/AES
  - 802.1x
  - TLS/TTLS
  - MAC filtering
- User authentication
  - CHAP/MSCHAP
  - PAP
  - EAP
  - Kerberos
  - Multifactor authentication
  - Two-factor authentication
  - Single sign-on
- Hashes
  - MD5
  - SHA

3.4 Compare and contrast physical security controls.

- Mantraps
- Network closets
- Video monitoring
  - IP cameras/CCTVs
- Door access controls
- Proximity readers/key fob
- Biometrics
- Keypad/cipher locks
- Security guard

3.5 Given a scenario, install and configure a basic firewall.

- Types of firewalls
  - Host-based
  - Network-based
  - Software vs hardware
  - Application aware/context aware
  - Small office/home office firewall
  - Stateful vs stateless inspection
  - UTM
- Settings/techniques
  - ACL
  - Virtual wire vs routed
  - DMZ

    - Implicit deny
    - Block/allow
        - Outbound traffic
        - Inbound traffic
    - Firewall placement
        - Internal/external

3.6 Explain the purpose of various network access control models.

- 802.1x
- Posture assessment
- Guest network
- Persistent vs non-persistent agents
- Quarantine network
- Edge vs access control

3.7 Summarize basic forensic concepts.

- First responder
- Secure the area
    - Escalate when necessary
- Document the scene
- eDiscovery
- Evidence/data collection
- Chain of custody
- Data transport
- Forensics report
- Legal hold

**

Practice Test Mode Section — Practice Test Questions without Answers for Network Security

1. Which of the following is the MOST important when considering business continuity after a disaster?

   A. RAID-6

   B. Network-based firewalls

   C. UTM appliances

   D. Off-site backups

2. Your organization has multiple remote offices with systems configured identically. Recently, helpdesk professionals have reported that one remote office has had a significantly large number of incidents where malware has infected user systems. The helpdesk has been able to clear this malware, but it has caused an increase in the workload. Which of the following is MOST likely needed at this remote location?

   A. 802.1x servers

   B. Guest network

   C. End-user training

   D. VLANs

3. You want to improve a system to increase its fault tolerance. What is needed?

   A. Higher bandwidth

   B. Reduced latency

   C. Redundancy

   D. High availability

4. An internal RAID-6 controller failed. Administrators replaced it with an external RAID-6 subsystem and reinstalled the operating system on the server. What else should the administrators do to restore the server to full functionality?

   A. Back up the data.

   B. Install a single point of failure.

   C. Add a UPS.

   D. Restore data from backups.

5. A network design has included two duplicate servers. What benefit(s) would this provide?

   A. High availability and the addition of a single point of failure

   B. High availability and fault tolerance

   C. Fault tolerance and decreased uptime

   D. Fault tolerance and caching

6. After a recent video went viral, a business saw a massive increase in traffic to its website. Many of the visitors are potential customers and the business wants to ensure the website continues to operate without any problems. What should the business address?

   A. High availability

   B. Traffic shaping

   C. Latency sensitivity

   D. Caching engines

7. Which of the following is the MOST important when considering business continuity after a disaster?

   A. DMZ

   B. Mantrap

C. Redundancy

D. Single point of failure

8. An attacker floods a switch with traffic hoping to redirect traffic to the attacker's computer. What type of attack does this describe?

   A. Smurfing

   B. VLAN hopping

   C. ARP poisoning

   D. Evil twin

9. Administrators are planning a new network that will process sensitive data. They want to ensure that systems on this network do not emanate any RF transmissions to computers in the existing network. The existing network only processes public or unclassified data. Which of the following standards provides guidance for this goal?

   A. SECCOM

   B. TEMPEST

   C. SECEM

   D. CCTV

10. Security experts have been analyzing your organization's network looking for potential issues. They discovered several internal computers have been sending GET and POST requests to a system on the Internet without any user interaction. Which of the following is the BEST explanation for this scenario?

   A. Vulnerability scanning

   B. VLAN hopping

   C. Compromised systems

   D. Insider threat

11. A security analyst performed a wireless survey and discovered an unauthorized wireless device. Of the following choices, what BEST describes this device?
    A. Rogue AP
    B. Botnet
    C. War driving
    D. VLAN hopping

12. An attacker has connected to an unused port on a switch and gained access to a restricted network created on the switch. What type of attack is this?
    A. Smurfing
    B. Rogue AP
    C. VLAN hopping
    D. ARP poisoning

13. What type of connector is commonly used with VoIP?
    A. RJ-11
    B. RJ-45
    C. ST
    D. F-connector

14. A system is being attacked with a flood of spoofed ICMP packets. What does this describe?
    A. ARP cache poisoning
    B. Rogue AP
    C. Sniffing
    D. Smurf attack

15. A malicious user has created a wireless network using the same SSID of a network operating in a coffee shop. He is using his wireless network to capture usernames and passwords as customers in the coffee shop access websites through his network. What type of attack is this?
    - A. War driving
    - B. Evil twin
    - C. WEP cracking
    - D. Buffer overflow

16. A company has a WPA2-Enterprise wireless network set up with an SSID of GetCertified. Users connect and then enter their credentials. Recently, a second network with the name of GetCertified2 appeared and users have been entering their credentials on this network. What is occurring?
    - A. A rogue access point is running.
    - B. An evil twin is running.
    - C. A war chalk attack is under way.
    - D. A WPA cracking attack is under way.

17. A telephone repair technician attempts to gain access to your server room to repair a phone problem. However, a manager verified that there isn't a phone problem and a telephone repairman was not called. What type of attack does this describe?
    - A. Social engineering
    - B. DoS
    - C. DDoS
    - D. Evil twin

18. You want to allow access to a network using the hardware address of a NIC. What would you implement?
    A. IP filtering
    B. Port filtering
    C. MAC filtering
    D. Spam filtering

19. You need to secure traffic for a new e-commerce website. Which of the following is the BEST choice?
    A. SSL
    B. TLS
    C. IPsec
    D. SFTP

20. You are helping a small business owner set up a WAP within her business. She wants to limit the number of devices that can connect to the WAP to five specific devices. Which of the following is the BEST choice to meet this goal?
    A. TLS security
    B. TKIP security
    C. WEP encryption
    D. MAC filtering

21. You need to segment traffic sent by the accounting department through a switch and ensure none of the traffic is sent to any non-accounting computers connected to the switch. Of the following choices, what could you use?
    A. Port mirroring
    B. Half-duplex

C. VLANs

D. Traffic shaping

22. You want to verify that malware has not modified files. Which of the following would you MOST likely use?

A. PAP or CHAP

B. TLS or SSL

C. AES or SSH

D. MD5 or SHA

23. There is a significant increase in the number of ransomware instances within your organization. Which of the following has the BEST chance of reducing these incidents?

A. Blocking port 443 at the firewall

B. Implementing SNMPv3

C. Segmenting the network with VLANs

D. Implementing web content filtering

24. A WAP is using WPA2-PSK. What type of encryption is it using?

A. TKIP

B. CCMP

C. DES

D. MAC

25. A WAP is using WPA2-PSK. What encryption is WPA2-PSK based on?

A. TKIP

B. TLS

C. AES

D. Kerberos

26. You want to create separate networks through a switch and reduce broadcast traffic sent to the different networks. What would you use?
    - A. VTP
    - B. RTP
    - C. VLANs
    - D. A router

27. Which of the following is a secure protocol used to manage network devices?
    - A. SNMPv3
    - B. SMTP
    - C. NTP
    - D. ARP

28. What is used in place of Telnet to provide better security?
    - A. SFTP
    - B. SCP
    - C. SSH
    - D. SSL

29. You are assisting a small business owner secure his wireless network. It is currently using WPA and has three computers that are authorized to connect. Of the following choices, what would provide the BEST improvement in security?
    - A. Disable MAC filtering and enable WPA2.
    - B. Enable SSID broadcast and use MAC address filtering.
    - C. Change the SSID name from the default and use WEP2.
    - D. Use MAC address filtering and WPA2.

30. You want to transfer files between two computers but ensure the files cannot be read if they are intercepted. What would you use?
    A. FTP
    B. SNMP
    C. HTTP
    D. SFTP

31. A technician moved a printer, unplugging it from one port and plugging it into another port in another room. Both ports connect to a switch with port security enabled. Which of the following is the MOST likely result?
    A. The switch would assign the printer a new IP address.
    B. The switch would assign the printer a new MAC address.
    C. The printer would work.
    D. The printer would cause the port to shut down.

32. A small business owner decided to allow employees to access the Internet from their work computers. Which of the following represents the GREATEST security risk from this policy change?
    A. Loss of productivity
    B. Loss of integrity due to hashing
    C. Tailgating
    D. Malware

33. An organization has several switches operating in a wiring closet. Of the following choices, what is the BEST physical security control to prevent attackers from accessing these switches?

    A. Mantrap

    B. Video monitoring

    C. Hashes

    D. Proximity cards and a proximity reader

34. Which of the following is a physical security control?

    A. MAC filtering

    B. Mantrap

    C. AES

    D. VLANs

35. Which of the following is a physical security control?

    A. Password policy

    B. Biometrics

    C. Tailgating

    D. Firewall

36. Which of the following is NOT a physical security control?

    A. CCTV

    B. ACL

    C. Cipher lock

    D. Security guard

37. Your organization recently purchased several laptops for employees. Employees will use these laptops when accessing the Internet. You are configuring a baseline image to install on these laptops and want to

include a security control to protect the laptops from external threats. Which of the following is the BEST choice?

A. Install a host-based firewall, and configure it to block all inbound connections.

B. Install a host-based firewall, and configure it to block all outbound connections.

C. Install a host-based firewall, and configure it to allow all inbound connections.

D. Install a host-based firewall, and configure it to allow all outbound connections.

38. You are assisting a homeowner install a video surveillance system in his home network. The owner wants to be able to access the video surveillance system remotely. However, the owner does not want to open any logical ports allowing access to his internal network. What would you do?

A. Disable the existing network firewall.

B. Implement an 802.1x server.

C. Create a DMZ and add the video surveillance system to the DMZ.

D. Disable any existing host-based firewalls.

39. What port needs to be opened on a firewall to allow outgoing DNS queries?

A. TCP 25

B. TCP 53

C. UDP 25

D. UDP 53

40. After a technician reconfigured a zone-based firewall, users began complaining that they lost functionality. The firewall should be configured to meet these requirements:

- Users within the 192.168.1.0/8 subnet should be able to connect to servers within the DMZ using any protocols.
- Users within the 192.168.0.0/24 subnet should be able to connect to servers within the DMZ, but only with HTTP or HTTPS.
- The rules within the firewall's ACL are currently set as shown in the following table.

Rule	Permission	Destination	Zone	Prot	Port
A	Deny	Any Trust	Any DMZ	Any	Any
B	Allow	192.168.0.0/16	Any DMZ	TCP	80
C	Allow	192.168.1.0/8	Any DMZ	Any	Any
D	Allow	192.168.0.0/16	Any DMZ	TCP	443

How should these rules be ordered to meet the requirements?

A. C, D, A, B

B. D, A, B, C

C. A, C, B, D

D. B, C, D, A

41. You are configuring an ACL on a firewall. Of the following choices, what could you include?

A. Certificate

B. Antivirus signatures

C. IP filtering

D. VLAN definition

42. You want to receive email from your ISP. What should be done on your firewall?

    A. Open outgoing port 25.

    B. Open incoming port 110.

    C. Set the firewall to use an implicit deny policy.

    D. Remove the ACL.

43. What type of appliance would you use to filter traffic based on IP addresses and ports within a network?

    A. Host-based firewall

    B. Network-based firewall

    C. Proxy server

    D. NAT

44. What port should you close in a firewall to block users from sending email through a firewall?

    A. 20

    B. 22

    C. 25

    D. 443

45. You need to set up a wireless network for customers so that they can access the Internet. However, you do not want the customers to be able to access the company's network. What should you set up?

    A. DMZ

    B. VTP

    C. 802.1x server

    D. Guest network

46. You need to implement port security. What protocol would you use?

    A. 802.3af

    B. 802.11i

    C. 802.1q

    D. 802.1x

47. A small business is allowing customers to access its wireless network so that they can access the Internet. A security expert recommends setting up a guest network instead. What benefit is provided by a guest network?

    A. Reduces bandwidth usage

    B. Protects servers in the DMZ

    C. Protects guests from malware

    D. Isolates company resources

48. An employee was accused of violating a security policy and a technician was directed to confiscate the employee's laptop computer. The technician collected the laptop computer and stored it on his desk overnight. Which of the following forensic concepts did the technician ignore?

    A. Beginning a chain of custody

    B. Securing the area

    C. Documenting the scene

    D. Protecting data during transport

49. While troubleshooting an issue on a user's computer, a technician discovers several videos that are not work related and might be illegal. What should the technician do?

    A. Contact the police.

    B. Create a forensic report.

    C. Escalate the event.

    D. Create a chain-of-custody document.

Review Mode Section — Practice Test Questions with Answers for Network Security

Objective: 3.1 Compare and contrast risk related concepts.

1. Which of the following is the MOST important when considering business continuity after a disaster?
   A. RAID-6
   B. Network-based firewalls
   C. UTM appliances
   D. Off-site backups

Answer: **D** is correct. Off-site backups ensure data is still available after a disaster. Of the given answers, this is the most important element. Other elements (not given as available answers) are redundancy and alternate locations.

A is incorrect. Although a redundant array of independent disks 6 (RAID-6) helps provide fault tolerance for disks, it won't necessarily help in a disaster. For example, if a fire destroys a server, it will also destroy the RAID-6. In contrast, the backups ensure the system can continue to operate.
B is incorrect. Network-based firewalls help protect a network when it is operational, but do not contribute to business continuity.
C is incorrect. A unified threat management (UTM) device is a single solution that combines multiple security controls, such as URL filtering and inspecting traffic for potentially malicious traffic.

2. Your organization has multiple remote offices with systems configured identically. Recently, helpdesk professionals have reported that one remote office has had a significantly large number of incidents where malware has infected user systems. The helpdesk has been able to clear this malware, but it has caused an increase in the workload. Which of the following is MOST likely needed at this remote location?
   A. 802.1x servers
   B. Guest network
   C. End-user training
   D. VLANs

Answer: **C** is correct. Because the systems are configured identically, the most likely issue is that users at one of the remote offices are not using safe computing practices, causing their systems to become infected. The best solution is better end-user training at this remote office.

A is incorrect. 802.1x is used for authentication. 802.1x servers can be used for port security, and for Wi-Fi Protected Access II-Enterprise (WPA2-Enterprise) as a Remote Authentication Dial-In User Service (RADIUS) server.

B is incorrect. A guest network allows customers to access the Internet without being able to access an internal network, but it wouldn't be used for employees. There isn't any indication in the scenario that customers are accessing the network.

D is incorrect. Virtual local area networks (VLANs) segregate traffic onto separate networks. However, it's unlikely a remote office needs separate networks and segmenting traffic won't block malware.

3. You want to improve a system to increase its fault tolerance. What is needed?

   A. Higher bandwidth

   B. Reduced latency

   C. Redundancy

   D. High availability

Answer: **C** is correct. Redundant components provide fault tolerance. As an example, a redundant array of independent disks (RAID) array using RAID-1 includes one redundant drive. The system can tolerate a fault in one drive due to the redundancy provided by the second drive.

A is incorrect. Increasing bandwidth does not provide fault tolerance. Increased bandwidth can be provided by upgrading components from 1 Gbps to 10 Gbps, but a failure in one of the components still results in a loss of service.
B is incorrect. Reducing latency does not provide fault tolerance, but it may result in better performance with less delays.
D is incorrect. High availability is a benefit of fault tolerance, but you actually need to add something (such as redundant drives or redundant servers) to provide both fault tolerance and high availability.

4. An internal RAID-6 controller failed. Administrators replaced it with an external RAID-6 subsystem and reinstalled the operating system on the server. What else should the administrators do to restore the server to full functionality?

   A. Back up the data.

   B. Install a single point of failure.

C. Add a UPS.

D. Restore data from backups.

Answer: **D** is correct. Because the redundant array of independent disks 6 (RAID-6) controller failed and was replaced with a different RAID-6 subsystem, the data must be restored with backups.

A is incorrect. If the data wasn't backed up prior to the failure, it's too late to back it up now.

B is incorrect. A RAID-6 removes disk drives as a single point of failure. A single point of failure is any component that can cause the entire system to fail if it fails, so you wouldn't want to add a single point of failure.

C is incorrect. An uninterruptible power supply (UPS) provides fault tolerance for power loss, but isn't needed when replacing a RAID subsystem.

5. A network design has included two duplicate servers. What benefit(s) would this provide?

   A. High availability and the addition of a single point of failure

   B. High availability and fault tolerance

   C. Fault tolerance and decreased uptime

   D. Fault tolerance and caching

Answer: **B** is correct. Two duplicate devices of any kind can be used in different designs to provide high availability and fault tolerance. High availability indicates that service provided by the devices will continue to be available even if a failure occurs. Fault tolerance indicates that a system can suffer a fault or a failure and continue to operate. As an example, load balancing balances the load among multiple servers, but it also provides high availability and fault tolerance with redundant servers.

A is incorrect. A single point of failure is a component that will cause the entire system to fail if it fails. High availability and fault tolerance methods attempt to remove a single point of failure, not add one.
C is incorrect. High availability and fault tolerance methods attempt to increase the time a system stays operational, not decrease the uptime.
D is incorrect. Duplicate servers would not necessarily cache data.

6. After a recent video went viral, a business saw a massive increase in traffic to its website. Many of the visitors are potential customers and the business wants to ensure the website continues to operate without any problems. What should the business address?
    A. High availability
    B. Traffic shaping
    C. Latency sensitivity
    D. Caching engines

Answer: **A** is correct. High availability refers to the ability of a system to stay operational when it is needed. Load balancing could be used to add additional website servers and balance the load among the different servers. This will ensure that the website will remain available to customers even if there is an increase in traffic.

B is incorrect. Traffic shaping is used to control bandwidth for specific types of traffic, such as reducing the amount of bandwidth available for audio or video streaming. Depending on the type of traffic used on the link, traffic shaping may be used to increase availability, but the goal is still high availability.
C is incorrect. Latency refers to the effect of delays on a system. For example, some systems such as video conferencing or Voice over IP

(VoIP) systems are highly sensitive to delays, while others can handle delays without any problem. However, this does not affect the overall availability of the website for customers.

D is incorrect. Caching engines are used on proxy servers when internal clients go to a website, not when external clients visit a website hosted by a company.

7. Which of the following is the MOST important when considering business continuity after a disaster?
    A. DMZ
    B. Mantrap
    C. Redundancy
    D. Single point of failure

Answer: **C** is correct. Redundancy provides fault tolerance and can ensure systems continue to operate after a disaster. Redundancy can include redundant locations, redundant connections, redundant servers, and redundant drives. Of the given answers, this is the most important element. Other elements (not given as available answers) are off-site backups and alternate locations.

A is incorrect. A demilitarized zone (DMZ) provides some protection for Internet-facing servers, but isn't directly related to business continuity.

B is incorrect. A mantrap is a physical security mechanism designed to control access to a secure area through a buffer zone. It helps prevent tailgating.

D is incorrect. Redundancy methods help eliminate any single point of failure. A single point of failure is any component that can cause the entire system to fail if it fails.

Objective: 3.2 Compare and contrast common network vulnerabilities and threats.

8. An attacker floods a switch with traffic hoping to redirect traffic to the attacker's computer. What type of attack does this describe?
   A. Smurfing
   B. VLAN hopping
   C. ARP poisoning
   D. Evil twin

Answer: **C** is correct. Address Resolution Protocol (ARP) poisoning attacks can redirect traffic to an attacker's system by sending false media access control (MAC) address updates to a switch.

A is incorrect. A smurf attack spoofs the source IP address of a ping packet with the IP address of the victim. It then broadcasts the ping on the network and all systems on the network then flood the victim with ping responses. It does not redirect traffic.
B is incorrect. Virtual local area network (VLAN) hopping is an attack on VLANs. When successful, it allows attackers to access different VLANs.
D is incorrect. An evil twin is a wireless network using the same service set identifier (SSID) as a legitimate wireless network. It doesn't redirect traffic, but instead depends on the user connecting to the evil twin.

9. Administrators are planning a new network that will process sensitive data. They want to ensure that systems on this network do not emanate any RF transmissions to computers in the existing network. The existing network only processes public or unclassified data. Which of the following standards provides guidance for this goal?

A. SECCOM

B. TEMPEST

C. SECEM

D. CCTV

Answer: **B** is correct. TEMPEST is a code name used by the U.S. government for emission security (EMSEC) and communication security (COMSEC). Any program that attempts to reduce electromagnetic interference (EMI) or radio frequency interference (RFI) also supports EMSEC and COMSEC and several countries have similar standards. Most documents indicate that TEMPEST is not an acronym.

A and C are incorrect. COMSEC and EMSEC are programs that attempt to reduce emissions. SECCOM and SECEM are not valid acronyms for TEMPEST-related programs.

D is incorrect. A closed-circuit television (CCTV) system does not include elements to reduce RF transmissions.

10. Security experts have been analyzing your organization's network looking for potential issues. They discovered several internal computers have been sending GET and POST requests to a system on the Internet without any user interaction. Which of the following is the BEST explanation for this scenario?

    A. Vulnerability scanning

    B. VLAN hopping

    C. Compromised systems

    D. Insider threat

Answer: **C** is correct. The most likely explanation is that some type of malware compromised the internal computers. The malware is now sending Hypertext Transfer Protocol (HTTP) GET commands requesting additional instructions, and sending POST commands that include data about the organization's internal network.

A is incorrect. Vulnerability scanning will scan a system or network for potential issues, but will not send commands from internal systems to the Internet.

B is incorrect. Virtual local area network (VLAN) hopping is an attack on VLANs. It does not include sending HTTP commands.

D is incorrect. If a single computer was sending these GET and POST commands, it might be an insider threat. However, because the scenario describes several computers sending the commands without any interaction, it is more likely that malware is causing the activity.

11. A security analyst performed a wireless survey and discovered an unauthorized wireless device. Of the following choices, what BEST describes this device?
    A. Rogue AP
    B. Botnet
    C. War driving
    D. VLAN hopping

Answer: **A** is correct. This unauthorized device is most likely a rogue access point (AP). If attackers can install a rogue AP, they can collect data from the network using a wireless device outside the organization.

B is incorrect. A botnet is a group of computers (often called zombies) controlled by someone external to the organization. It is not a single device within the organization.

C is incorrect. War driving is the practice of driving (or sometimes walking) around an area looking for wireless signals. The security analyst might have used war driving techniques to locate the rogue AP.

D is incorrect. Virtual local area network (VLAN) hopping is an attack on VLANs and when successful, it allows attackers to access different VLANs. It is not related to wireless attacks.

12. An attacker has connected to an unused port on a switch and gained access to a restricted network created on the switch. What type of attack is this?

    A. Smurfing

    B. Rogue AP

    C. VLAN hopping

    D. ARP poisoning

Answer: **C** is correct. Virtual local area network (VLAN) hopping is an attack on VLANs and when successful, it allows attackers to access different VLANs. VLANs are configured on switches.

A is incorrect. A smurf attack spoofs the source IP address of a ping packet with the IP address of the victim. It then broadcasts the ping on the network, and all systems on the network then flood the victim with ping responses. It does not exploit VLANs.

B is incorrect. A rogue access point (AP) is an unauthorized wireless AP. Although a rogue AP can be plugged into an unused port, that won't give the AP access to the restricted network.

D is incorrect. Address Resolution Protocol (ARP) poisoning attacks can redirect traffic to an attacker's system by sending false media access control (MAC) address updates to a switch. They won't grant the attacker access to a restricted network.

13. What type of connector is commonly used with VoIP?
    - A. RJ-11
    - B. RJ-45
    - C. ST
    - D. F-connector

Answer: **B** is correct. Voice over Internet Protocol (VoIP) commonly uses twisted-pair connected with a Registered Jack-45 (RJ-45) connector.

A is incorrect. RJ-11 is used with phone lines.
C is incorrect. A straight tip (ST) connector is used with fiber connections, but fiber is not commonly used with VoIP mostly because the majority of network connections use twisted-pair instead of fiber.
D is incorrect. An F-connector is used with Radio Guide-6 (RG-6) coaxial cable, but RG-6 is not commonly used with VoIP.

14. A system is being attacked with a flood of spoofed ICMP packets. What does this describe?
    - A. ARP cache poisoning
    - B. Rogue AP
    - C. Sniffing
    - D. Smurf attack

Answer: **D** is correct. A smurf attack spoofs the source IP address of a ping packet with the IP address of the victim. It then broadcasts the ping on the network and all systems on the network then flood the victim with ping responses. Ping uses Internet Control Message Protocol (ICMP).

A is incorrect. Address Resolution Protocol (ARP) poisoning attacks redirect traffic to an attacker's system by sending false media access control (MAC) address updates to a switch. They do not flood an attacked system with spoofed ICMP packets.
B is incorrect. A rogue access point (AP) is an unauthorized wireless access point that allows an attacker to collect data. It does not send spoofed ICMP packets.
C is incorrect. A sniffing attack captures packets with a sniffer (also called a protocol analyzer).

15. A malicious user has created a wireless network using the same SSID of a network operating in a coffee shop. He is using his wireless network to capture usernames and passwords as customers in the coffee shop access websites through his network. What type of attack is this?
    A. War driving
    B. Evil twin
    C. WEP cracking
    D. Buffer overflow

Answer: **B** is correct. An evil twin is a wireless network using the same service set identifier (SSID) as a legitimate wireless network. The attacker can capture and analyze all of the users' traffic.

A is incorrect. War driving is the practice of driving around looking for wireless networks. Attackers often look for unprotected networks, or weakly protected networks, and hack into them.

C is incorrect. Wired Equivalent Privacy (WEP) is a weak wireless protocol that can easily be cracked (sometimes called WEP cracking).
D is incorrect. A buffer overflow is an error caused when an application receives unexpected data that it cannot handle. An attacker may send data to a system to cause a buffer overflow in a buffer overflow attack.

16. A company has a WPA2-Enterprise wireless network set up with an SSID of GetCertified. Users connect and then enter their credentials. Recently, a second network with the name of GetCertified2 appeared and users have been entering their credentials on this network. What is occurring?
    A. A rogue access point is running.
    B. An evil twin is running.
    C. A war chalk attack is under way.
    D. A WPA cracking attack is under way.

Answer: **A** is correct. A rogue access point (AP) is an unauthorized wireless access point (WAP) set up within a network. In this case, an attacker is trying to trick users into thinking the rogue access point is a company network by using a similar service set identifier (SSID). The question mentions that Wi-Fi Protected Access II (WPA2) Enterprise is being used. This uses an 802.1x authentication server and requires users to enter a valid username and password. The attacker can mimic the functionality of the legitimate network and if users connect, they may be tricked into entering their credentials, which are then captured by the attacker.

B is incorrect. An evil twin will have the same SSID as a legitimate wireless network. In this case, the SSIDs are different, so it is not an evil twin.

C is incorrect. War chalking is the practice of locating wireless networks and marking their location with chalk.

D is incorrect. Wi-Fi Protected Access (WPA) cracking is the practice of cracking WPA encryption. Although this is possible, it is much harder to crack than WEP cracking. WPA2 is not susceptible to WPA cracking.

17. A telephone repair technician attempts to gain access to your server room to repair a phone problem. However, a manager verified that there isn't a phone problem and a telephone repairman was not called. What type of attack does this describe?

    A. Social engineering

    B. DoS

    C. DDoS

    D. Evil twin

Answer: **A** is correct. Social engineering occurs when attackers attempt to trick users into doing something they would not normally do, or providing some information that they would not normally provide. In this case, an attacker was likely trying to impersonate a technician to convince an employee to provide him access to a restricted area. The attacker could just as easily have tried to impersonate a pest control employee, a power company employee, or just about anyone else if the impersonation is believable and will allow the attacker access to the restricted area. Social engineering is often accomplished with nontechnical means, but a phishing attempt with email is also referred to as social engineering.

B is incorrect. A denial-of-service (DoS) attack attempts to disrupt service provided by a system. DoS attacks are technical in nature.
C is incorrect. A Distributed DoS (DDoS) is a DoS attack from multiple sources at the same time. DDoS attacks are technical in nature.
D is incorrect. An evil twin is a wireless network set up by a malicious user with the same service set identifier (SSID) as a legitimate wireless network.

Objective: 3.3 Given a scenario, implement network hardening techniques.

18. You want to allow access to a network using the hardware address of a NIC. What would you implement?
    A. IP filtering
    B. Port filtering
    C. MAC filtering
    D. Spam filtering

Answer: **C** is correct. Media access control (MAC) address filters can block or allow traffic based on the hardware address of a network interface card (NIC). The hardware address is also known as the MAC address or physical address.

A is incorrect. An IP filter can filter traffic based on specific IP addresses or network IDs, but not the MAC address.
B is incorrect. Port filters filter protocol traffic using well-known ports. For example, outgoing email can be blocked by blocking Simple Mail Transfer Protocol (SMTP) port 25.
D is incorrect. A spam filter filters unwanted or unsolicited email.

19. You need to secure traffic for a new e-commerce website. Which of the following is the BEST choice?

    A. SSL

    B. TLS

    C. IPsec

    D. SFTP

Answer: **B** is correct. Transport Layer Security (TLS) is the best choice to secure Hypertext Transfer Protocol (HTTP) traffic.

A is incorrect. Secure Sockets Layer (SSL) is the second best choice, but it has been compromised, so TLS is a better choice.
C is incorrect. Internet Protocol security (IPsec) is a secure transport encryption protocol. However, an e-commerce website would use HTTP, and IPsec is rarely (if ever) used to encrypt HTTP.
D is incorrect. Secure Shell (SSH) is a secure transport encryption protocol. However, an e-commerce website would use HTTP, and SSH is rarely (if ever) used to encrypt HTTP.

20. You are helping a small business owner set up a WAP within her business. She wants to limit the number of devices that can connect to the WAP to five specific devices. Which of the following is the BEST choice to meet this goal?

    A. TLS security

    B. TKIP security

    C. WEP encryption

    D. MAC filtering

Answer: **D** is correct. Media access control (MAC) filtering is the best choice to limit the wireless access point (WAP) to support only five specific devices.

A is incorrect. Transport Layer Security (TLS) is a secure encryption protocol, but it does not differentiate between devices, so it couldn't limit the WAP connections to only five.
B is incorrect. Temporal Key Integrity Protocol (TKIP) is an older security algorithm used with wireless networks and does not differentiate between devices, so it couldn't limit the WAP connections to only five.
C is incorrect. Wired Equivalent Privacy (WEP) is compromised and should not be used.

21. You need to segment traffic sent by the accounting department through a switch and ensure none of the traffic is sent to any non-accounting computers connected to the switch. Of the following choices, what could you use?
    A. Port mirroring
    B. Half-duplex
    C. VLANs
    D. Traffic shaping

Answer: **C** is correct. Virtual local area networks (VLANs) will segment traffic. Any traffic (including broadcast traffic) on one VLAN will not be sent to another VLAN.

A is incorrect. Port mirroring creates a monitoring port and sends all traffic sent through a switch to a specific port used for monitoring.

B is incorrect. Half-duplex refers to the mode of operation for the cable. Data can be sent or received but not sent and received at the same time. In contrast, full-duplex allows data to be sent and received on the same cable at the same time.
D is incorrect. Traffic shaping controls bandwidth for specific types of traffic, such as reducing the amount of bandwidth available for audio or video streaming. It doesn't segment traffic.

22. You want to verify that malware has not modified files. Which of the following would you MOST likely use?
    A. PAP or CHAP
    B. TLS or SSL
    C. AES or SSH
    D. MD5 or SHA

Answer: **D** is correct. Message Digest 5 (MD5) and Secure Hash Algorithm (SHA) are hashing algorithms and hashing algorithms can detect changes in files (or verify the files have not lost integrity).

A is incorrect. Password Authentication Protocol (PAP) and Challenge Handshake Authentication Protocol (CHAP) are used for authentication. They cannot detect changes in files.
B is incorrect. Transport Layer Security (TLS) and Secure Sockets Layer (SSL) are transport encryption protocols. They cannot detect changes in files.
C is incorrect. Advanced Encryption Standard (AES) and Secure Shell (SSH) are encryption protocols. They aren't hashing algorithms and cannot detect changes in files.

23. There is a significant increase in the number of ransomware instances within your organization. Which of the following has the BEST chance of reducing these incidents?

    A. Blocking port 443 at the firewall

    B. Implementing SNMPv3

    C. Segmenting the network with VLANs

    D. Implementing web content filtering

Answer: **D** is correct. Web content filtering can detect malware coming into the network and is the best choice of the available answers. Ransomware is a type of malware that takes control of computers or data and attempts to extort money from users.

A is incorrect. Port 443 is the default port for Hypertext Transfer Protocol Secure (HTTPS). It is unlikely malware is being delivered via HTTPS, so this is unlikely to help. However, it will decrease functionality for users.
B is incorrect. Simple Network Management Protocol (SNMP) is used to manage network devices and does not block malware. SNMPv3 is the newest version and the most secure.
C is incorrect. Virtual local area networks (VLANs) segment traffic. They do not block malware.

24. A WAP is using WPA2-PSK. What type of encryption is it using?

    A. TKIP

    B. CCMP

    C. DES

    D. MAC

Answer: **B** is correct. Wi-Fi Protected Access II (WPA2) includes mandatory support for Counter Mode with Cipher Block Chaining Message Authentication Code Protocol (CCMP). CCMP is based on Advanced Encryption Standard (AES).

A is incorrect. Temporal Key Integrity Protocol (TKIP) is an older encryption protocol used with WPA, but not WPA2.
C is incorrect. The Data Encryption Standard (DES) is on older encryption standard. It has been cracked and is not used with wireless technologies.
D is incorrect. Media access control (MAC) is not an encryption type.

25. A WAP is using WPA2-PSK. What encryption is WPA2-PSK based on?
    A. TKIP
    B. TLS
    C. AES
    D. Kerberos

Answer: **C** is correct. Wi-Fi Protected Access II (WPA2) includes mandatory support for Counter Mode with Cipher Block Chaining Message Authentication Code Protocol (CCMP). CCMP is based on Advanced Encryption Standard (AES).

A is incorrect. Temporal Key Integrity Protocol (TKIP) is an older encryption protocol used with WPA, but not WPA2.
B is incorrect. Transport Layer Security (TLS) is a secure encryption protocol, but WPA2-Pre-shared key (WPA2-PSK) is not based on TLS.
D is incorrect. Kerberos is a single sign-on (SSO) authentication protocol using tickets.

26. You want to create separate networks through a switch and reduce broadcast traffic sent to the different networks. What would you use?

    A. VTP

    B. RTP

    C. VLANs

    D. A router

Answer: **C** is correct. Virtual local area networks (VLANs) are created on switches. VLANs segregate traffic onto separate networks and broadcast traffic is not sent between the VLANs.

A is incorrect. VLAN Trunk Protocol (VTP) is used to share VLAN information among multiple Cisco switches in a network.
B is incorrect. Real-time Transport Protocol (RTP) is used with Voice over Internet Protocol (VoIP) and is not related to creating separate networks.
D is incorrect. A router can be used to create separate networks and broadcast traffic is not passed through a router to the different networks. However, the scenario requires the use of a switch.

27. Which of the following is a secure protocol used to manage network devices?

    A. SNMPv3

    B. SMTP

    C. NTP

    D. ARP

Answer: **A** is correct. Simple Network Management Protocol (SNMP) is used to manage network devices. SNMPv3 is the newest version and the most secure.

B is incorrect. Simple Mail Transfer Protocol (SMTP) is used to send email over port 25, not manage network devices.
C is incorrect. Network Time Protocol (NTP) is used to synchronize clocks on network devices ensuring they all have the same time.
D is incorrect. The Address Resolution Protocol (ARP) resolves media access control (MAC) addresses to IP addresses and the arp command-line program shows the ARP cache.

28. What is used in place of Telnet to provide better security?

    A. SFTP

    B. SCP

    C. SSH

    D. SSL

Answer: **C** is correct. Secure Shell (SSH) is used in place of Telnet. Telnet sends data over a network in cleartext, but SSH encrypts the data.

A is incorrect. Secure File Transfer Protocol (SFTP) is used to transfer files and cannot be used in place of Telnet. SFTP is encrypted with SSH.
B is incorrect. Secure Copy Protocol (SCP) is a secure method of transferring files over a network and cannot be used in place of Telnet.
D is incorrect. Secure Sockets Layer (SSL) provides encryption for many different protocols, but it cannot be used in place of Telnet.

29. You are assisting a small business owner secure his wireless network. It is currently using WPA and has three computers that are authorized to connect. Of the following choices, what would provide the BEST improvement in security?

    A. Disable MAC filtering and enable WPA2.

    B. Enable SSID broadcast and use MAC address filtering.

    C. Change the SSID name from the default and use WEP2.

    D. Use MAC address filtering and WPA2.

Answer: **D** is correct. Of the choices given, using media access control (MAC) filtering and Wi-Fi Protected Access version 2 (WPA2) provides the best security. MAC address filtering can be used to restrict access to only the clients with specific MAC addresses (but a dedicated attacker can beat this). WPA2 security ensures that only clients that have the pre-shared key can connect.

A is incorrect. Although MAC address filtering can be beaten by a dedicated attacker, having it provides more security than disabling it.
B is incorrect. Manipulating service set identifier (SSID) broadcast provides very little security. It can hide a network from users, making it more difficult to connect, but attackers using a wireless sniffer can still see it.
C is incorrect. Changing the SSID from its default is a good security practice, but there is no such thing as WEP2.

30. You want to transfer files between two computers but ensure the files cannot be read if they are intercepted. What would you use?

    A. FTP

    B. SNMP

C. HTTP

D. SFTP

Answer: **D** is correct. Secure File Transfer Protocol (SFTP) uses Secure Shell (SSH) to encrypt data sent over the network and is a secure way to transfer files over a network.

A is incorrect. File Transfer Protocol (FTP) is a common protocol used to transfer files over a network, but it transfers data in cleartext. If the files are intercepted, they can be read.
B is incorrect. Simple Network Management Protocol (SNMP) is used for managing devices on networks, not to transfer files.
C is incorrect. Hypertext Transfer Protocol (HTTP) is used to transfer web-based files over a network, but it is not secure unless it is encrypted as HTTP Secure (HTTPS). Secure Sockets Layer (SSL) or Transport Layer Security (TLS) is used to encrypt HTTP as HTTPS.

31. A technician moved a printer, unplugging it from one port and plugging it into another port in another room. Both ports connect to a switch with port security enabled. Which of the following is the MOST likely result?

    A. The switch would assign the printer a new IP address.

    B. The switch would assign the printer a new MAC address.

    C. The printer would work.

    D. The printer would cause the port to shut down.

Answer: **D** is correct. Port security includes assigning specific media access control (MAC) addresses to ports. If a device with a different MAC is connected, the switch shuts down the port to prevent communication. Although not an available answer, port security includes disabling unused ports, so it's also possible that the printer wouldn't work simply because the port is disabled.

A is incorrect. Switches do not assign IP addresses. Dynamic Host Configuration Protocol (DHCP) assigns IP addresses.
B is incorrect. Switches do not assign MAC addresses. MAC addresses are semi permanently assigned to network interface cards (NICs).
C is incorrect. With port security enabled, the printer would not work unless the second port is configured with the printer's MAC address. Because the printer is being moved to another room, this is highly unlikely.

32. A small business owner decided to allow employees to access the Internet from their work computers. Which of the following represents the GREATEST security risk from this policy change?
    A. Loss of productivity
    B. Loss of integrity due to hashing
    C. Tailgating
    D. Malware

Answer: **D** is correct. The greatest security risk of those listed from this policy change is malicious software (malware). Users can inadvertently infect their systems just by visiting a site that performs a drive-by download. Every system should have anti-malware software installed and users should receive training on security risks from malware.
A is incorrect. Although this policy change may affect productivity, this is not a security risk.
B is incorrect. Hashing protocols, such as Message Digest 5 (MD5) and Secure Hash Algorithm version 3 (SHA-3) help ensure integrity. However, this is not related to this question.

C is incorrect. Tailgating (also called piggybacking) occurs when one user follows closely behind another user without using credentials. It is unrelated to Internet access. Mantraps help prevent tailgating.

Objective: 3.4 Compare and contrast physical security controls.

33. An organization has several switches operating in a wiring closet. Of the following choices, what is the BEST physical security control to prevent attackers from accessing these switches?

    A. Mantrap

    B. Video monitoring

    C. Hashes

    D. Proximity cards and a proximity reader

Answer: **D** is correct. A proximity reader can detect proximity cards that are close (in close proximity). Organizations issue proximity cards to authorized users and code them to open specific doors. Without the proper card, personnel are not able to gain access.

A is incorrect. A mantrap helps prevent tailgating, but tailgating isn't a problem in wiring closets.

B is incorrect. Video monitoring might record who entered a wiring closet, but it doesn't prevent access.

C is incorrect. Hashes are created from hashing algorithms such as Message Digest 5 (MD5) and Secure Hash Algorithm version 3 (SHA-3), but a hash is simply a number. It cannot prevent access to a room.

34. Which of the following is a physical security control?

A. MAC filtering

B. Mantrap

C. AES

D. VLANs

Answer: **B** is correct. A mantrap is a physical security control designed to prevent tailgating. A physical security control is one that you can touch.

A, C, and D are incorrect. Media access control (MAC) filtering, Advanced Encryption Standard (AES), and virtual local area networks (VLANs) are all technical controls. They are implemented with technology.

35. Which of the following is a physical security control?

A. Password policy

B. Biometrics

C. Tailgating

D. Firewall

Answer: **B** is correct. Biometrics, when used to control entry into a secure area, is a physical security control designed to control access. A physical security control is one that you can touch.

A is incorrect. A written password policy is an administrative control and it defines requirements for passwords. A technical password policy enforces the written policy using technology.

C is incorrect. Tailgating (also called piggybacking) occurs when one user follows closely behind another user without using credentials. A mantrap is a physical security control designed to prevent tailgating.

D is incorrect. A firewall is a technical control.

36. Which of the following is NOT a physical security control?

    A. CCTV

    B. ACL

    C. Cipher lock

    D. Security guard

Answer: **B** is correct. An access control list (ACL) is a list of rules in a router or firewall. A physical security control is one that you can touch, but you cannot touch the ACL.

A is incorrect. A closed-circuit television (CCTV) is a physical security control.

C is incorrect. A cipher lock is a physical security control.

D is incorrect. A security guard is a physical security control.

Objective: 3.5 Given a scenario, install and configure a basic firewall.

37. Your organization recently purchased several laptops for employees. Employees will use these laptops when accessing the Internet. You are configuring a baseline image to install on these laptops and want to include a security control to protect the laptops from external threats. Which of the following is the BEST choice?

    A. Install a host-based firewall, and configure it to block all inbound connections.

    B. Install a host-based firewall, and configure it to block all outbound connections.

    C. Install a host-based firewall, and configure it to allow all inbound connections.

    D. Install a host-based firewall, and configure it to allow all outbound connections.

Answer: **D** is correct. Of the available choices, the best one is to install a host-based firewall and configure it to allow all outbound connections. Although not available as a choice, you would also configure the access control list (ACL) to allow specific incoming traffic and block other unwanted traffic. Similarly, you can configure the access control list to allow specific outgoing traffic and block all other traffic.

A is incorrect. If you block all inbound connections, the firewall will block all incoming traffic and the laptop won't have any network connectivity.
B is incorrect. If you block all outbound connections, the firewall will block all outgoing traffic and the laptop won't have any network connectivity.
C is incorrect. If you configure the firewall to allow all inbound connections, it does not protect the laptop from external threats.

38. You are assisting a homeowner install a video surveillance system in his home network. The owner wants to be able to access the video surveillance system remotely. However, the owner does not want to open any logical ports allowing access to his internal network. What would you do?
    A. Disable the existing network firewall.
    B. Implement an 802.1x server.
    C. Create a DMZ and add the video surveillance system to the DMZ.
    D. Disable any existing host-based firewalls.

Answer: **C** is correct. By creating a demilitarized zone (DMZ) and adding the video surveillance system to the DMZ, it allows remote access to the system without opening any additional ports to the internal network.

A is incorrect. Disabling the network firewall eliminates security from the firewall and is not desirable. Also, unless a router is blocking traffic, this effectively opens all ports into the internal network.

B is incorrect. An 802.1x server requires users to authenticate before they are granted access to a network. It won't reduce the need to open ports to access the video surveillance CCTV system remotely.

D is incorrect. Disabling host-based firewalls weakens security, and won't necessarily grant access to the video surveillance system.

39. What port needs to be opened on a firewall to allow outgoing DNS queries?

    A. TCP 25

    B. TCP 53

    C. UDP 25

    D. UDP 53

Answer: **D** is correct. Domain Name System (DNS) uses User Datagram Protocol (UDP) port 53 for DNS queries from DNS clients to DNS servers. DNS uses Transmission Control Protocol (TCP) port 53 when doing zone transfers between DNS servers.

A and C are incorrect. DNS does not use port 25. Simple Mail Transfer Protocol (SMTP) uses Transmission Control Protocol (TCP) port 25.

B is incorrect. DNS uses TCP port 53 for zone transfers when doing zone transfers between DNS servers.

40. After a technician reconfigured a zone-based firewall, users began complaining that they lost functionality. The firewall should be configured to meet these requirements:

- Users within the 192.168.1.0/8 subnet should be able to connect to servers within the DMZ using any protocols.
- Users within the 192.168.0.0/24 subnet should be able to connect to servers within the DMZ, but only with HTTP or HTTPS.
- The rules within the firewall's ACL are currently set as shown in the following table.

Rule	Permission	Destination	Zone	Prot	Port
A	Deny	Any Trust	Any DMZ	Any	Any
B	Allow	192.168.0.0/16	Any DMZ	TCP	80
C	Allow	192.168.1.0/8	Any DMZ	Any	Any
D	Allow	192.168.0.0/16	Any DMZ	TCP	443

How should these rules be ordered to meet the requirements?

A. C, D, A, B

B. D, A, B, C

C. A, C, B, D

D. B, C, D, A

Answer: **D** is correct. The implicit deny rule (denying all traffic that hasn't been explicitly allowed), should be placed at the end. In the table, the implicit deny rule is labeled A, so A should be last. In this scenario, any other order for the remaining rules is acceptable as long as A is last.

A is incorrect. Placing the B rule last will block all Hypertext Transfer Protocol (HTTP) traffic from the 192.168.0.0/16 subnet. HTTP uses Transmission Control Protocol (TCP) port 80.
B is incorrect. Placing the C rule last will block all traffic from the 192.168.1.0/8 subnet.
C is incorrect. Placing the D rule last will block all HTTP Secure (HTTPS) traffic from the 192.168.0.0/16 subnet. HTTPS uses TCP port 443.

41. You are configuring an ACL on a firewall. Of the following choices, what could you include?
    A. Certificate
    B. Antivirus signatures
    C. IP filtering
    D. VLAN definition

Answer: **C** is correct. A firewall can filter traffic based on rules in an access control list (ACL). ACLs can filter traffic based on IP addresses (IP filtering), ports (port filtering), or protocols (using protocol IDs).

A is incorrect. Certificates are used for encryption protocols such as Secure Sockets Layer (SSL) or Transport Layer Security (TLS), but are not included in an ACL.
B is incorrect. Antivirus signatures are used to detect malicious software, but are not in an ACL.
D is incorrect. Virtual local area networks (VLANs) are defined on switches, not firewalls.

42. You want to receive email from your ISP. What should be done on your firewall?

    A. Open outgoing port 25.

    B. Open incoming port 110.

    C. Set the firewall to use an implicit deny policy.

    D. Remove the ACL.

Answer: **B** is correct. Post Office Protocol version 3 (POP3) is used to receive email from an Internet Service Provider (ISP) and POP3 uses port 110 by default. Opening port 110 would allow POP3 traffic. Some ISPs use Internet Message Access Protocol (IMAP) and if so, port 143 would need to be opened.

A is incorrect. Simple Mail Transfer Protocol (SMTP) is used to send email. Opening outgoing port 25 would allow you to send email through the firewall, not receive it from the ISP.

C is incorrect. Firewalls use an implicit deny philosophy by default. Only traffic with an explicit rule to allow it through is passed by the firewall. Other traffic that doesn't have an explicit rule to allow it is implicitly denied.

D is incorrect. Removing the access control list (ACL) would block all traffic. The rules within the ACL identify what traffic to allow, so if the ACL is removed, the firewall would not allow any traffic.

43. What type of appliance would you use to filter traffic based on IP addresses and ports within a network?

    A. Host-based firewall

    B. Network-based firewall

C. Proxy server

D. NAT

Answer: **B** is correct. A packet-filtering firewall can filter traffic based on the IP address (or network ID), ports, and some protocols using a protocol ID. A network-based firewall filters network traffic. Other filtering is also possible, such as the use of media access control (MAC) address filters and stateful inspection filters. A packet-filtering firewall makes a decision about allowing or blocking a packet based entirely on the contents of a single packet. A stateful inspection firewall evaluates all the traffic and determines if the packet is part of an existing session.

A is incorrect. A host-based firewall (sometimes referred to as a software firewall) filters traffic for a single system, not the entire network.
C is incorrect. A proxy server can filter traffic based on keywords or website addresses, but not IP addresses and ports.
D is incorrect. Network Address Translation (NAT) is a protocol used to translate public and private IP addresses and does not filter traffic.

44. What port should you close in a firewall to block users from sending email through a firewall?

A. 20

B. 22

C. 25

D. 443

Answer: **C** is correct. Simple Mail Transfer Protocol (SMTP) is used to send email over Transmission Control Protocol (TCP) port 25, so outgoing TCP port 25 should be closed.

A is incorrect. Port 20 is used for the File Transfer Protocol (FTP) along with port 21.

B is incorrect. Secure Shell (SSH) encrypts some protocols and it uses port 22.

D is incorrect. Hypertext Transfer Protocol Secure (HTTPS) uses port 443.

Objective: 3.6 Explain the purpose of various network access control models.

45. You need to set up a wireless network for customers so that they can access the Internet. However, you do not want the customers to be able to access the company's network. What should you set up?

    A. DMZ

    B. VTP

    C. 802.1x server

    D. Guest network

Answer: **D** is correct. A guest network allows customers to access the Internet without being able to access an internal network.

A is incorrect. A demilitarized zone (DMZ) provides some protection for Internet-facing servers, but won't grant customers access to the Internet.

B is incorrect. The VLAN Trunk Protocol (VTP) is a Cisco protocol that transmits VLAN information to all switches on the network. It will not provide customers access to the Internet.

C is incorrect. An 802.1x server can require users to authenticate before granting them access to a network. However, customers would not have user accounts, so would not be able to authenticate.

46. You need to implement port security. What protocol would you use?

    A. 802.3af

    B. 802.11i

    C. 802.1q

    D. 802.1x

Answer: **D** is correct. 802.1x is used for port security. It can be used for port security on wired devices or wireless devices. As an example, Wi-Fi Protected Access II-Enterprise (WPA2-Enterprise) can use Remote Authentication Dial-In User Service (RADIUS) as an 802.1x authentication server.

A is incorrect. 802.3af describes Power over Ethernet (PoE), which provides power over an Ethernet cable (such as Category 6 cable) to a device.

B is incorrect. 802.11i describes Wi-Fi Protected Access II (WPA2), which supersedes Wired Equivalent Privacy (WEP).

C is incorrect. 802.1q defines virtual local area networks (VLANs).

47. A small business is allowing customers to access its wireless network so that they can access the Internet. A security expert recommends setting up a guest network instead. What benefit is provided by a guest network?

    A. Reduces bandwidth usage

    B. Protects servers in the DMZ

    C. Protects guests from malware

    D. Isolates company resources

Answer: **D** is correct. A guest network isolates company resources, but also allows customers to access the Internet.

A is incorrect. Granting more users access to a network will increase bandwidth usage, not decrease it.
B is incorrect. Firewalls protect servers in a demilitarized zone (DMZ). A guest network won't assist with this.
C is incorrect. A guest network won't protect users from malware. If they have access, this will increase their chances of being exposed to malware.

Objective: 3.7 Summarize basic forensic concepts.

48. An employee was accused of violating a security policy and a technician was directed to confiscate the employee's laptop computer. The technician collected the laptop computer and stored it on his desk overnight. Which of the following forensic concepts did the technician ignore?
    A. Beginning a chain of custody
    B. Securing the area
    C. Documenting the scene
    D. Protecting data during transport

Answer: **A** is correct. A chain of custody provides assurances that evidence has been controlled and handled properly after collection. The employee should have secured the laptop after confiscating it and created a chain-of-custody document to identify how the laptop was controlled.
B and C are incorrect. The technician was told to confiscate the laptop computer. Forensic experts or management personnel were responsible for securing the area and documenting the scene.

D is incorrect. Data was not transported, other than the data on the laptop computer, so the technician did not ignore any data transport guidelines.

49. While troubleshooting an issue on a user's computer, a technician discovers several videos that are not work related and might be illegal. What should the technician do?
    A. Contact the police.
    B. Create a forensic report.
    C. Escalate the event.
    D. Create a chain-of-custody document.

Answer: **C** is correct. The technician should escalate the incident based on the organization's policies. In most cases, the technician would escalate the incident to a manager or supervisor.

A is incorrect. It is not appropriate for the technician to contact the police unless there is some type of threat to people. Also, the technician doesn't know if the videos are illegal. Management might choose to call the police later.

B is incorrect. Forensic experts would create a forensic report after performing a forensic investigation. However, there is no indication an investigation has been performed.

D is incorrect. The technician should create a chain-of-custody document if evidence was collected, but no evidence was collected in this scenario.

Chapter 4 Troubleshooting

Troubleshooting topics are 24 percent of the CompTIA Network + exam. The objectives in this domain are:

4.1 Given a scenario, implement the following network troubleshooting methodology.

- Identify the problem
    - Gather information
    - Duplicate the problem, if possible
    - Question users
    - Identify symptoms
    - Determine if anything has changed
    - Approach multiple problems individually
- Establish a theory of probable cause
    - Question the obvious
    - Consider multiple approaches
        - Top-to-bottom/bottom-to-top OSI model
        - Divide and conquer
- Test the theory to determine cause
    - Once theory is confirmed, determine next steps to resolve problem
    - If theory is not confirmed, re-establish new theory or escalate
- Establish a plan of action to resolve the problem and identify potential effects
- Implement the solution or escalate as necessary
- Verify full system functionality and if applicable implement preventative measures
- Document findings, actions, and outcomes

4.2 Given a scenario, analyze and interpret the output of troubleshooting tools.

- Command line tools
    - Ipconfig
    - Netstat
    - Ifconfig
    - ping/ping6/ping -6
    - tracert/tracert -6/traceroute6/traceroute -6
    - nbtstat
    - nslookup
    - arp
    - mac address lookup table
    - pathping
- Line testers

- Certifiers
- Multimeter
- Cable tester
- Light meter
- Toner probe
- Speed test sites
- Looking glass sites
- WiFi analyzer
- Protocol analyzer

4.3 Given a scenario, troubleshoot and resolve common wireless issues.

- Signal loss
- Interference
- Overlapping channels
  - Mismatched channels
- Signal-to-noise ratio
- Device saturation
- Bandwidth saturation
- Untested updates
- Wrong SSID
- Power levels
- Open networks
- Rogue access point
- Wrong antenna type
- Incompatibilities
- Wrong encryption
- Bounce
- MIMO
- AP placement
- AP configurations
  - LWAPP
  - Thin vs thick
- Environmental factors
  - Concrete walls
  - Window film
  - Metal studs
- Wireless standard related issues
  - Throughput
  - Frequency
  - Distance
  - Channels

4.4 Given a scenario, troubleshoot and resolve common copper cable issues.

- Shorts

- Opens
- Incorrect termination (mismatched standards)
  - Straight-through
  - Crossover
- Cross-talk
  - Near end
  - Far end
- EMI/RFI
- Distance limitations
- Attenuation/Db loss
- Bad connector
- Bad wiring
- Split pairs
- Tx/Rx reverse
- Cable placemen
- Bad SFP/GBIC - cable or transceiver

4.5 Given a scenario, troubleshoot and resolve common fiber cable issues.

- Attenuation/Db loss
- SFP/GBIC - cable mismatch
- Bad SFP/GBIC - cable or transceiver
- Wavelength mismatch
- Fiber type mismatch
- Dirty connectors
- Connector mismatch
- Bend radius limitations
- Distance limitations

4.6 Given a scenario, troubleshoot and resolve common network issues.

- Incorrect IP configuration/default gateway
- Broadcast storms/switching loop
- Duplicate IP
- Speed and duplex mismatch
- End-to-end connectivity
- Incorrect VLAN assignment
- Hardware failure
- Misconfigured DHCP
- Misconfigured DNS
- Incorrect interface/interface misconfiguration
- Cable placement
- Interface errors
- Simultaneous wired/wireless connections
- Discovering neighboring devices/nodes
- Power failure/power anomalies

- MTU/MTU black hole
- Missing IP routes
- NIC teaming misconfiguration
    - Active-active vs active-passive
    - Multicast vs broadcast

4.7 Given a scenario, troubleshoot and resolve common security issues.

- Misconfigured firewall
- Misconfigured ACLs/applications
- Malware
- Denial of service
- Open/closed ports
- ICMP related issues
    - Ping of death
    - Unreachable default gateway
- Unpatched firmware/OSs
- Malicious users
    - Trusted
    - Untrusted users
    - Packet sniffing
- Authentication issues
    - TACACS/RADIUS misconfigurations
    - Default passwords/settings
- Improper access/backdoor access
- ARP issues
- Banner grabbing/OUI
- Domain/local group configurations
- Jamming

4.8 Given a scenario, troubleshoot and resolve common WAN issues.

- Loss of internet connectivity
- Interface errors
- Split-horizon
- DNS issues
- Interference
- Router configurations
- Customer premise equipment
    - Smart jack/NIU
    - Demarc
    - Loopback
    - CSU/DSU
    - Copper line drivers/repeaters
- Company security policy
    - Throttling
    - Blocking
    - Fair access policy/utilization limits

- Satellite issues
- Latency

**

Practice Test Mode Section — Practice Test Questions without Answers for Troubleshooting

1. You become aware of a network problem. One user within the HR department is unable to access the company website on the Internet and another user is unable to access a file server on the network. After troubleshooting, you realize you cannot reach any of the HR computers through a network switch. What should you do next?

   A. Identify the problem.

   B. Establish a theory of probable cause.

   C. Establish a plan of action to resolve the problem and identify potential effects.

   D. Document findings, actions, and outcomes.

2. You are asked to check into a problem a user is having accessing the company intranet web server managed by another department. You've verified that other users are having the same problem. Of the following choices, what is the most logical next step?

   A. Establish a plan of action to resolve the problem.

   B. Ask the server administrator to reboot the server.

   C. Ask the server administrator if the server had any recent changes.

   D. Restore the server from backups.

3. You are troubleshooting a network problem that is preventing a user from accessing any resources outside the network. You theorize that the default gateway was configured incorrectly and test the system with ipconfig to verify your theory. What should you do next?

A. Identify the problem.

B. Establish a plan of action to resolve the problem and identify potential effects.

C. Implement the solution or escalate as necessary.

D. Document findings, actions, and outcomes.

4. You have been assisting a user with a network problem. After you've implemented a solution to the problem, what should you do next?

   A. Assist the next user's problem as quickly as possible.

   B. Establish a theory of probable cause.

   C. Document findings, actions, and outcomes.

   D. Verify full system functionality and if applicable implement preventative measures.

5. Users are receiving duplicate IP addresses on your network. You have only one authorized DHCP server, but you suspect someone has installed a wireless access point that is issuing IP addresses. Using a sniffer, you've verified that a rogue DHCP server is issuing IP addresses. Based on the CompTIA troubleshooting model, what should you do next?

   A. Identify the problem.

   B. Establish a theory of probable cause.

   C. Establish a plan of action to resolve the problem.

   D. Document findings, actions, and outcomes.

6. While troubleshooting a networking connectivity problem for a user, you discover that all users on a single segment have lost connectivity. Which of the following is the MOST appropriate action to take next?
    A. Determine if anything has changed.
    B. Establish a plan of action to resolve the problem and identify potential effects.
    C. Implement the solution or escalate as necessary.
    D. Verify full system functionality.

7. Homer complains that he cannot print a document to a specific printer. After investigating the problem, you discover that other users are able to print documents to the same printer. Of the following choices, what is the BEST next step?
    A. Power cycle the printer.
    B. Establish a plan of action to resolve the problem.
    C. Ask Homer if can access any network resources.
    D. Document the problem with the printer.

8. Several computers lost network connectivity and you determined the problem is due to a bad CAT6 cable. The cable is within a server wall between a switch and a router. You know which cable it is from the switch, but you're having trouble locating the other end of the cable. Which of the following tools will help you locate the faulty cable?
    A. Toner probe
    B. Multimeter
    C. Cable tester
    D. Protocol analyzer

9. You suspect that a twisted-pair cable is damaged and has a split wire. What can you use to check it?
   A. Toner probe
   B. Cable tester
   C. OTDR
   D. Crimper

10. You suspect that an attacker is sending malformed packets to a web server in an attempt to cause it to crash. What would you use to capture and inspect the packets sent to this server?
    A. TDR
    B. Certifier
    C. Butt set
    D. Sniffer

11. You need to trace a single red wire through an area that has multiple red wires going through it. What would make your job easier?
    A. Cable tester
    B. Certifier
    C. Toner probe
    D. TDR

12. Your organization wants to determine how much bandwidth is being consumed by P2P sharing services. What tool can you use?
    A. Certifier
    B. Protocol analyzer
    C. Crimper
    D. OTDR

13. While troubleshooting a problem with an FTP server, you capture some traffic with a protocol analyzer. You want to filter the capture so that it only shows FTP traffic. Which of the following ports should you include in the capture filter? (Select TWO.)

    A. 20

    B. 21

    C. 22

    D. 23

14. You need to move a cable connecting a server from one switch to another. What can you use to verify you have the correct cable?

    A. Certifier

    B. Packet sniffer

    C. Punch down tool

    D. Toner probe

15. You maintain a wireless network that is using MAC filtering to restrict access. You suspect that attackers have discovered MAC addresses and are spoofing them to gain access. What would they have used to discover these MAC addresses?

    A. Firewall

    B. Protocol analyzer

    C. Multimeter

    D. OTDR

16. Which of the following commands can you use to test connectivity with a remote system?

    A. Ping

    B. Ipconfig

C. Arp

D. Route

17. Which of the following types of information are you likely to obtain when using the tracert command?

    A. Physical address of systems

    B. MAC address of systems

    C. IP address for each hop

    D. IP address for local system

18. You want to determine if your computer can resolve a web server name to an IP address. Which of the following commands will work?

    A. Nslookup

    B. Ipconfig

    C. Netstat

    D. Route

19. Which of the following is a command-line tool you can use to view TCP/IP configuration for a NIC?

    A. Nslookup

    B. Nbtstat

    C. Ifconfig

    D. Ping

20. You want to determine how long it takes a packet to get to and from a router. What can you use?

    A. Ipconfig

    B. Traceroute

    C. Nslookup

    D. Netstat

21. You suspect your system is being attacked on TCP port 5555. What could you use to determine if this port is being used and to identify the source of the connection?
    A. netstat -e
    B. netstat -es tcp
    C. netstat -nap tcp
    D. netstat -tcp

22. What command can you use to determine the IP address that is assigned to a computer?
    A. Netstat
    B. Traceroute
    C. Ipconfig
    D. Ping

23. You are troubleshooting a connectivity issue with a server across a WAN link. Which of the following commands will give you the most information about the path to this server?
    A. Ping
    B. Nslookup
    C. Arp
    D. Tracert

24. A system has an incorrect DNS entry in cache. What can you use to remove this entry?
    A. Ipconfig /displaydns
    B. Ipconfig /flushdns
    C. Nslookup /removedns
    D. Nslookup /flushdns

25. You are troubleshooting a network connectivity issue within your organization's network. You used tracert to determine the source of the problem, but the output only gave you a "Request timed out" result. What should you do to ensure tracert gives you more information?

    A. Enable routers to allow echo messages.

    B. Enable ping.

    C. Enable ICMP traffic on border firewalls.

    D. Enable IGMP traffic on internal firewalls.

26. You want to determine the MAC address of five systems in a small network. What can you do?

    A. Ping each and then use the arp command.

    B. Use nslookup and then ping each IP address.

    C. Use the route command and then run tracert.

    D. Ping each and then use the ipconfig command.

27. What is the function of ARP?

    A. Resolve IP addresses to MAC addresses.

    B. Resolve MAC addresses to IP addresses.

    C. Resolve host names to IP addresses.

    D. Resolve IP addresses to host names.

28. You want to check connectivity of a website on the Internet at the Network layer of the OSI model. What would you use?

    A. Nbtstat

    B. Dig

    C. Route

    D. Ping

29. You want to view a listing of active TCP connections. What command would you use?
    A. Dig
    B. Ipconfig
    C. Arp
    D. Netstat

30. What can you use to verify an IP address conflict on a network?
    A. Dig
    B. Ipconfig
    C. Arp
    D. Netstat

31. What can you use to check the number of active connections on your computer?
    A. Netstat
    B. Tracert
    C. Dig
    D. Nslookup

32. Homer is able to connect his smartphone to the organization's wireless network while he's in the lobby. However, when sitting at his desk, his smartphone keeps disconnecting from the network, even though he has a strong wireless signal. Which of the following is the MOST likely cause of this problem?
    A. Faulty wiring
    B. Cross-talk
    C. Wrong SSID
    D. Bounce

33. After replacing a faulty WAP, you discover that users working in the accounting department are having intermittent problems, but other users can connect to the network without any problem. Before replacing the WAP, users in the accounting department didn't have any problems. What is the MOST likely reason for this problem?
    A. WAP placement is causing problems.
    B. Wrong SSID was configured.
    C. An incorrect media converter was installed.
    D. Accounting department systems are using the incorrect wireless protocol.

34. When Bart connects to the wireless network, he can normally connect to a general server with data he uses for his job. After connecting to the wireless network today, he was unable to find his data, but instead saw several shared folders that weren't familiar to him. Which of the following is the MOST likely cause for this?
    A. Bart connected to the network with the wrong SSID.
    B. Bart connected to the network with an incorrect channel.
    C. Bart connected to a network with excessive bounce.
    D. Bart connected to the network with the wrong antenna.

35. You are configuring three 802.11g wireless access points for a business in the United States. What channels should you use to avoid interference?
    A. 1, 6, 11
    B. 1, 6, 13
    C. 5, 6, 7
    D. 1, 2, 3

36. When installing multiple wireless access points, what will help ensure the best performance?
    A. Disabling SSID broadcast
    B. Enabling WPA2
    C. Using overlapping channels
    D. Using nonoverlapping channels

37. A wireless network is experiencing interference from telephones using the 2.4-GHz frequency range. Which of the following can be used to avoid this interference? (Select TWO.)
    A. 802.11a
    B. 802.11b
    C. 802.11g
    D. 802.11ac

38. An organization has three wireless networks running in the same environment. What channels should they use?
    A. 1, 2, 3
    B. 1, 4, 8
    C. 1, 6, 11
    D. 9, 10, 11

39. You are preparing to connect two networks together in different locations. The only place you can run the cables is in a power duct side by side with power. What type of cable should you use to ensure there are no problems?
    A. Either UTP or SMF
    B. Either UTP or MMF
    C. Either SMF or MMF
    D. Either UTP or STP

40. You are troubleshooting a wired printer and notice that the link light on the NIC is not lit. You test the printer on a different RJ-45 port and it works. What is the MOST likely problem?
    A. Faulty NIC
    B. Signal bounce
    C. Faulty wiring
    D. Faulty media converter

41. After replacing a cable for a user's computer, the system is unable to connect to the network. You checked the port on the switch and verified it is enabled and configured correctly and you verified the 1-Gbps NIC on the computer is using auto sense. What is the MOST likely problem?
    A. Open wire on the cable
    B. Mismatched speed
    C. Mismatched duplex mode
    D. EMI

42. A technician is planning on running several twisted-pairs to a switch. He decides to bundle the cables tightly together to make it easier to run all the cables at the same time. What type of problem can this cause?
    A. Cross-talk
    B. EMI
    C. DB loss
    D. TX RX reversal

43. You are troubleshooting an intermittent connection issue with a computer. You've traced the twisted-pair cable and see it is running through several open power junction boxes. You've measured the length of the cable and determined it is 110 feet long. What is the MOST likely problem?

    A. Cable length
    B. Electromagnetic interference
    C. Plenum safety
    D. Open in the cable

44. You are troubleshooting an intermittent connection with a computer. Upon inspection, you notice that a large part of the jacket has been removed on the cable close to the jack, and the pairs are untwisted. What types of problem can this cause?

    A. Cross-talk
    B. DB loss
    C. TX RX reversal
    D. Duplex mismatch

45. You are preparing to connect several networking devices together in an environment that has a high amount of interference. What type of cables provides the BEST protection?

    A. MMF and UTP
    B. UTP and STP
    C. STP and MMF
    D. STP and Plenum-safe

46. A new technician gave you a twisted-pair cable saying it doesn't work. When he used it to connect to a 100-Mbps switch, the link light never lit. However, when you use this cable to connect a computer to a 1,000 Mbps switch, the connection does work. What is the MOST likely reason?

    A. The 1,000-Mbps switch is using PoE, but the 100-Mbps switch is not using PoE.

    B. The cable has the wrong LC connector for the 100-Mbps switch.

    C. The cable is wired as a crossover cable.

    D. The cable is wired for 1,000 Mbps, not 100 Mbps.

47. You need to plug in a fiber-optic cable to an RJ-45 jack. What, if anything, can be used to allow this to work?

    A. Nothing. This is not possible.

    B. Media converter

    C. ST connector

    D. SC connector

48. You are troubleshooting an intermittent connection issue with a computer. After tracing the wire, you've verified it is running through a fluorescent lighting fixture. Could this be causing the problem and if so, why?

    A. No

    B. Yes, due to EMI

    C. Yes, due to cross-talk

    D. Yes, due to duplex mismatch

49. A technician recently moved a desktop computer used within a manufacturing plant. After moving it, users report intermittent connectivity problems with this computer. Reviewing the logs, you've verified that the problems are only occurring when the manufacturing equipment is running. What is the MOST likely cause of the problem?

    A. STP cable

    B. GBIC mismatch

    C. EMI

    D. Duplex mismatch

50. You are troubleshooting a network outage. You suspect that a fiber cable with a small service loop is the cause of the problem. What problem can a small service loop cause in this scenario?

    A. Excessive EMI

    B. Bend radius exceeded

    C. Wavelength mismatch

    D. Low signal power

51. You are tasked with connecting a DWDM system to a router. After connecting it, you verify that the router is receiving a good signal. However, the router is not transmitting data through the connected interface. Which of the following is the MOST likely cause for this problem?

    A. The fiber cable is faulty.

    B. A mismatch with the GBIC.

    C. The DWDM system is not configured to transmit the correct wavelength.

    D. The wrong SSID is assigned.

52. A technician saw a cable with one end plugged into a switch but the other end unconnected. He plugged the cable into an open port on the switch. Afterwards, all users connected through this switch are complaining of connectivity problems. What is the likely cause?

    A. Switching loop

    B. Bad/missing routes

    C. Wrong gateway

    D. Wrong DNS

53. You are inspecting a switch and you notice that most of the LEDs are blinking green, but one is blinking orange. Of the following choices, what is the MOST likely reason?

    A. Port configured to wrong port speed

    B. Port connected with a crossover cable

    C. Port configured with wrong subnet mask

    D. Switching loop

54. You are assisting a user who is troubleshooting a network connectivity problem. The user is unable to reach the GetCertifiedGetAhead.com website using a web browser, but is able to ping the website using the website's IP address. What is the MOST likely problem?

    A. DHCP

    B. Default gateway

    C. DNS

    D. Router

55. Several devices are connected to a network via a switch. All of the devices except one are able to communicate with network resources. This one device has an APIPA address. What is the MOST likely reason?

    A. The computer is assigned a duplicate IP address.

    B. The computer is not a DHCP client.

    C. STP is not running on this computer.

    D. The port on the switch for this computer is disabled.

56. Several users are complaining that they are unable to communicate on the network, though they could yesterday. You discover all these users are connected to the same switch and all the LEDs on this switch are blinking rapidly. What is the MOST likely problem?

    A. A broadcast storm is causing interference.

    B. Traffic is being segregated by the switch.

    C. An incorrect default gateway is assigned.

    D. The users are connected on different VLAN segments.

57. You recently installed a new AP on a wireless network. All devices can communicate with each other on the wireless network. However, none of the devices can access the Internet. What is the MOST likely problem?

    A. The AP has the incorrect SSID.

    B. Devices are configured with the incorrect SSID.

    C. The AP has the incorrect gateway.

    D. The edge router has the incorrect gateway.

58. Network 1 includes multiple computers in the 10.10.10.16/28 range. Homer has called into the helpdesk complaining that he can't access

the Internet. He says that he configured the NIC, but he suspects it needs to be replaced. You determine that his NIC has the following settings:

IP address: 10.10.10.17

Subnet mask: 255.255.255.240

Default gateway: 10.10.10.32

Speed: 100 Mbps

Duplex: Full

What is the cause of the problem?

A. The NIC has an incorrect IP address.

B. The NIC has an incorrect default gateway.

C. The NIC is configured with the incorrect speed.

D. The NIC is configured with the incorrect subnet mask.

59. Network 1 includes multiple computers in the 10.10.10.16/28 range. Homer has called into the helpdesk complaining that he can't access the Internet. He says that he configured the NIC, but he suspects it needs to be replaced. You determine that his NIC has the following settings:

IP address: 10.10.10.16

Subnet mask: 255.255.255.240

Default gateway: 10.10.10.28

Speed: 10 Gbps

Duplex: Full

What is the cause of the problem?

A. The NIC has an incorrect IP address.

B. The NIC has an incorrect default gateway.

C. The NIC is configured with the incorrect speed.

D. The NIC is configured with the incorrect subnet mask.

60. You have just removed malware from a user's computer and completed a full scan to ensure it doesn't have any additional malware on it. When checking it out, you determine that the computer is unable to access some websites. Which of the following is the MOST likely cause?

A. The computer has an incorrect default gateway assigned.

B. The local hosts file has been modified.

C. The computer has an incorrect subnet mask assigned.

D. The DHCP reservation has been modified.

61. Maggie enters the following command: **telnet server1 80** against a remote server. Which of the following BEST describes the purpose of this command?

A. Identify if server1 is running a service using port 80 and is reachable.

B. Launch an attack on server1 sending 80 separate packets in a short period of time.

C. Use Telnet to remotely administer server1.

D. Use Telnet to start an RDP session.

62. Routers in your wide area network (WAN) are using RIPv2. Which of the following can prevent switching loops with these routers?

A. Split-horizon route advertisement

B. BGP

C. OSPF

D. Convergence

63. What identifies the line where responsibility for a communications link lies with either the provider or the customer?

A. Demarc

B. MDF

C. IDF

D. CSU/DSU

64. Which of the following indicates one of the primary weaknesses with satellite connections?

A. Cost of physical media

B. Latency

C. Distance limitations

D. Compatibility

65. Of the following choices, what can you use to connect networks without the use of physical cables between the networks?

A. DSL

B. OC-24

C. Satellite

D. SONET

66. A company is leasing a T-1 line. What would the T-1 connect to at the company's building?

A. Server

B. 110 block

C. Smart jack

D. Wireless router

67. What would you connect with a CSU/DSU?

A. WAP

B. T-1

C. POTS lines

D. Wireless devices

Review Mode Section — Practice Test Questions with Answers for Troubleshooting

Objective: 4.1 Given a scenario, implement the following network troubleshooting methodology.

1. You become aware of a network problem. One user within the HR department is unable to access the company website on the Internet and another user is unable to access a file server on the network. After troubleshooting, you realize you cannot reach any of the HR computers through a network switch. What should you do next?

   A. Identify the problem.

   B. Establish a theory of probable cause.

   C. Establish a plan of action to resolve the problem and identify potential effects.

   D. Document findings, actions, and outcomes.

Answer: **B** is correct. Based on the information given, the next troubleshooting step is to establish a theory of probable cause. This is based on the CompTIA troubleshooting model.

A is incorrect. The first troubleshooting step is to identify the problem by gathering information and identifying symptoms, and the scenario indicates the problem has been identified.
C is incorrect. Establishing a plan of action is done after establishing and testing a theory.
D is incorrect. Documentation is the last step.

2. You are asked to check into a problem a user is having accessing the company intranet web server managed by another department. You've verified that other users are having the same problem. Of the following choices, what is the most logical next step?
    A. Establish a plan of action to resolve the problem.
    B. Ask the server administrator to reboot the server.
    C. Ask the server administrator if the server had any recent changes.
    D. Restore the server from backups.

Answer: **C** is correct. The first step in troubleshooting is identifying the problem. This includes gathering information, duplicating the problem (if possible), questioning users, identifying symptoms, and determining if anything has changed. Of these, the only thing the scenario hasn't addressed is checking to see if anything has changed. The next step would be to establish a theory of probable cause.

A is incorrect. Additional information is needed before establishing a plan of action.
B is incorrect. You might choose to boot the server, as a method to implement a solution, but you shouldn't implement a solution before fully identifying the problem.
D is incorrect. Restoring the server from backups would be implementing a solution, but you shouldn't implement a solution before fully identifying the problem.

3. You are troubleshooting a network problem that is preventing a user from accessing any resources outside the network. You theorize that the default gateway was configured incorrectly and test the system with ipconfig to verify your theory. What should you do next?

   A. Identify the problem.

   B. Establish a plan of action to resolve the problem and identify potential effects.

   C. Implement the solution or escalate as necessary.

   D. Document findings, actions, and outcomes.

Answer: **B** is correct. The CompTIA troubleshooting model specifies that you should establish a plan of action to resolve the problem after establishing and testing a theory. In this case, the solution would be to reconfigure the default gateway correctly.

A is incorrect. The first step is to identify the problem and this was done by gathering information and identifying the symptoms.
C is incorrect. Before implementing the solution, a plan of action is established to determine any potential effects.
D is incorrect. The last step of the CompTIA troubleshooting model is documentation.

4. You have been assisting a user with a network problem. After you've implemented a solution to the problem, what should you do next?

   A. Assist the next user's problem as quickly as possible.

   B. Establish a theory of probable cause.

   C. Document findings, actions, and outcomes.

   D. Verify full system functionality and if applicable implement preventative measures.

Answer: **D** is correct. Based on the CompTIA troubleshooting model, you should verify the system is fully functional after implementing a solution.

A is incorrect. You should not begin working on the next problem until you have completely finished the current problem.
B is incorrect. Establishing a theory of probable cause is done early in the CompTIA troubleshooting process, immediately after identifying the problem.
C is incorrect. Documentation is the last step.

5. Users are receiving duplicate IP addresses on your network. You have only one authorized DHCP server, but you suspect someone has installed a wireless access point that is issuing IP addresses. Using a sniffer, you've verified that a rogue DHCP server is issuing IP addresses. Based on the CompTIA troubleshooting model, what should you do next?
    A. Identify the problem.
    B. Establish a theory of probable cause.
    C. Establish a plan of action to resolve the problem.
    D. Document findings, actions, and outcomes.

Answer: **C** is correct. Based on the information given, the next troubleshooting step is to establish a plan of action to resolve the problem. In this scenario, you would establish a plan of action to locate the rogue Dynamic Host Configuration Protocol (DHCP) server. DHCP could be running on a wireless access point or on a different device.

A is incorrect. You've identified the problem as duplicate IP addresses.
B is incorrect. You've established and verified a theory of a rogue DHCP server issuing duplicate IP addresses.

D is incorrect. You would document your findings, actions, and outcomes after resolving the problem.

6. While troubleshooting a networking connectivity problem for a user, you discover that all users on a single segment have lost connectivity. Which of the following is the MOST appropriate action to take next?

   A. Determine if anything has changed.

   B. Establish a plan of action to resolve the problem and identify potential effects.

   C. Implement the solution or escalate as necessary.

   D. Verify full system functionality.

Answer: **A** is correct. The first step in troubleshooting is identifying the problem. This includes gathering information, duplicating the problem (if possible), questioning users, identifying symptoms, and determining if anything has changed. Of these, the only thing the scenario hasn't addressed is checking to see if anything has changed. The next step would be to establish a theory of probable cause.

B is incorrect. You would establish a plan of action, only after establishing and testing a theory.
C is incorrect. You would implement the solution after establishing a plan of action.
D is incorrect. You would verify full system functionality after implementing a solution.

7. Homer complains that he cannot print a document to a specific printer. After investigating the problem, you discover that other users are able to print documents to the same printer. Of the following choices, what is the BEST next step?
   A. Power cycle the printer.
   B. Establish a plan of action to resolve the problem.
   C. Ask Homer if can access any network resources.
   D. Document the problem with the printer.

Answer: **C** is correct. If other users can access the printer, the best choice of the available answers is to ask the user if he has *any* network access. This is part of the first step in the CompTIA troubleshooting model—identify the problem.

A is incorrect. You wouldn't implement a solution before identifying the problem. Additionally, other people can print, so cycling the power on the printer (turning it off and back on) isn't necessary.
B is incorrect. You would establish a plan of action to resolve the problem after you have identified the problem, established a theory of probable cause, and tested the theory.
D is incorrect. Documentation is the last step in the CompTIA troubleshooting model. Additionally, the problem isn't with the printer because other users can print to it.

Objective: 4.2 Given a scenario, analyze and interpret the output of troubleshooting tools.

8. Several computers lost network connectivity and you determined the problem is due to a bad CAT6 cable. The cable is within a server wall between a switch and a router. You know which cable it is from the switch, but you're having trouble locating the other end of the cable. Which of the following tools will help you locate the faulty cable?
   A. Toner probe
   B. Multimeter
   C. Cable tester
   D. Protocol analyzer

Answer: **A** is correct. A toner probe is the best choice of the available answers. It includes a tone generator and a speaker. You connect the tone generator onto one end of the cable to place a tone on the cable. You can then go to the other end of the cable in another room. The speaker has a probe you can touch to individual cables and the tone plays on the speaker when you've found the correct cable.

B is incorrect. A multimeter is useful for measuring voltage. You can also use it to measure continuity (an open or a short) if you have both ends of the cable available.

C is incorrect. A cable tester can verify that a cable is wired accurately. It isn't useful if you're trying to locate the other end of the cable.

D is incorrect. A protocol analyzer (also called a sniffer) can capture and analyze packets. It won't help you locate the physical end of a cable.

9. You suspect that a twisted-pair cable is damaged and has a split wire. What can you use to check it?
   A. Toner probe
   B. Cable tester
   C. OTDR
   D. Crimper

Answer: **B** is correct. Cable testers verify that a cable is wired accurately and doesn't have any breaks in it. It can be used to test a cable that you suspect is bad, or a cable that has just been wired.

A is incorrect. A toner probe is useful for tracing wires, but it isn't the best tool to check for a damaged cable.
C is incorrect. An optical time domain reflectometer (OTDR) is used to test fiber, not twisted-pair cables.
D is incorrect. A crimper would be used to attach a Registered Jack-45 (RJ-45) connector to a twisted-pair cable, not check it.

10. You suspect that an attacker is sending malformed packets to a web server in an attempt to cause it to crash. What would you use to capture and inspect the packets sent to this server?
    A. TDR
    B. Certifier
    C. Butt set
    D. Sniffer

Answer: **D** is correct. A sniffer (also called a protocol analyzer) can capture packets and these packets can then be inspected to look for any abnormalities, possibly indicating an attack.

A is incorrect. A time domain reflectometer (TDR) can identify the location of a break in a cable, but it doesn't do any analysis of packets.
B is incorrect. A cable certifier verifies that a cable meets specifications, such as ensuring that it can transfer data at a specific speed. A cable certifier cannot capture packets.
C is incorrect. Telephone technicians use a butt set to verify that a telephone line is working.

11. You need to trace a single red wire through an area that has multiple red wires going through it. What would make your job easier?
    A. Cable tester
    B. Certifier
    C. Toner probe
    D. TDR

Answer: **C** is correct. A toner probe allows you to place a tone on one end of a wire and then locate the other end by finding the wire that has the corresponding tone.

A is incorrect. A cable tester can verify that a cable is wired correctly, but it isn't useful when you need to trace a wire.
B is incorrect. A certifier verifies that a cable is working and can transmit data based on specifications.
D is incorrect. A time domain reflectometer (TDR) identifies the exact location of a break in a long cable.

12. Your organization wants to determine how much bandwidth is being consumed by P2P sharing services. What tool can you use?

    A. Certifier

    B. Protocol analyzer

    C. Crimper

    D. OTDR

Answer: **B** is correct. Peer-to-peer (P2P) traffic uses specific ports and a protocol analyzer (also called a sniffer) can capture traffic and determine how much of the traffic is using these ports. A protocol analyzer can even determine which IP addresses are generating the most P2P traffic.

A is incorrect. Certifiers are used to verify that cables meet required specifications.
C is incorrect. A crimper is used to attach a connector to a cable such as a Registered Jack-45 (RJ-45) connector to a twisted-pair cable.
D is incorrect. An optical time domain reflectometer (OTDR) is used to identify the location of a break in a fiber-optic cable.

13. While troubleshooting a problem with an FTP server, you capture some traffic with a protocol analyzer. You want to filter the capture so that it only shows FTP traffic. Which of the following ports should you include in the capture filter? (Select TWO.)

    A. 20

    B. 21

    C. 22

    D. 23

Answer: **A** and **B** are correct. File Transfer Protocol (FTP) uses ports 20 and 21. By filtering the capture to only show traffic with these ports, you will limit the capture to only show FTP traffic.

C is incorrect. Secure Shell (SSH) uses port 22.
D is incorrect. Telnet uses port 23.

14. You need to move a cable connecting a server from one switch to another. What can you use to verify you have the correct cable?
    A. Certifier
    B. Packet sniffer
    C. Punch down tool
    D. Toner probe

Answer: **D** is correct. A toner probe includes two components, a tone generator and a speaker. You connect the tone generator onto one end of the cable to place a tone on the cable. You can then go to the other end of the cable in another room. The speaker has a probe you can touch to individual cables and the tone plays on the speaker when you've found the correct cable.

A is incorrect. A certifier can verify that a cable is accurately wired, and can operate at a specific speed.
B is incorrect. A packet sniffer (also called a protocol analyzer) can capture and inspect packets going over a network.
C is incorrect. Punch down tools are used to terminate cables to jacks, or connect cables to wiring blocks such as a 110 block.

15. You maintain a wireless network that is using MAC filtering to restrict access. You suspect that attackers have discovered MAC addresses and are spoofing them to gain access. What would they have used to discover these MAC addresses?
    A. Firewall
    B. Protocol analyzer
    C. Multimeter
    D. OTDR

Answer: **B** is correct. A protocol analyzer (also called a sniffer) can capture and analyze packets to discover the allowed media access control (MAC) addresses. Wireless attackers use wireless sniffers to capture wireless traffic to identify specific information, such as the service set identifier (SSID) and allowed MAC addresses.

A is incorrect. The firewall provides some protection against attacks, but the attackers would not use it to discover MAC addresses.
C is incorrect. Technicians use multimeters to take measurements such as voltage measurements or continuity checks.
D is incorrect. An optical time domain reflectometer (OTDR) can identify the location of a break in a fiber-optic cable.

16. Which of the following commands can you use to test connectivity with a remote system?
    A. Ping
    B. Ipconfig
    C. Arp
    D. Route

Answer: **A** is correct. The ping command will check connectivity with remote systems using either the name of the remote system or its IP address. It sends out an Internet Control Message Protocol (ICMP) Echo Request to another system. If the other system is operational and not blocking ICMP, it will respond with an ICMP Echo Reply. If you receive a response, it provides verification that the other system is operational. Many firewalls block ICMP traffic, so if you do not receive a response, it doesn't necessarily mean that the remote system is not operational. It could be that ICMP was blocked. Try it by pinging a computer in your network.

B is incorrect. Ipconfig will show the Transmission Control Protocol/Internet Protocol (TCP/IP) configuration information for a system.
C is incorrect. Arp will show the media access control (MAC) address to IP address mapping for systems in the Address Resolution Protocol (ARP) cache.
D is incorrect. Route allows you to view or manipulate the routing table within a system.

17. Which of the following types of information are you likely to obtain when using the tracert command?
    - A. Physical address of systems
    - B. MAC address of systems
    - C. IP address for each hop
    - D. IP address for local system

Answer: **C** is correct. The tracert (or traceroute) command identifies the IP address of each of the hops between two systems. Each hop represents a router and the round trip time (RTT) shows how long it takes to get to and from the two systems. Try it with **tracert GetCertifiedGetAhead.com**.

A, B, and D are incorrect. You can identify the physical address or media access control (MAC) address, and the IP address of the local system with the **ipconfig /all** command, but not with the tracert command.

18. You want to determine if your computer can resolve a web server name to an IP address. Which of the following commands will work?

    A. Nslookup

    B. Ipconfig

    C. Netstat

    D. Route

Answer: **A** is correct. The nslookup command can check to see if a Domain Name System (DNS) server can resolve a web server name, or any server name, to an IP address.

B is incorrect. Ipconfig can show Transmission Control Protocol/Internet Protocol (TCP/IP) configuration information, but it can't check name resolution.

C is incorrect. Netstat shows different protocol statistics for a system and can list open ports.

D is incorrect. The route command can show known routes and the address of the default gateway, but doesn't resolve host names of web servers.

19. Which of the following is a command-line tool you can use to view TCP/IP configuration for a NIC?

    A. Nslookup

    B. Nbtstat

C. Ifconfig

D. Ping

Answer: **C** is correct. The ifconfig command will show Transmission Control Protocol/Internet Protocol (TCP/IP) configuration for a network interface card (NIC) on Unix/Linux-based systems.

A is incorrect. Nslookup is used to query Domain Name System (DNS) servers and verify that host names can be resolved to an IP address.
B is incorrect. Nbtstat is used to display statistics for Network Basic Input/Output System (NetBIOS) over TCP/IP connections, but it doesn't show TCP/IP configuration.
D is incorrect. Ping can check connectivity with remote systems and is often the next command used after verifying the TCP/IP configuration with ipconfig.

20. You want to determine how long it takes a packet to get to and from a router. What can you use?

    A. Ipconfig

    B. Traceroute

    C. Nslookup

    D. Netstat

Answer: **B** is correct. The traceroute command shows the round trip time (RTT) for each router (or hop) in the path it traces.

A is incorrect. Ipconfig shows Transmission Control Protocol/Internet Protocol (TCP/IP) configuration information but not the RTT.
C is incorrect. Nslookup can query Domain Name System (DNS) servers for name resolution, but doesn't list the RTT for routers.

D is incorrect. The netstat command shows network statistics and open connections.

21. You suspect your system is being attacked on TCP port 5555. What could you use to determine if this port is being used and to identify the source of the connection?

    A. netstat -e

    B. netstat -es tcp

    C. netstat -nap tcp

    D. netstat -tcp

Answer: **C** is correct. The **netstat -nap tcp** command would meet your needs. It includes three switches identified as *n*, *a*, and *p*. The *a* switch lists all open connections, the *n* switch puts them in numerical order, and the *p* switch specifies the Transmission Control Protocol (TCP) protocol. Try it on your computer.

A and B are incorrect. The netstat -e command lists overall statistics for a system and when combined with *s* (as *-es*) it lists the statistics for each protocol.

D is incorrect. Netstat -tcp isn't a valid command.

22. What command can you use to determine the IP address that is assigned to a computer?

    A. Netstat

    B. Traceroute

    C. Ipconfig

    D. Ping

Answer: **C** is correct. The ipconfig command will show basic Transmission Control Protocol/Internet Protocol (TCP/IP) configuration, including the IP address, and can show detailed information with the /all switch (**ipconfig /all**). Try it.

A is incorrect. Netstat is useful to display network statistics and open connections.
B is incorrect. Traceroute will display all the hops between two systems.
D is incorrect. Ping can check connectivity with a remote system, but it doesn't show the local address.

23. You are troubleshooting a connectivity issue with a server across a WAN link. Which of the following commands will give you the most information about the path to this server?
    A. Ping
    B. Nslookup
    C. Arp
    D. Tracert

Answer: **D** is correct. Tracert will give you the most information about the path to a remote system.
A is incorrect. Ping gives you information about connectivity to the remote host, but doesn't provide details about the hops between two systems.
B is incorrect. You would use nslookup to see if a Domain Name System (DNS) server can resolve host names to IP addresses.
C is incorrect. The arp command shows the media access control (MAC) address to IP address mapping for known systems. It doesn't give any information for hosts beyond the router.

24. A system has an incorrect DNS entry in cache. What can you use to remove this entry?
    A. Ipconfig /displaydns
    B. Ipconfig /flushdns
    C. Nslookup /removedns
    D. Nslookup /flushdns

Answer: **B** is correct. The **ipconfig /flushdns** command will remove any entries in the Domain Name System (DNS) cache that were resolved from a DNS server. Try it with the following three commands: **ipconfig /displaydns**, **ipconfig /flushdns**, **ipconfig /displaydns**.

A is incorrect. The **ipconfig /displaydns** command shows the entries in the DNS cache.

C and D are incorrect. Nslookup can be used to verify that a DNS server can resolve a host name to an IP address, but it does not support /removedns or /flushdns switches.

25. You are troubleshooting a network connectivity issue within your organization's network. You used tracert to determine the source of the problem, but the output only gave you a "Request timed out" result. What should you do to ensure tracert gives you more information?
    A. Enable routers to allow echo messages.
    B. Enable ping.
    C. Enable ICMP traffic on border firewalls.
    D. Enable IGMP traffic on internal firewalls.

Answer: **A** is correct. By enabling routers to pass echo messages (such as Echo Reply in and Echo Request out), it will allow tracert echo commands to pass through the routers and provide more information. Unix-based systems typically use tracert commands with User Datagram Protocol (UDP). In contrast, Windows systems use traceroute echo commands with Internet Control Message Protocol (ICMP).

B is incorrect. Tracert is more robust than ping and ping is a different command. Also, ping uses ICMP rather than UDP.
C is incorrect. Because you're only troubleshooting a problem within the network, you don't need to manipulate rules on border firewalls.
D is incorrect. Tracert uses UDP, not Internet Group Management Protocol (IGMP).

26. You want to determine the MAC address of five systems in a small network. What can you do?

    A. Ping each and then use the arp command.

    B. Use nslookup and then ping each IP address.

    C. Use the route command and then run tracert.

    D. Ping each and then use the ipconfig command.

Answer: **A** is correct. When you ping each system, the Address Resolution Protocol (ARP) protocol will resolve the IP address to its media access control (MAC) address and store it in the ARP cache. You can then use the arp command to display the mappings. Try it with the **arp -a** command.

B is incorrect. Nslookup will query Domain Name System (DNS) and the ping command checks connectivity, but neither shows the MAC address.

C is incorrect. The route command shows the routing table and the tracert command can trace a path to other systems, though neither shows the MAC address.

D is incorrect. The **ipconfig /all** command will show the MAC address of the local system, but not remote systems.

27. What is the function of ARP?
    A. Resolve IP addresses to MAC addresses.
    B. Resolve MAC addresses to IP addresses.
    C. Resolve host names to IP addresses.
    D. Resolve IP addresses to host names.

Answer: **A** is correct. The Address Resolution Protocol (ARP) resolves IP addresses to media access control (MAC) addresses. You can view ARP cache with the arp command.

B is incorrect. Reverse ARP (RARP) provides an IP address to a client that has a MAC address. However, it is more common to use Dynamic Host Configuration Protocol (DHCP) to dynamically issue IP addresses instead of RARP.

C is incorrect. Domain Name System (DNS) resolves host names to IP addresses with the use of A records for IPv4 addresses and AAAA records for Internet Protocol version 6 (IPv6) addresses.

D is incorrect. DNS resolves IP addresses to host names with Pointer (PTR) records.

28. You want to check connectivity of a website on the Internet at the Network layer of the OSI model. What would you use?
    A. Nbtstat
    B. Dig

C. Route

D. Ping

Answer: **D** is correct. You can use ping to check connectivity with any system, including one on the Internet. Ping uses Internet Control Message Protocol (ICMP), which operates on the Network layer (Layer 3) of the Open Systems Interconnection (OSI) model. Additionally, IP addresses are defined on the Network layer.

A is incorrect. Nbtstat is used for Network Basic Input/Output System (NetBIOS), but NetBIOS is not used on the Internet.
B is incorrect. Dig can help you determine if you can resolve the name of a website with an IP address, but it does not check connectivity.
C is incorrect. Route can help you determine the default gateway used to reach the website.

29. You want to view a listing of active TCP connections. What command would you use?

    A. Dig

    B. Ipconfig

    C. Arp

    D. Netstat

Answer: **D** is correct. The netstat command shows a listing of open Transmission Control Protocol (TCP) connections and can also show network statistics for specific protocols when used with additional switches. Try it with the netstat -a command.

A is incorrect. You can use the dig command to query Domain Name System (DNS) servers and verify you can resolve names to IP addresses.

B is incorrect. Ipconfig shows the current Transmission Control Protocol/Internet Protocol (TCP/IP) configuration information.
C is incorrect. Arp shows media access control (MAC) address to IP address mappings held in the ARP cache.

30. What can you use to verify an IP address conflict on a network?
    A. Dig
    B. Ipconfig
    C. Arp
    D. Netstat

Answer: **C** is correct. The arp command shows the media access control (MAC) to IP address mapping for known systems and can be used to verify an IP address conflict. An IP address should always map to a single media access control (MAC) address.

A is incorrect. The dig command is used to query and verify Domain Name System (DNS) functionality.
B is incorrect. The ipconfig command will display Transmission Control Protocol/Internet Protocol (TCP/IP) configuration information.
D is incorrect. The netstat command will show network statistics and identify open connections.

31. What can you use to check the number of active connections on your computer?
    A. Netstat
    B. Tracert
    C. Dig
    D. Nslookup

Answer: **A** is correct. The network statistics tool (netstat) can be used to check the number of active connections on a computer. Try it with the **netstat -a** command.

B is incorrect. Tracert can trace a path through routers, or hops, on a network.
C and D are incorrect. Dig and nslookup are used to verify functionality with Domain Name System (DNS).

Objective: 4.3 Given a scenario, troubleshoot and resolve common wireless issues.

32. Homer is able to connect his smartphone to the organization's wireless network while he's in the lobby. However, when sitting at his desk, his smartphone keeps disconnecting from the network, even though he has a strong wireless signal. Which of the following is the MOST likely cause of this problem?
    A. Faulty wiring
    B. Cross-talk
    C. Wrong SSID
    D. Bounce

Answer: **D** is correct. The most likely cause is signal bounce. Some surfaces reflect signals causing wireless signals to bounce off them. This can cause a device to receive signals from multiple directions causing interference between them.

A is incorrect. Smartphones do not use wiring.
B is incorrect. Cross-talk occurs when a signal from one cable crosses over to another cable. However, this question is only related to a wireless signal.

C is incorrect. If the device were using the wrong service set identifier (SSID), it wouldn't be able to connect at all, or it would have connected to a different network.

33. After replacing a faulty WAP, you discover that users working in the accounting department are having intermittent problems, but other users can connect to the network without any problem. Before replacing the WAP, users in the accounting department didn't have any problems. What is the MOST likely reason for this problem?
    A. WAP placement is causing problems.
    B. Wrong SSID was configured.
    C. An incorrect media converter was installed.
    D. Accounting department systems are using the incorrect wireless protocol.

Answer: **A** is correct. The most likely reason is the placement of the wireless access point (WAP). It may be that the WAP was placed in a location that prevents the signal from reaching the users in the accounting department, or that the antenna on the WAP was placed in such a manner that weakens the signal for users in the accounting department.

B is incorrect. If users in the accounting department were using the wrong service set identifier (SSID), they wouldn't be able to connect at all, or they would have connected to a different network.
C is incorrect. Media converters connect dissimilar media and connectors, such as a fiber-optic cable to a Registered Jack-45 (RJ-45) jack. They are not used with wireless networks.
D is incorrect. The accounting department users had no problem before the WAP was installed, so it's unlikely they now have the incorrect wireless

protocol. Additionally, having the incorrect wireless protocol (such as 802.11g instead of 802.11ac) wouldn't cause intermittent problems.

34. When Bart connects to the wireless network, he can normally connect to a general server with data he uses for his job. After connecting to the wireless network today, he was unable to find his data, but instead saw several shared folders that weren't familiar to him. Which of the following is the MOST likely cause for this?
    A. Bart connected to the network with the wrong SSID.
    B. Bart connected to the network with an incorrect channel.
    C. Bart connected to a network with excessive bounce.
    D. Bart connected to the network with the wrong antenna.

Answer: **A** is correct. The most likely reason is that Bart connected to the network with the wrong service set identifier (SSID). By connecting to a different wireless network, he is seeing folders available on the network. Normally, using the wrong SSID would result in no connectivity. However, an organization might create a guest network with minimal resources, using a different SSID.

B is incorrect. It isn't possible to connect to an access point with the incorrect channel. Also, devices will normally adjust to the correct channel automatically.

C is incorrect. Bounce causes intermittent connections due to bounced wireless signals interfering with other signals.

D is incorrect. It isn't possible for a user to connect to a network with the wrong antenna.

35. You are configuring three 802.11g wireless access points for a business in the United States. What channels should you use to avoid interference?
    A. 1, 6, 11
    B. 1, 6, 13
    C. 5, 6, 7
    D. 1, 2, 3

Answer: **A** is correct. Channels 1, 6, and 11 are recommended for use in North America to avoid interference.

B is incorrect. North America only uses channels 1 through 11, so channel 13 isn't valid in North America. Most of the rest of the world uses up to 13 channels and Japan uses 14 channels.
C is incorrect. Channels 5, 6, and 7 will each overlap with each other, causing interference.
D is incorrect. Channels 1, 2, and 3 will each overlap with each other, causing interference.

36. When installing multiple wireless access points, what will help ensure the best performance?
    A. Disabling SSID broadcast
    B. Enabling WPA2
    C. Using overlapping channels
    D. Using nonoverlapping channels

Answer: **D** is correct. Nonoverlapping channels should be used to prevent interference. For the 2.4-GHz frequency band, you should use channels 1, 6, and 11 because these channels do not overlap with either other.

A is incorrect. Disabling the service set identifier (SSID) makes it more difficult for clients to discover the access point, so it does not provide better performance.

B is incorrect. Wi-Fi Protected Access II (WPA2) provides the strongest encryption and should be used for security, but it does not contribute to performance.

C is incorrect. Overlapping channels can result in interference similar to how one FM radio station can interfere with another if the two stations use frequencies that are close to each other, or if you tune a radio to a frequency between the two.

37. A wireless network is experiencing interference from telephones using the 2.4-GHz frequency range. Which of the following can be used to avoid this interference? (Select TWO.)

    A. 802.11a

    B. 802.11b

    C. 802.11g

    D. 802.11ac

Answer: **A** and **D** are correct. 802.11a uses the 5-GHz frequency range and 802.11ac can use either the 2.4-GHz or the 5-GHz frequency range.

B and C are incorrect. 802.11b and 802.11g both use the 2.4-GHz frequency range.

38. An organization has three wireless networks running in the same environment. What channels should they use?

    A. 1, 2, 3

    B. 1, 4, 8

    C. 1, 6, 11

    D. 9, 10, 11

Answer: **C** is correct. Channels 1, 6, and 11 do not overlap with each other and should be used when multiple wireless access points (WAPs) are used in the same environment. When channels overlap, it's possible for the transmission from one WAP to interfere with the transmission from another WAP. This is similar to how two radio stations that use frequencies close to each other can interfere with each other; you can tune to one radio station but hear music from the other radio station. Most WAPs use channel 6 by default, and if there are several wireless networks in the area (such as in an apartment building or suburban neighborhood), changing the WAP to channel 1 or 11 can sometimes improve performance by eliminating interference from other WAPs.

A is incorrect. Channels 1, 2, and 3 are adjacent to each other. This overlap results in interference.
B is incorrect. Channels 1, 4, and 8 will overlap, resulting in interference.
D is incorrect. Channels 9, 10, and 11 are adjacent to each other. This overlap results in interference.

Objective: 4.4 Given a scenario, troubleshoot and resolve common copper cable issues.

39. You are preparing to connect two networks together in different locations. The only place you can run the cables is in a power duct side by side with power. What type of cable should you use to ensure there are no problems?
    A. Either UTP or SMF
    B. Either UTP or MMF
    C. Either SMF or MMF
    D. Either UTP or STP

Answer: **C** is correct. Single mode fiber (SMF) or multimode fiber (MMF) should be used to prevent electromagnetic interference (EMI) problems that can occur by running the cable side by side with the power. Fiber cable is immune to EMI.

A and B are incorrect. Unshielded twisted-pair (UTP) does not provide any protection against interference.
D is incorrect. Shielded twisted-pair (STP) provides some protection against EMI, but fiber is immune to EMI and is a better choice.

40. You are troubleshooting a wired printer and notice that the link light on the NIC is not lit. You test the printer on a different RJ-45 port and it works. What is the MOST likely problem?
    A. Faulty NIC
    B. Signal bounce
    C. Faulty wiring
    D. Faulty media converter

Answer: **C** is correct. Because the device works when plugged into a different Registered Jack-45 (RJ-45) port, it indicates the first RJ-45 port has faulty wiring.

A is incorrect. The printer's network interface card (NIC) functions when plugged into a different port, so it is not faulty.
B is incorrect. Signal bounce is a problem with wireless signals when surfaces reflect signals causing wireless signals to bounce off them. It is not related to wired systems.
D is incorrect. A media converter is used to connect dissimilar media and connectors, such as fiber-optic cable to an RJ-45 jack. It is unrelated to this question.

41. After replacing a cable for a user's computer, the system is unable to connect to the network. You checked the port on the switch and verified it is enabled and configured correctly and you verified the 1-Gbps NIC on the computer is using auto sense. What is the MOST likely problem?

    A. Open wire on the cable

    B. Mismatched speed

    C. Mismatched duplex mode

    D. EMI

Answer: **A** is correct. The most likely problem is the cable, which was just replaced. It could be a bad connector, bad wiring, or an open, a short, or a split cable.

B and C are incorrect. The question states the port on the switch is enabled and configured correctly and the network interface card (NIC) on the computer is using auto sense. Auto sense on the computer will automatically match the speed and duplex mode of the switch if the cable is good.
D is incorrect. There is no indication that electromagnetic interference (EMI) is the problem.

42. A technician is planning on running several twisted-pairs to a switch. He decides to bundle the cables tightly together to make it easier to run all the cables at the same time. What type of problem can this cause?

    A. Cross-talk

    B. EMI

    C. DB loss

    D. TX RX reversal

Answer: **A** is correct. When cables are run together, there is the potential for cross-talk where data from one cable crosses over to another. The twists in a cable help prevent cross-talk, but if the cables are bundled tightly together, the risk of cross-talk increases.

B is incorrect. Electromagnetic interference (EMI) comes from external sources such as from a power source or a fluorescent light.
C is incorrect. Decibel (db) loss, or signal loss, occurs when the cable runs are too long. For example, most twisted-pair cable is limited to a maximum length of 100 meters.
D is incorrect. Wiring within a cable can have the transmit wires (TX) swapped with the receive wires (RX) to create a crossover cable. This is unrelated to cross-talk that can occur when cables are bundled tightly together.

43. You are troubleshooting an intermittent connection issue with a computer. You've traced the twisted-pair cable and see it is running through several open power junction boxes. You've measured the length of the cable and determined it is 110 feet long. What is the MOST likely problem?
    A. Cable length
    B. Electromagnetic interference
    C. Plenum safety
    D. Open in the cable

Answer: **B** is correct. Electromagnetic interference (EMI) can come from power sources, such as a cable run through an open power junction box, or side by side with a power cable. EMI can also come from fluorescent lighting fixtures.

A is incorrect. Most twisted-pair cable runs can be 100 meters (about 330 feet) and using a time-domain reflectometer (TDR) is one way to measure the distance, but 110 feet is not too long. If the cable is too long, it can result in decibel (db) loss, or signal loss.

C is incorrect. Plenum safety refers to the fire-retardant jacket over a cable and is not related to EMI.

D is incorrect. If there was an open, or break, in the cable, the problem would not be intermittent.

44. You are troubleshooting an intermittent connection with a computer. Upon inspection, you notice that a large part of the jacket has been removed on the cable close to the jack, and the pairs are untwisted. What types of problem can this cause?

    A. Cross-talk

    B. DB loss

    C. TX RX reversal

    D. Duplex mismatch

Answer: **A** is correct. The twists in a cable help prevent cross-talk and noise on a cable. Although the pairs needs to be untwisted a little to connect them to the correct pin, when they are untwisted too much it can eliminate the canceling effect provided by the twists and contribute to cross-talk.

B is incorrect. Decibel (db) loss, or signal loss, occurs when the cable runs are too long. Most twisted-pair cable is limited to a maximum length of 100 meters, but this is unrelated to the twists.

C is incorrect. Untwisting the cables won't change the wiring so that transmit wires (TX) are swapped with the receive wires (RX).
D is incorrect. Untwisting the wires will not affect the duplex mode (full-duplex or half-duplex) of the cable.

45. You are preparing to connect several networking devices together in an environment that has a high amount of interference. What type of cables provides the BEST protection?
    A. MMF and UTP
    B. UTP and STP
    C. STP and MMF
    D. STP and Plenum-safe

Answer: **C** is correct. Shielded twisted-pair (STP) and multimode fiber (MMF) provide protection against interference. STP uses shielding and fiber cable is immune. Interference can come from electromagnetic interference (EMI), such as power sources or fluorescent lights, or radio frequency interference (RFI) from RF signals.

A and B are incorrect. Unshielded twisted-pair (UTP) does not provide any protection against interference.
D is incorrect. Plenum-safe cable has a fire-retardant jacket, but the jacket does not provide protection against interference.

46. A new technician gave you a twisted-pair cable saying it doesn't work. When he used it to connect to a 100-Mbps switch, the link light never lit. However, when you use this cable to connect a computer to a 1,000 Mbps switch, the connection does work. What is the MOST likely reason?

    A. The 1,000-Mbps switch is using PoE, but the 100-Mbps switch is not using PoE.

    B. The cable has the wrong LC connector for the 100-Mbps switch.

    C. The cable is wired as a crossover cable.

    D. The cable is wired for 1,000 Mbps, not 100 Mbps.

Answer: **C** is correct. Newer switches (such as 1,000-Mbps or 10-Gbps switches) include auto medium dependent interface crossover (MDIX). They can automatically detect if the connection is made with a crossover cable and automatically adjust the connection to either MDI or MDIX. Older switches that support 10 Mbps or 100 Mbps do not include this capability and will not work if the wrong cable is used.

A is incorrect. Power over Ethernet (PoE) is used to provide power to access points over Ethernet cable when commercial power is not readily available. It is not connection-specific.

B is incorrect. Twisted-pair cable uses Registered Jack-45 (RJ-45) connectors and will be the same for a 100-Mbps switch or a 1,000-Mbps switch. A Lucent Connector (LC) connector is used for fiber cable.

D is incorrect. Cables are not wired differently for 1,000 Mbps than they are for 100 Mbps.

47. You need to plug in a fiber-optic cable to an RJ-45 jack. What, if anything, can be used to allow this to work?

    A. Nothing. This is not possible.

    B. Media converter

    C. ST connector

    D. SC connector

Answer: **B** is correct. A media converter is used to connect dissimilar media and connectors. There are media converters that will connect fiber-optic cable to a Registered Jack-45 (RJ-45) jack. Media converters are sometimes called transceivers because they can transmit and receive data.

A is incorrect. It is possible to achieve this with a media converter.
C is incorrect. A straight tip (ST) connector is used to connect a fiber cable to a fiber jack with a push and twist-on connection.
D is incorrect. A Standard Connector (SC) connector is used to connect a fiber cable to a fiber jack. It is sometimes called Subscriber Connector or square connector.

48. You are troubleshooting an intermittent connection issue with a computer. After tracing the wire, you've verified it is running through a fluorescent lighting fixture. Could this be causing the problem and if so, why?

    A. No

    B. Yes, due to EMI

    C. Yes, due to cross-talk

    D. Yes, due to duplex mismatch

Answer: **B** is correct. Electromagnetic interference (EMI) can come from fluorescent lighting fixtures, and unshielded twisted-pair cable should not be run through or over a fluorescent light fixture.

A is incorrect. Running cable over fluorescent light fixtures or through power junctions can cause problems related to EMI.

C is incorrect. Cross-talk occurs when two cables are side by side and signals from one cable cross over to the other cable. The twists in twisted-pair cable reduce cross-talk. Fluorescent lights do not carry data and cross-talk can't come from a fluorescent light.

D is incorrect. Duplex mismatch is when one device in the connection is set to one duplex mode (such as full-duplex) and the second device is set to a different duplex mode (such as half-duplex). Devices typically use auto negotiation and use the slower duplex mode.

49. A technician recently moved a desktop computer used within a manufacturing plant. After moving it, users report intermittent connectivity problems with this computer. Reviewing the logs, you've verified that the problems are only occurring when the manufacturing equipment is running. What is the MOST likely cause of the problem?
    A. STP cable
    B. GBIC mismatch
    C. EMI
    D. Duplex mismatch

Answer: **C** is correct. Manufacturing equipment can cause electromagnetic interference (EMI) and because the computer is only having problems when the equipment is running, the most likely cause of the given answers is EMI. When the computer was moved, it's likely cables were rerouted to accommodate the move.

A is incorrect. Shielded twisted-pair (STP) cable can help block EMI, but STP cable wouldn't cause the problems described in the scenario.
B is incorrect. A Gigabit interface converter (GBIC) acts as a transceiver connecting twisted-pair with fiber cable. A GBIC mismatch would prevent any connectivity, not cause intermittent connectivity.
D is incorrect. A duplex mismatch would prevent any connectivity, not cause intermittent connectivity.

Objective: 4.5 Given a scenario, troubleshoot and resolve common fiber cable issues.

50. You are troubleshooting a network outage. You suspect that a fiber cable with a small service loop is the cause of the problem. What problem can a small service loop cause in this scenario?
    A. Excessive EMI
    B. Bend radius exceeded
    C. Wavelength mismatch
    D. Low signal power

Answer: **B** is correct. A small service loop can result in fiber damage due to bend radius limitations. A service loop is the excess cable at the end of a cable designed to accommodate future cabling system changes. If it is too small, it can damage the fiber by exceeding the bend radius specifications.

A is incorrect. Fiber is immune to electromagnetic interference (EMI), and EMI is unrelated to service loops.
C is incorrect. Devices at both ends of a cable need to be configured with the proper wavelength. The fiber cable isn't configured with a wavelength.
D is incorrect. A service loop is unrelated to the signal power.

51. You are tasked with connecting a DWDM system to a router. After connecting it, you verify that the router is receiving a good signal. However, the router is not transmitting data through the connected interface. Which of the following is the MOST likely cause for this problem?

    A. The fiber cable is faulty.

    B. A mismatch with the GBIC.

    C. The DWDM system is not configured to transmit the correct wavelength.

    D. The wrong SSID is assigned.

Answer: **C** is correct. If the dense wavelength division multiplexing (DWDM) system is not configured to transmit the correct wavelength, the router interface won't recognize the transmission. However, the router will still be receiving a signal, just at a wavelength that the router interface can't decipher. This is similar to a broadband cable system that transmits both TV channel transmissions and Internet data. Your TV expects TV channel signals and your computer expects Internet data. If a fault causes these to be swapped, both your TV and your computer will receive data, but not in a usable form.

A is incorrect. If the fiber cable was faulty, the router would not be receiving a good signal.

B is incorrect. A Gigabit interface converter (GBIC) acts as a transceiver connecting twisted-pair with fiber cable. If it was used and there was a mismatch, the router would not receive any signal.

D is incorrect. Wireless systems use a service set identifier (SSID), but a wired router connected to a DWDM system doesn't use a wireless network.

Objective: 4.6 Given a scenario, troubleshoot and resolve common network issues.

52. A technician saw a cable with one end plugged into a switch but the other end unconnected. He plugged the cable into an open port on the switch. Afterwards, all users connected through this switch are complaining of connectivity problems. What is the likely cause?
    A. Switching loop
    B. Bad/missing routes
    C. Wrong gateway
    D. Wrong DNS

Answer: **A** is correct. A switching loop can occur if two ports are connected together with a cable and the switch is not protected with Spanning Tree Protocol (STP) or the newer Rapid STP (RSTP). When a broadcast is received on the switch, it will go out all ports. The cable connecting the two ports together loops the broadcast back into the switch where it's again sent out all ports. This continues forever, causing a broadcast storm and effectively blocking regular traffic. STP and RSTP protect against switching loops.

B is incorrect. Bad or missing routes can affect traffic through a router, but this is unrelated to connecting two ports of a switch.

C is incorrect. The gateway is the IP address of a router on the same network, but this is unrelated to a switch.

D is incorrect. Domain Name System (DNS) is used for resolving host names to IP addresses and is unrelated to a switch.

53. You are inspecting a switch and you notice that most of the LEDs are blinking green, but one is blinking orange. Of the following choices, what is the MOST likely reason?
    - A. Port configured to wrong port speed
    - B. Port connected with a crossover cable
    - C. Port configured with wrong subnet mask
    - D. Switching loop

Answer: **A** is correct. A different color light-emitting diode (LED) indicates that the port is configured with a different speed or a different duplex mode than other ports. This can also occur if the connected device is using a different speed than other devices connected to the switch. For example, if a computer's network interface card (NIC) only supports 100 Mbps, but the switch supports 100 Mbps and 1,000 Mbps, the switch will auto negotiate to the slower speed and the LED will be a different color. Similarly, the LED may be one color for full-duplex mode and another color for half-duplex mode.

B is incorrect. A crossover cable will either work or not work. The LED color will not indicate a crossover cable is used.
C is incorrect. The subnet mask will not affect connectivity to the switch, but it will affect connectivity with other devices.
D is incorrect. A switching loop may cause a broadcast storm if two ports are connected to each other on a switch, but the symptom will be all ports blinking rapidly. Spanning Tree Protocol (STP) or Rapid STP (RSTP) will protect against a switching loop.

54. You are assisting a user who is troubleshooting a network connectivity problem. The user is unable to reach the GetCertifiedGetAhead.com website using a web browser, but is able to ping the website using the website's IP address. What is the MOST likely problem?

    A. DHCP

    B. Default gateway

    C. DNS

    D. Router

Answer: **C** is correct. If you can ping the IP address of a system, but not reach it with the name, it indicates that Domain Name System (DNS) is not resolving names to IP addresses. The reason may be that the client's DNS server's IP address is configured incorrectly, the DNS server is down, or the DNS server is unreachable.

A is incorrect. Dynamic Host Configuration Protocol (DHCP) dynamically assigns Transmission Control Protocol/Internet Protocol (TCP/IP) configuration information such as an IP address and other options. It is possible that DHCP is assigning the wrong DNS address, but in this question, you don't even know if the user's system is a DHCP client.

B is incorrect. If the user is unable to get out of the network, the problem might be with the default gateway. However, a ping to the IP address is successful, so the default gateway is working.

D is incorrect. The default gateway is the near side of a router providing a path out of the network. Because a ping using the IP address is working, routing is working.

55. Several devices are connected to a network via a switch. All of the devices except one are able to communicate with network resources. This one device has an APIPA address. What is the MOST likely reason?

    A. The computer is assigned a duplicate IP address.

    B. The computer is not a DHCP client.

    C. STP is not running on this computer.

    D. The port on the switch for this computer is disabled.

Answer: **D** is correct. The most likely reason of those given is that the port on the switch for this computer is disabled. This will block all traffic, including Dynamic Host Configuration Protocol (DHCP) traffic. If a DHCP server does not respond, a computer will assign itself an Automatic Private IP Addressing (APIPA) address.

A is incorrect. If a computer is assigned a duplicate IP address, it will try to use this IP address and not be able to communicate on the network, or assign itself an IP address of 0.0.0.0 and not be able to communicate on the network. It will not assign itself an APIPA address.

B is incorrect. DHCP clients that do not receive a response from a DHCP server assign themselves an APIPA address. Because the computer has an APIPA address, it is a DHCP client, but the real issue is that the computer cannot communicate through the switch.

C is incorrect. Spanning Tree Protocol (STP) is installed on switches to prevent switching loop problems, not on computers.

56. Several users are complaining that they are unable to communicate on the network, though they could yesterday. You discover all these users are connected to the same switch and all the LEDs on this switch are blinking rapidly. What is the MOST likely problem?

    A. A broadcast storm is causing interference.

    B. Traffic is being segregated by the switch.

    C. An incorrect default gateway is assigned.

    D. The users are connected on different VLAN segments.

Answer: **A** is correct. All of the light-emitting diodes (LEDs) blinking rapidly (often in unison) indicates a broadcast storm. A broadcast storm occurs when broadcasts result in repeated collisions. Each collision requires the broadcast to be retransmitted, which results in more collisions. A common culprit is a cable connecting two ports on a switch that isn't protected with Spanning Tree Protocol (STP) or Rapid STP (RSTP). When the switch isn't protected, the cable can cause a switching loop.

B is incorrect. Segregating traffic through a switch is done by creating virtual local area networks (VLANs). Broadcasts are not sent to different VLAN segments, so VLANs would not give these symptoms.

C is incorrect. The default gateway is the address of an interface on a router providing a path out of a network. In this case, the problem is with the switch before the traffic reaches the router.

D is incorrect. The problem is describing a broadcast storm, and broadcasts from VLAN segments are not propagated to other VLAN segments.

57. You recently installed a new AP on a wireless network. All devices can communicate with each other on the wireless network. However, none of the devices can access the Internet. What is the MOST likely problem?

    A. The AP has the incorrect SSID.

    B. Devices are configured with the incorrect SSID.

    C. The AP has the incorrect gateway.

    D. The edge router has the incorrect gateway.

Answer: **C** is correct. The most likely problem is that the access point (AP) has the incorrect gateway. This would prevent it from reaching the edge router and accessing the Internet.

A and B are incorrect. If the AP or other devices had the incorrect service set identifier (SSID), they wouldn't be able to communicate with each other.

D is incorrect. Because the AP was replaced, it is much more likely to be the problem, rather than the edge router. Also, the edge router typically would know multiple paths on the Internet and not have a single gateway.

58. Network 1 includes multiple computers in the 10.10.10.16/28 range. Homer has called into the helpdesk complaining that he can't access the Internet. He says that he configured the NIC, but he suspects it needs to be replaced. You determine that his NIC has the following settings:

    IP address: 10.10.10.17

    Subnet mask: 255.255.255.240

    Default gateway: 10.10.10.32

    Speed: 100 Mbps

Duplex: Full

What is the cause of the problem?

A. The NIC has an incorrect IP address.

B. The NIC has an incorrect default gateway.

C. The NIC is configured with the incorrect speed.

D. The NIC is configured with the incorrect subnet mask.

Answer: **B** is correct. The NIC has an incorrect default gateway. Valid IP addresses in the 10.10.10.16/28 range are 10.10.10.17 through 10.10.10.30. 10.10.10.32/24 is in a different network, so it would be unreachable if the default gateway is set to this address.

A is incorrect. The IP address is valid because it is in the range of 10.10.10.17 through 10.10.10.30.

C is incorrect. The speed of the network isn't given, so it's not possible to determine if the speed set on the NIC (100 Mbps) is correct or incorrect.

D is incorrect. A subnet mask of 255.255.255.240 is valid for a /28 Classless Inter-Domain Routing (CIDR) notation.

59. Network 1 includes multiple computers in the 10.10.10.16/28 range. Homer has called into the helpdesk complaining that he can't access the Internet. He says that he configured the NIC, but he suspects it needs to be replaced. You determine that his NIC has the following settings:

    IP address: 10.10.10.16

    Subnet mask: 255.255.255.240

    Default gateway: 10.10.10.28

    Speed: 10 Gbps

    Duplex: Full

What is the cause of the problem?

A. The NIC has an incorrect IP address.

B. The NIC has an incorrect default gateway.

C. The NIC is configured with the incorrect speed.

D. The NIC is configured with the incorrect subnet mask.

Answer: **A** is correct. The NIC has the incorrect IP address. Valid IP addresses in the 10.10.10.16/28 range are 10.10.10.17 through 10.10.10.30. 10.10.10.16/24 is the network ID of the network and cannot be assigned as an address to any single system.

B is incorrect. The default gateway is valid because it is in the range of 10.10.10.17 through 10.10.10.30.

C is incorrect. The speed of the network isn't given, so it's not possible to determine if the speed set on the NIC (100 Mbps) is correct or incorrect.

D is incorrect. A subnet mask of 255.255.255.240 is valid for a /28 CIDR notation.

Objective: 4.7 Given a scenario, troubleshoot and resolve common security issues.

60. You have just removed malware from a user's computer and completed a full scan to ensure it doesn't have any additional malware on it. When checking it out, you determine that the computer is unable to access some websites. Which of the following is the MOST likely cause?

    A. The computer has an incorrect default gateway assigned.

    B. The local hosts file has been modified.

    C. The computer has an incorrect subnet mask assigned.

    D. The DHCP reservation has been modified.

Answer: **B** is correct. The most likely cause of those given is that the local hosts file has been modified. The hosts file holds name to IP address mappings and takes precedence over other name resolution methods.

A is incorrect. If the computer had an incorrect default gateway, it couldn't access any websites. However, the scenario indicates the computer is unable to access *some* websites, indicating it can access some others.
C is incorrect. If the computer had an incorrect subnet mask, it couldn't access any websites. However, the scenario indicates the computer is unable to access *some* websites, indicating it can access some others.
D is incorrect. A Dynamic Host Configuration Protocol (DHCP) reservation assigns a specific IP address to a computer based on its media access control (MAC) address. Even if a computer didn't get a reserved IP address, it wouldn't affect name resolution.

61. Maggie enters the following command: **telnet server1 80** against a remote server. Which of the following BEST describes the purpose of this command?
    A. Identify if server1 is running a service using port 80 and is reachable.
    B. Launch an attack on server1 sending 80 separate packets in a short period of time.
    C. Use Telnet to remotely administer server1.
    D. Use Telnet to start an RDP session.

Answer: **A** is correct. This command sends a query to server1 over port 80 and if the server is running a service on port 80, it will connect. This is a common beginning command for a banner-grabbing attempt.

B is incorrect. This command does not send 80 separate packets.

C is incorrect. If 80 was omitted in the command, Telnet would attempt to connect using its default port of 23 and attempt to create a Telnet session.

D is incorrect. Remote Desktop Protocol (RDP) uses port 3389 and is not relevant in this scenario.

Objective: 4.8 Given a scenario, troubleshoot and resolve common WAN issues.

62. Routers in your wide area network (WAN) are using RIPv2. Which of the following can prevent switching loops with these routers?

    A. Split-horizon route advertisement

    B. BGP

    C. OSPF

    D. Convergence

Answer: **A** is correct. Distance-vector routing protocols such as Routing Information Protocol version 2 (RIPv2) can use split-horizon route advertisement as a method to prevent routing loops. It prevents the router from advertising a route on the same interface where the router learned the route.

B is incorrect. The Border Gateway Protocol (BGP) is useful if an organization maintains multiple links to the Internet. It can help ensure that a wide area network (WAN) can use alternate links if necessary.

C is incorrect. Open Shortest Path First (OSPF) is a link-state routing protocol that identifies the shortest path based on the current status (or current state of the link).

D is incorrect. Convergence is the state of routers when they have learned the same routing information within a network.

63. What identifies the line where responsibility for a communications link lies with either the provider or the customer?

    A. Demarc

    B. MDF

    C. IDF

    D. CSU/DSU

Answer: **A** is correct. Demarc is short for demarcation and it marks the point where responsibility for a communications link shifts from a telecommunications company to the customer.

B is incorrect. A main distribution frame (MDF) is a frame used to connect cables from external sources to internal equipment, but it isn't necessarily the demarc point.

C is incorrect. An intermediate distribution frame (IDF) is internal to a company and includes cross connects for cables. It will often be an intermediate point between the MDF and other devices that need the connection.

D is incorrect. A Channel Service Unit/Data Service Unit (CSU/DSU) is commonly used to connect T-1 lines.

64. Which of the following indicates one of the primary weaknesses with satellite connections?

    A. Cost of physical media

    B. Latency

    C. Distance limitations

    D. Compatibility

Answer: **B** is correct. Latency is the time it takes for signals to travel to the destination and often indicates a delay. Satellite signals have to travel to space and back, which can result in a high latency or delay.

A is incorrect. Physical media refers to the physical cable, but satellite connections primarily use transmitted signals to and from satellites. In other words, there is minimal cost for physical media when using satellite connections.

C is incorrect. Satellite connections are useful when connecting networks over great distances without physical media, so distance limitations are not a weakness. Instead, distance limitations are one of its primary strengths.

D is incorrect. There are multiple protocols available that can be used with satellite connections, so compatibility is not a weakness.

65. Of the following choices, what can you use to connect networks without the use of physical cables between the networks?
    A. DSL
    B. OC-24
    C. Satellite
    D. SONET

Answer: **C** is correct. Satellite connections allow you to connect networks separated by large distances without physical media between the networks. Wireless standards such as 802.11a/b/g/n also connect networks without physical media, but were not listed as an option.

A is incorrect. A digital subscriber line (DSL) uses a physical connection to provide Internet access through a telephone company's wired network.

B is incorrect. Optical Carrier 24 (OC-24) is one of many OC specifications and each of the OC specifications use fiber cable. For example, OC-1 has transmission speeds of up to 51.84 Mbps and OC-24 has transmissions speeds up to 1244.16 Mbps.

D is incorrect. Synchronous Optical Networking (SONET) is a protocol used with fiber connections for wide area networks (WANs).

66. A company is leasing a T-1 line. What would the T-1 connect to at the company's building?

    A. Server

    B. 110 block

    C. Smart jack

    D. Wireless router

Answer: **C** is correct. A smart jack is a network interface device used to terminate a T-1 connection. The smart jack also represents the demarcation point (often called demarc point), or the line of responsibility between the customer and the communications company providing access to the T-1 line.

A is incorrect. A T-1 line would pass through a smart jack, then a Channel Service Unit/Data Service Unit (CSU/DSU), then a router before reaching any servers.

B is incorrect. A 110 block is replacing the 66 block as a connection point for telephone wires and computer connections, but it is not used for a T-1.

D is incorrect. A T-1 line does not connect directly to a wireless router.

67. What would you connect with a CSU/DSU?

A. WAP

B. T-1

C. POTS lines

D. Wireless devices

Answer: **B** is correct. A Channel Service Unit/Data Service Unit (CSU/DSU) is used to connect hardware devices such as routers, to transmission lines such as T-1 lines.

A is incorrect. A wireless access point (WAP) is used to bridge wireless clients to a wired network.
C is incorrect. A CSU/DSU is not used with plain old telephone service (POTS) lines.
D is incorrect. A CSU/DSU is not used to connect wireless devices.

»Get Certified »Get Ahead

Chapter 5 Industry Standards, Practices, and Network Theory

Industry Standards, Practices, and Network Theory topics are 16 percent of the CompTIA Network + exam. The objectives in this domain are:

5.1 Analyze a scenario and determine the corresponding OSI layer.

- Layer 1 – Physical
- Layer 2 – Data Link
- Layer 3 – Network
- Layer 4 – Transport
- Layer 5 – Session
- Layer 6 – Presentation
- Layer 7 – Application

5.2 Explain the basics of network theory and concepts.

- Encapsulation/de-encapsulation
- Modulation techniques
    - Multiplexing
    - De-multiplexing
    - Analog and digital techniques
    - TDM
- Numbering systems
    - Binary
    - Hexadecimal
    - Octal
- Broadband/base band
- Bit rates vs baud rate
- Sampling size
- CDMA
- CSMA/CD and CSMA/CA
- Carrier detect/sense
- Wavelength
- TCP/IP suite
    - ICMP
    - UDP
    - TCP
- Collision

5.3 Given a scenario, deploy the appropriate wireless standard.

- 802.11a
- 802.11b

- 802.11g
- 802.11n
- 802.11ac

5.4 Given a scenario, deploy the appropriate wired connectivity standard.

- Ethernet standards
    - 10BaseT
    - 100BaseT
    - 1000BaseT
    - 1000BaseTX
    - 10GBaseT
    - 100BaseFX
    - 10Base2
    - 10GBaseSR
    - 10GBaseER
    - 10GBaseSW
    - IEEE 1905.1-2013
        - Ethernet over HDMI
        - Ethernet over power line
- Wiring standards
    - EIA/TIA 568A/568B
- Broadband standards
    - DOCSIS

5.5 Given a scenario, implement the appropriate policies or procedures.

- Security policies
    - Consent to monitoring
- Network policies
- Acceptable use policy
- Standard business documents
    - SLA
    - MOU
    - MSA
    - SOW

5.6 Summarize safety practices.

- Electrical safety
    - Grounding
- ESD
    - Static
- Installation safety
    - Lifting equipment
    - Rack installation
    - Placement
    - Tool safety
- MSDS
- Emergency procedures

    - Building layout
    - Fire escape plan
    - Safety/emergency exits
    - Fail open/fail close
    - Emergency alert system
- Fire suppression systems
- HVAC

5.7 Given a scenario, install and configure equipment in the appropriate location using best practices.

- Intermediate distribution frame
- Main distribution frame
- Cable management
    - Patch panels
- Power management
    - Power converters
    - Circuits
    - UPS
    - Inverters
    - Power redundancy
- Device placement
- Air flow
- Cable trays
- Rack systems
    - Server rail racks
    - Two-post rack
    - Four-post racks
    - Free-standing racks
- Labeling
    - Port labeling
    - System labeling
    - Circuit labeling
    - Naming conventions
    - Patch panel labeling
- Rack monitoring
- Rack security

5.8 Explain the basics of change management procedures.

- Document reason for a change
- Change request
    - Configuration procedures
    - Rollback process
    - Potential impact
    - Notification
- Approval process
- Maintenance window
    - Authorized downtime

- Notification of change
- Documentation
    - Network configurations
    - Additions to network
    - Physical location changes

5.9 Compare and contrast the following ports and protocols.

- 80 HTTP
- 443 HTTPS
- 137-139 NetBIOS
- 110 POP
- 143 IMAP
- 25 SMTP
- 5060/5061 SIP
- 2427/2727 MGCP
- 5004/5005 RTP
- 1720 H.323
- TCP
    - Connection-oriented
- UDP
    - Connectionless

5.10 Given a scenario, configure and apply the appropriate ports and protocols.

- 20,21 FTP
- 161 SNMP
- 22 SSH
- 23 Telnet
- 53 DNS
- 67,68 DHCP
- 69 TFTP
- 445 SMB
- 3389 RDP

**

Practice Test Mode Section — Practice Test Questions without Answers for Industry Standards, Practices, and Network Theory

1. You are troubleshooting a network issue using a protocol analyzer. You discover that a network device is sending data that have errors in some frames. On which of the following OSI layers is this problem located?
    A. Layer 1
    B. Layer 2
    C. Layer 3
    D. Layer 4

2. You are troubleshooting a network issue using a protocol analyzer. You discover that a switch is sending data that have errors in some PDUs. On which of the following OSI layers is this problem located?
    A. Physical
    B. Data Link
    C. Network
    D. Transport

3. A helpdesk technician is helping a user troubleshoot network connectivity with a laptop computer. The helpdesk technician discovered that the wireless switch on the laptop was set to off and turned it on to resolve the problem. On which OSI layer was this problem located?
    A. Layer 1
    B. Layer 3

C. Layer 5

D. Layer 7

4. A user complains that the Internet is down. After some discussion, you discover the user is unable to reach any Internet resources. At which layer of the OSI model would you MOST likely begin troubleshooting?

A. Application

B. Physical

C. Network

D. Transport

5. Ten computers are connected in a network via a switch. However, two computers are unable to communicate with any other computers in this network. Using a sniffer, you capture some traffic that includes the following output:

SRC MAC	**SRC IP**	**DST MAC**	**DST IP**
15:c3:45:2c:6f:01	192.168.5.5	01:15:2d:6f:c3:45	192.168.5.55
22:2c:6f:01:c3:45	192.168.5.5	05:c3:45:2d:9f:01	192.168.5.56

On which layer of the OSI model is this problem located?

A. Physical

B. Transport

C. Data Link

D. Network

6. Which of the following PDUs does a connectionless protocol use?

A. Datagrams

B. Frames

C. Bits

D. Packets

7. Which of the following is the Network layer of the OSI model?

A. 2

B. 3

C. 4

D. 5

8. A device operates on Layer 7 of the OSI model. Which layer is this?

A. Application

B. Network

C. Session

D. Physical

9. On which layer of the OSI model are specifications such as 1000BaseT or 10GBaseT defined?

A. Application

B. Session

C. Network

D. Physical

10. On which layer of the OSI model are IPv4 and IPv6 addresses defined?

A. Data Link

B. Transport

C. Network

D. Physical

11. A computer has an address of 192.168.1.5. On which layer of the OSI model is this address used?

    A. Layer 1

    B. Layer 2

    C. Layer 3

    D. Layer 4

12. Of the following choices, which one is located on the Transport layer?

    A. TCP

    B. Physical address

    C. 10GBaseT

    D. 802.11n

13. Which of the following protocols is located on Layer 4 of the OSI model?

    A. IPv6

    B. ICMP

    C. 802.11n

    D. UDP

14. On which layer of the OSI model are VLANs defined?

    A. Physical

    B. Data Link

    C. Network

    D. Transport

15. Given the following choices, which is the BEST choice to identify the layer of the OSI model where a NIC operates?

    A. 1

    B. 3

    C. 4

    D. 7

16. You are troubleshooting a network problem. You determine that you can ping the default gateway, but you cannot ping the IP address of servers on other networks. On which layer of the OSI model does the problem MOST likely exist?

    A. 1

    B. 2

    C. 3

    D. 7

17. On which layer(s) of the OSI model do wireless protocols operate?

    A. Physical

    B. Physical and Data Link

    C. Data Link

    D. Data Link and Network

18. Of the following choices, which one operates on Layer 1 of the OSI model and will always forward broadcast traffic?

    A. Switch

    B. Router

    C. Hub

    D. NIC

19. Which of the following is associated with the Transport layer of the OSI model?

    A. Reliable delivery of packets

    B. VLANs

    C. IP subnets

    D. NICs

20. Which of the following devices uses CSMA/CA?

    A. Layer 3 switch

    B. Router

    C. Hub

    D. Wireless access point

21. Which of the following standards uses timers to force devices to wait after detecting a collision on a congested network?

    A. RTS/CTS

    B. CDMA

    C. CSMA/CA

    D. CSMA/CD

22. Which of the following is a valid wireless standard that supports high-definition video streaming?

    A. 802.11a

    B. 802.11b

    C. 802.11g

    D. 802.11ac

23. You are assisting a business owner who is troubleshooting an existing WLAN. You discover that the maximum speed is 11 Mbps. Which of the following standards is this network MOST likely running?
    A. 802.11a
    B. 802.11b
    C. 802.11g
    D. 802.11ac

24. You've been asked to help a small business owner create a wireless network. She wants to create a network that will support newer wireless devices and provide the maximum transfer rate. What would you recommend?
    A. A wireless router that supports 802.11a
    B. A wireless router that supports 802.11b
    C. A wireless router that supports 802.11g
    D. A wireless router that supports 802.11n

25. You've been asked to help a small business owner identify a WAP to support multiple wireless devices in his business. After checking, you've found that some of these devices use 2.4 GHz and some of the devices use 5 GHz. What would you recommend?
    A. A wireless router that supports 802.11a
    B. A wireless router that supports 802.11b
    C. A wireless router that supports 802.11g
    D. A wireless router that supports 802.11n

26. You've been asked to help a small business owner create a wireless network. He wants to install a network with the greatest throughput. What would you recommend?

    A. A wireless router that supports 802.11a

    B. A wireless router that supports 802.11b

    C. A wireless router that supports 802.11g

    D. A wireless router that supports 802.11n

27. You want to install a wireless network using the same frequency band as 802.11a. What, if anything, can you use?

    A. None. 802.11a operates on a frequency that isn't used by other wireless standards.

    B. 802.11b

    C. 802.11g

    D. 802.11n

28. Which of the following standards supports multimode fiber?

    A. 1000BaseLR

    B. 1000BaseSR

    C. 1000BaseT

    D. 1000BaseER

29. You are replacing an older computer with a new one and connecting it to a legacy SCADA network. Unfortunately, the connection isn't working. You verify the CAT3 cable used with the original computer is wired properly and doesn't have any breaks. Which of the following is a logical next step?

A. Verify the new computer is compatible with 10BaseT.

B. Verify the new computer is compatible with 10Base2.

C. Verify the new computer is compatible with 10Base5.

D. Verify the new computer is compatible with 100BaseFX.

30. Which of the following standards was designed to be used with SONET equipment?

    A. 10GBaseSW

    B. 10GBaseSR

    C. 10GBaseCX4

    D. 10GBaseT

31. You need to purchase cable for a 10GBaseSR connection. What should you get?

    A. SMF

    B. MMF

    C. CAT5e

    D. CAT6a

32. You are designing a 10-Gigabit network for a high-speed data center. All of the cable runs will be 10 meters or less. Which of the following cable types provides the BEST choice?

    A. 10GGaseER

    B. 10GGaseLR

    C. 10GBaseSR

    D. 100BaseFX

33. Which of the following standards would be used within a data center to provide 10 Gigabit Ethernet with the least cost?
    A. 10GBaseR
    B. 10GBaseT
    C. 10GBaseW
    D. 10GBaseX

34. Which of the following is a valid LAN technology that provides the highest data rate?
    A. 10BaseT
    B. 100BaseT
    C. 1000BaseT
    D. 10GBaseT

35. Which of the following is a valid LAN technology that can be used for the greatest distance?
    A. 10GBaseT
    B. 10GBaseER
    C. 10GBaseLR
    D. 10GBaseSR

36. Users are reporting errors accessing some websites. You've verified that you can access GetCertifiedGetAhead.com, but you are unable to access websites that require you to log on. What is the MOST likely problem?
    A. TCP port 53 is blocked at the network firewall.
    B. UDP port 67 is blocked at the network firewall.
    C. TCP port 80 is blocked at the network firewall.
    D. TCP port 443 is blocked at the network firewall.

37. Before new employees receive an account and password, they are required to read and sign a document acknowledging they understand their responsibilities. Which of the following BEST describes this document?

    A. AUP

    B. MOU

    C. SLA

    D. SOW

38. An organization wants to ensure that employees understand the guidelines related to their use of network resources. What is used to describe this?

    A. ACL

    B. DoS

    C. Incident response

    D. AUP

39. Your organization has contracted with a service provider to provide connectivity between headquarters and several remote locations. The connections should meet minimum speeds, but after measuring it, administrators discovered the speeds are significantly lower. Which of the following documents is MOST likely to allow the organization to hold the service provider responsible for providing higher speeds?

    A. MLA

    B. MOU

    C. SLA

    D. AUP

40. Your organization has hired a contractor to review your network with a goal of improving availability of the internal network and running applications. Which of the following will document the scope of work for the contractor?

    A. MLA
    B. MOU
    C. SLA
    D. SOW

41. Your company recently purchased another company. Several administrators have inspected the server room at the new company and raised safety concerns. Specifically, they state that the server room has a system that can remove all oxygen from the room and threaten the lives of anyone in the room. What is the purpose of this system?

    A. ESD prevention
    B. Safety of personnel
    C. Temperature control
    D. Fire suppression

42. A technician has had prolonged contact with a cleaning agent and is getting a rash. Which of the following will provide the best information in this scenario?

    A. SLA
    B. MOU
    C. SOW
    D. MSDS

43. Which of the following identifies where you would connect equipment from an external service provider with an organization's equipment?

    A. 110 block

    B. 66 block

    C. MDF

    D. IDF

44. Bart is troubleshooting a problem and he determines the problem is with a switch. The switch is connecting multiple office computers on the second floor and north side of the building. All switches terminate in the server room. Which of the following will make it the easiest for Bart to locate the switch?

    A. Connecting via a 110 block

    B. Using cable trays

    C. Using naming conventions

    D. Using patch panels

45. You are tasked with implementing an approved change to a server. Users have been notified that there will be an outage of approximately 1 hour long, which is the approved maintenance window. What should you do if you are unable to complete the change within the allotted time?

    A. Roll back the drivers.

    B. Test the change on the test server.

    C. Roll back the changes.

    D. Increase the maintenance window.

46. After a recent software update, a user is no longer able to access a 3D printer through a company-created application. After investigation, you discover that the update installed incompatible drivers on the user's system. Of the following choices, what will MOST likely restore the user's system capabilities?

    A. Install a new operating system on the user's system.

    B. Roll back the drivers.

    C. Test the drivers on a test system.

    D. Request authorized downtime for the printer.

47. Which of the following scenarios is a valid reason to request authorized downtime?

    A. A major upgrade for a test server

    B. To reboot a desktop system

    C. To test drivers on a test system

    D. A minor upgrade for a production server

48. An organization wants users to be able to access websites for research and to make purchases. What ports must be opened on the firewall? (Choose all that apply.)

    A. 22

    B. 80

    C. 143

    D. 443

49. Which of the following protocols provides the highest level of security for traffic sent over a network?

    A. HTTP

    B. Telnet

    C. SIP

    D. HTTPS

50. A user is accessing the Internet with a web browser. What port does a web browser use by default?

    A. 67

    B. 80

    C. 143

    D. 3389

51. Which of the following protocols does NOT retransmit lost packets?

    A. TCP

    B. UDP

    C. HTTP

    D. FTP

52. Which of the following ports are used for email? (Choose all that apply.)

    A. 25

    B. 53

    C. 143

    D. 3389

53. Which of the following identifies a valid difference between IPv4 TCP and UDP?

    A. The TCP header uses flags, but the UDP header does not use flags.

    B. The UDP header uses flags, but the TCP header does not use flags.

    C. UDP is connection-oriented, but TCP is connectionless.

    D. UDP provides guaranteed delivery, but TCP only makes a best effort to deliver traffic.

54. What port needs to be opened on a firewall to allow outgoing DNS traffic through?

    A. 25

    B. 53

    C. 80

    D. 443

55. Which port is used by DNS?

    A. 21

    B. 22

    C. 25

    D. 53

56. Which of the following ports are commonly used for FTP traffic?

    A. 20 and 21

    B. 25 and 143

    C. 67 and 68

    D. 80 and 443

57. What port does RDP use?

    A. 22

    B. 67

    C. 143

    D. 3389

58. You need to connect to a remote system using RDP. Which of the following ports must be opened on the firewall?

    A. 53

    B. 3389

    C. 67

    D. 445

59. Which of the following protocols uses port 22?

    A. FTP

    B. SSH

    C. SMTP

    D. RDP

60. Administrators have stored small text files on a server, which hold router and switch configuration scripts. They use TFTP to connect to the server and download the scripts when necessary. However, they can no longer connect to this server using TFTP. Which of the following is the MOST likely reason?

    A. Port 67 is blocked on a router.

    B. Port 161 is blocked on a router.

    C. Port 20 is blocked on a router.

    D. Port 69 is blocked on a router.

61. You are checking a firewall and see that port 161 is open. What protocol would be using this port?

    A. IMAP

    B. SNMP

    C. DNS

    D. SSH

Review Mode Section — Practice Test Questions with Answers for Industry Standards, Practices, and Network Theory

Objective: 5.1 Analyze a scenario and determine the corresponding OSI layer.

1. You are troubleshooting a network issue using a protocol analyzer. You discover that a network device is sending data that have errors in some frames. On which of the following OSI layers is this problem located?
    A. Layer 1
    B. Layer 2
    C. Layer 3
    D. Layer 4

Answer: **B** is correct. Frames are sent by switches on Layer 2 (the Data Link layer) of the Open Systems Interconnection (OSI) model. This scenario indicates a device is sending out protocol data units (PDUs) as frames, but the frames have errors. A switch sends out frames on Layer 2. Note that you could simplify this question with "Which layer sends PDUs as frames?"

A is incorrect. Layer 1 (the Physical layer) sends data out as bits. Basic hardware such as hubs and cables operate on this layer.
C is incorrect. Layer 3 (the Network layer) sends data out as packets. Routers and Layer 3 switches operate on this layer.
D is incorrect. Layer 4 (the Transport layer) sends data out as packets.

2. You are troubleshooting a network issue using a protocol analyzer. You discover that a switch is sending data that have errors in some PDUs. On which of the following OSI layers is this problem located?
    A. Physical
    B. Data Link
    C. Network
    D. Transport

Answer: **B** is correct. A switch operates on the Data Link layer (Layer 2) of the Open Systems Interconnection (OSI) model. The protocol data unit (PDU) used by a switch is a frame. This scenario indicates the switch is sending out frames with errors. Note that you could simplify this question with "On which layer does a switch operate?"

A is incorrect. The Physical layer (Layer 1) sends data out as bits. Basic hardware such as hubs and cables operate on this layer.
C is incorrect. The Network layer (Layer 3) sends data out as packets. Routers and Layer 3 switches operate on this layer.
D is incorrect. The Transport layer (Layer 4) sends data out as packets.

3. A helpdesk technician is helping a user troubleshoot network connectivity with a laptop computer. The helpdesk technician discovered that the wireless switch on the laptop was set to off and turned it on to resolve the problem. On which OSI layer was this problem located?
    A. Layer 1
    B. Layer 3
    C. Layer 5
    D. Layer 7

Answer: **A** is correct. The problem was a basic connectivity issue with the wireless network interface card (NIC) disabled. The NIC operates on Layer 1 (the Physical Layer), so the problem was on Layer 1.

B is incorrect. Layer 3 (the Network layer) includes IP addressing, but not basic connectivity.

C is incorrect. Layer 5 (the Session layer) includes advanced protocols, but not basic connectivity.

D is incorrect. Layer 7 (the Application layer) includes advanced functions, but not basic connectivity.

4. A user complains that the Internet is down. After some discussion, you discover the user is unable to reach any Internet resources. At which layer of the OSI model would you MOST likely begin troubleshooting?
   A. Application
   B. Physical
   C. Network
   D. Transport

Answer: **B** is correct. This is most likely a connectivity issue, so it is most appropriate to begin troubleshooting at the Physical layer (Layer 1) of the Open Systems Interconnection (OSI) model. This includes checking the system to see if it has connectivity with the network.

A is incorrect. The Application layer (Layer 7) includes higher-order protocols, but they wouldn't be used if you don't have network connectivity.

C is incorrect. The Network layer (Layer 3) includes IP addresses and while the system might not have an IP address, this isn't generally the best place to start looking.

D is incorrect. Transmission Control Protocol (TCP) and User Datagram Protocol (UDP) protocols operate on the Transport layer (Layer 4), but this wouldn't be the place to start.

5. Ten computers are connected in a network via a switch. However, two computers are unable to communicate with any other computers in this network. Using a sniffer, you capture some traffic that includes the following output:

SRC MAC	SRC IP	DST MAC	DST IP
15:c3:45:2c:6f:01	192.168.5.5	01:15:2d:6f:c3:45	192.168.5.55
22:2c:6f:01:c3:45	192.168.5.5	05:c3:45:2d:9f:01	192.168.5.56

On which layer of the OSI model is this problem located?

A. Physical

B. Transport

C. Data Link

D. Network

Answer: **D** is correct. The problem is occurring on the Network layer (Layer 3) of the Open Systems Interconnection (OSI) model. The table shows that two different computers have the same source IP address. You can tell that they are different computers because they have different source media access control (MAC) addresses.

A is incorrect. The Physical layer (Layer 1) sends data out as bits, but this question is using IP and MAC addresses.

B is incorrect. The Transport layer (Layer 4) uses Transmission Control Protocol (TCP) or User Datagram Protocol (UDP) ports to identify traffic, but the scenario doesn't mention ports.
C is incorrect. The Data Link layer (Layer 2) uses media access control (MAC) addresses, but the scenario doesn't indicate any problem with the MAC addresses.

6. Which of the following PDUs does a connectionless protocol use?
   A. Datagrams
   B. Frames
   C. Bits
   D. Packets

Answer: **A** is correct. User Datagram Protocol (UDP) uses datagrams or segments and is a connectionless protocol. This is on Layer 4 (the Transport Layer) of the Open Systems Interconnection (OSI) model.

B is incorrect. Frames are on Layer 2 (the Data Link layer).
C is incorrect. Bits are on Layer 1 (the Physical layer).
D is incorrect. Packets are on Layer 3 (the Network layer).

7. Which of the following is the Network layer of the OSI model?
   A. 2
   B. 3
   C. 4
   D. 5

Answer: **B** is correct. The Network layer is Layer 3 of the Open Systems Interconnection (OSI) model.

A is incorrect. Layer 2 is the Data Link layer.

C is incorrect. Layer 4 is the Transport layer.

D is incorrect. Layer 5 is the Session layer.

8. A device operates on Layer 7 of the OSI model. Which layer is this?
   - A. Application
   - B. Network
   - C. Session
   - D. Physical

Answer: **A** is correct. Layer 7 of the Open Systems Interconnection (OSI) model is the Application layer.

B is incorrect. The Network layer is Layer 3.

C is incorrect. The Session layer is Layer 5.

D is incorrect. The Physical layer is Layer 1.

9. On which layer of the OSI model are specifications such as 1000BaseT or 10GBaseT defined?
   - A. Application
   - B. Session
   - C. Network
   - D. Physical

Answer: **D** is correct. Cabling specification protocols such as 1000BaseT and 10GBaseT are Physical layer (Layer 1) protocols in the Open Systems Interconnection (OSI) model.

A is incorrect. Cabling is not defined on the Application layer (Layer 7) of the OSI model.

B is incorrect. Cabling is not defined on the Session layer (Layer 5) of the OSI model.

C is incorrect. Cabling is not defined on the Network layer (Layer 3) of the OSI model.

10. On which layer of the OSI model are IPv4 and IPv6 addresses defined?
    A. Data Link
    B. Transport
    C. Network
    D. Physical

Answer: **C** is correct. IP addresses are defined on the Network layer (Layer 3) of the Open Systems Interconnection (OSI) model. Internet Protocol version 4 (IPv4) and Internet Protocol version 6 (IPv6) addresses are not defined on different layers.

A is incorrect. Media access control (MAC) addresses are defined on the Data Link layer (Layer 2).

B is incorrect. Transport protocols such as Transmission Control Protocol (TCP) and User Datagram Protocol (UDP) are defined on the Transport layer (Layer 4).

D is incorrect. Cabling specifications are defined on the Physical layer (Layer 1) and data is sent out as 1s and 0s.

11. A computer has an address of 192.168.1.5. On which layer of the OSI model is this address used?
    A. Layer 1
    B. Layer 2
    C. Layer 3
    D. Layer 4

Answer: **C** is correct. This is an IP address and IP addresses are used and identified on Layer 3 (Network layer) of the Open Systems Interconnection (OSI) model.

A is incorrect. Cable specifications are defined on Layer 1 (Physical layer).
B is incorrect. Media access control (MAC) addresses are defined on Layer 2 (Data Link layer).
D is incorrect. Transport protocols such as Transmission Control Protocol (TCP) and User Datagram Protocol (UDP) are defined on the Transport layer (Layer 4).

12. Of the following choices, which one is located on the Transport layer?
    A. TCP
    B. Physical address
    C. 10GBaseT
    D. 802.11n

Answer: **A** is correct. TCP is defined on the Transport layer (Layer 4) of the Open Systems Interconnection (OSI) model. User Datagram Protocol (UDP) is also defined on this layer.

B is incorrect. The physical address, also called the media access control (MAC) address, is defined on the Data Link layer (Layer 2).
C is incorrect. The 10GBaseT specification is defined on the Physical layer (Layer 1).
D is incorrect. The wireless 802.11n protocol is defined on Layers 1 and 2.

13. Which of the following protocols is located on Layer 4 of the OSI model?

    A. IPv6

    B. ICMP

    C. 802.11n

    D. UDP

Answer: **D** is correct. User Datagram Protocol (UDP) is on Layer 4 (the Transport layer) of the Open Systems Interconnection (OSI) model. Transmission Control Protocol (TCP) is also defined on this layer.

A is incorrect. Internet Protocol version 6 (IPv6) and Internet Protocol version 4 (IPv4) operate on Layer 3 (the Network layer).
B is incorrect. Internet Control Message Protocol (ICMP) operates on Layer 3 (Network layer).
C is incorrect. Wireless protocols such as 802.11n operate on Layers 1 and 2 (the Physical and Data Link layers).

14. On which layer of the OSI model are VLANs defined?

    A. Physical

    B. Data Link

    C. Network

    D. Transport

Answer: **B** is correct. Virtual local area networks (VLANs) are defined on the Data Link layer (Layer 2) of the Open Systems Interconnection (OSI) model.

A is incorrect. Cabling specification protocols are defined on the Physical layer (Layer 1).

C is incorrect. IP addresses are defined on the Network layer (Layer 3).

D is incorrect. Transmission Control Protocol (TCP) and User Datagram Protocol (UDP) are two protocols defined on the Transport layer (Layer 4).

15. Given the following choices, which is the BEST choice to identify the layer of the OSI model where a NIC operates?

    A. 1

    B. 3

    C. 4

    D. 7

Answer: **A** is correct. Network interface cards (NICs) operate on Layers 1 and 2 (Physical and Data Link layers) of the Open Systems Interconnection (OSI) model. This includes both wired and wireless NICs.

B, C, and D are incorrect. NICs do not operate on Layer 3 (the Network layer), Layer 4 (the Transport layer), or Layer 7 (the Application layer).

16. You are troubleshooting a network problem. You determine that you can ping the default gateway, but you cannot ping the IP address of servers on other networks. On which layer of the OSI model does the problem MOST likely exist?

    A. 1

    B. 2

    C. 3

    D. 7

Answer: **C** is correct. The problem most likely exists on Layer 3 (the Network layer) of the Open Systems Interconnection (OSI) model. The system is able to access the resources on the local network (the default gateway), but cannot access resources beyond the router on different IP networks. The router (which includes the default gateway) operates on the Network layer.

A and B are incorrect. The NIC operates on Layers 1 and 2 (Physical and Data Link layers), but it is operating because you can ping the default gateway with the IP address.
D is incorrect. Higher layers are not involved when pinging an IP address, so the problem is not on Layer 7 (the Application layer). However, Domain Name System (DNS) operates on Layer 7 and resolves host names to IP addresses. If you could ping the IP address of the remote system but it failed when you pinged the name, the problem could be related to DNS on Layer 7.

17. On which layer(s) of the OSI model do wireless protocols operate?
    A. Physical
    B. Physical and Data Link
    C. Data Link
    D. Data Link and Network

Answer: **B** is correct. Wireless protocols (such as 802.11 a/b/g/n) operate on both Layers 1 and 2 (Physical and Data Link layers) of the Open Systems Interconnection (OSI) model. This is similar to how wired network interface cards (NICs) operate on Layers 1 and 2.

A and C are incorrect. Wireless protocols operate on both the Physical layer and the Data Link layer, so the best answer is to identify each of the layers (Physical and Data Link), rather than only one.
D is incorrect. Wireless protocols do not operate on the Network layer.

18. Of the following choices, which one operates on Layer 1 of the OSI model and will always forward broadcast traffic?
    - A. Switch
    - B. Router
    - C. Hub
    - D. NIC

Answer: **C** is correct. A hub operates on Layer 1 of the Open Systems Interconnection (OSI) model and always forwards broadcast traffic.

A is incorrect. Switches normally forward broadcast traffic, but they can be used to configure virtual local area networks (VLANs) and will not forward broadcast traffic between the VLANs.
B is incorrect. Routers do not forward broadcast traffic. A broadcast domain refers to a group of devices on a network that can receive broadcast traffic from each other and routers create separate broadcast domains.
D is incorrect. Network interface cards (NICs) process broadcast traffic, but do not forward it.

19. Which of the following is associated with the Transport layer of the OSI model?
    - A. Reliable delivery of packets
    - B. VLANs
    - C. IP subnets
    - D. NICs

Answer: **A** is correct. The Transport layer (Layer 4) of the Open Systems Interconnection (OSI) model is associated with the reliable delivery of packets and Transmission Control Protocol (TCP) operates on this layer.

User Datagram Protocol (UDP) also operates on the Transport layer, but it does not provide guaranteed delivery.

B is incorrect. Virtual local area networks (VLANs) are created with switches and operate on Layer 2 (Data Link).
C is incorrect. IP subnets are identified on Layer 3 (Network layer). Routers route data between IP subnets.
D is incorrect. Network interface cards (NICs) operate on Layers 1 and 2 (Physical and Data Link).

Objective: 5.2 Explain the basics of network theory and concepts.

20. Which of the following devices uses CSMA/CA?
    A. Layer 3 switch
    B. Router
    C. Hub
    D. Wireless access point

Answer: **D** is correct. A wireless access point (WAP) uses Carrier Sense Multiple Access/Collision Avoidance (CSMA/CA). Some implementations of 802.11 wireless protocols also use Request To Send (RTS) and Clear To Send (CTS) to manage traffic on a network.

A and B are incorrect. Wired devices such as Layer 3 switches and routers use Carrier Sense Multiple Access/Collision Detection (CSMA/CD), instead of CSMA/CA.
C is incorrect. A hub uses CSMA/CD.

21. Which of the following standards uses timers to force devices to wait after detecting a collision on a congested network?
    A. RTS/CTS
    B. CDMA
    C. CSMA/CA
    D. CSMA/CD

Answer: **D** is correct. Carrier Sense Multiple Access/Collision Detection (CSMA/CD) uses standoff timers forcing devices to wait a random amount of time after detecting a collision.

A is incorrect. Standards using Request To Send (RTS) and Clear To Send (CTS) avoid collisions by negotiating when it is clear to send data. Some implementations of 802.11 wireless protocols also use RTS and CTS to manage traffic on a network.
B is incorrect. Code division multiple access (CDMA) is used for multiplexing signals with transmitters sending data over different frequencies within the same band. It is commonly used with 3G cellular transmissions.
C is incorrect. Carrier Sense Multiple Access/Collision Avoidance (CSMA/CA) avoids collisions.

Objective: 5.3 Given a scenario, deploy the appropriate wireless standard.

22. Which of the following is a valid wireless standard that supports high-definition video streaming?
    A. 802.11a
    B. 802.11b

C. 802.11g

D. 802.11ac

Answer: **D** is correct. 802.11ac is a wireless networking standard that supports a wireless local area network (WLAN) with a throughput of at least 1 Gbps. This supports high-definition video streaming and other transmissions that consume a lot of bandwidth.

A is incorrect. 802.11a has a maximum speed of 54 Mbps, which isn't enough to support high-definition video streaming.
B is incorrect. 802.11b has a maximum speed of 11 Mbps, which isn't enough to support high-definition video streaming.
C is incorrect. 802.11g has a maximum speed of 54 Mbps, which isn't enough to support high-definition video streaming.

23. You are assisting a business owner who is troubleshooting an existing WLAN. You discover that the maximum speed is 11 Mbps. Which of the following standards is this network MOST likely running?

    A. 802.11a

    B. 802.11b

    C. 802.11g

    D. 802.11ac

Answer: **B** is correct. The maximum speed of 802.11b is 11 Mbps in a wireless local area network (WLAN).

A is incorrect. The maximum speed of 802.11a is 54 Mbps.
C is incorrect. The maximum speed of 802.11g is 54 Mbps.
D is incorrect. The maximum speed of 802.11ac is 866.7 Mbps per channel. With eight channels, that's about 6.933 Gbps.

24. You've been asked to help a small business owner create a wireless network. She wants to create a network that will support newer wireless devices and provide the maximum transfer rate. What would you recommend?

    A. A wireless router that supports 802.11a

    B. A wireless router that supports 802.11b

    C. A wireless router that supports 802.11g

    D. A wireless router that supports 802.11n

Answer: **D** is correct. 802.11n is a newer wireless protocol supported by newer wireless devices. It provides the highest available bandwidth with a transfer rate of 600 Mbps or higher using multiple-input, multiple-output (MIMO) technologies.

A is incorrect. 802.11a is an older wireless protocol and it has a maximum transfer rate of 54 Mbps.

B is incorrect. 802.11b is an older wireless protocol and it has a maximum transfer rate of 11 Mbps.

C is incorrect. 802.11g has a maximum transfer rate of 11 Mbps.

25. You've been asked to help a small business owner identify a WAP to support multiple wireless devices in his business. After checking, you've found that some of these devices use 2.4 GHz and some of the devices use 5 GHz. What would you recommend?

    A. A wireless router that supports 802.11a

    B. A wireless router that supports 802.11b

    C. A wireless router that supports 802.11g

    D. A wireless router that supports 802.11n

Answer: **D** is correct. 802.11n uses both 2.4 GHz and 5 GHz and is backward compatible with other wireless protocols using either of the frequencies.

A is incorrect. 802.11a uses 5.0 GHz only.

B is incorrect. 802.11b uses 2.4 GHz only.

C is incorrect. 802.11g uses 2.4 GHz only.

26. You've been asked to help a small business owner create a wireless network. He wants to install a network with the greatest throughput. What would you recommend?

    A. A wireless router that supports 802.11a

    B. A wireless router that supports 802.11b

    C. A wireless router that supports 802.11g

    D. A wireless router that supports 802.11n

Answer: **D** is correct. 802.11n supports a throughput of 600 Mbps or higher using multiple-input, multiple-output (MIMO) technologies.

A is incorrect. The maximum transfer rate of 802.11a is 54 Mbps.

B is incorrect. The maximum transfer rate of 802.11b is 11 Mbps.

C is incorrect. The maximum transfer rate of 802.11g is 54 Mbps.

27. You want to install a wireless network using the same frequency band as 802.11a. What, if anything, can you use?

    A. None. 802.11a operates on a frequency that isn't used by other wireless standards.

    B. 802.11b

    C. 802.11g

    D. 802.11n

Answer: **D** is correct. 802.11a operates on 5 GHz and 802.11n operates on both 2.4 GHz and 5 GHz.

A is incorrect. 802.11a isn't the only wireless standard using 5 GHz.
B is incorrect. 802.11b only uses 2.4 GHz.
C is incorrect. 802.11g only uses 2.4 GHz.

Objective: 5.4 Given a scenario, deploy the appropriate wired connectivity standard.

28. Which of the following standards supports multimode fiber?
    A. 1000BaseLR
    B. 1000BaseSR
    C. 1000BaseT
    D. 1000BaseER

Answer: **B** is correct. 1000BaseSR and10GBaseSR (short range) uses multimode fiber (MMF) and is the best choice. MMF is used for shorter distances and has a lower cost for the cable, the connectors, and the lasers used to put the signal onto the fiber.

A is incorrect. 10GBaseLR (long range) uses single mode fiber (SMF) and has a specified range of up to 10 km (6.2 miles). SMF has a higher cost for the cable, the connectors, and the lasers.
C is incorrect. 1000BaseT uses twisted-pair cable.
D is incorrect. 10GBaseER (extended range) uses SMF and can be used for the greatest distances, up to 30 kilometers (about 18 miles) using standard materials. SMF has a higher cost for the cable, the connectors, and the lasers.

29. You are replacing an older computer with a new one and connecting it to a legacy SCADA network. Unfortunately, the connection isn't working. You verify the CAT3 cable used with the original computer is wired properly and doesn't have any breaks. Which of the following is a logical next step?
    A. Verify the new computer is compatible with 10BaseT.
    B. Verify the new computer is compatible with 10Base2.
    C. Verify the new computer is compatible with 10Base5.
    D. Verify the new computer is compatible with 100BaseFX.

Answer: **A** is correct. You should verify the new computer is compatible with 10BaseT. CAT3 cable is commonly used with phone lines, but it was also used in early implementations of Ethernet. Because the scenario indicates the original computer connected to the legacy Supervisory Control and Data Acquisition (SCADA) network is using CAT3 cable, it indicates the network is using the 10BaseT standard.

B and C are incorrect. 10Base2 and 10Base5 use coaxial-type cables, but CAT3 is a twisted-pair cable.
D is incorrect. 100BaseFX uses fiber cable.

30. Which of the following standards was designed to be used with SONET equipment?
    A. 10GBaseSW
    B. 10GBaseSR
    C. 10GBaseCX4
    D. 10GBaseT

Answer: **A** is correct. The 10BaseW standards (including 10BaseSW, 10BaseLW, and 10BaseEW) were designed work with existing Synchronous Optical Networking (SONET) equipment.

B is incorrect. The 10BaseR standards include 10BaseSR (short range), 10BaseLR (long range), and 10BaseER (extended range). These were not designed specifically to work with existing SONET equipment.
C is incorrect. 10BaseCX4 uses copper with maximum range of 15 km (about 49 feet), but SONET uses optical media (fiber) and transmits data over farther distances.
D is incorrect. 10GbaseT uses twisted-pair cable, not fiber used by SONET.

31. You need to purchase cable for a 10GBaseSR connection. What should you get?
    A. SMF
    B. MMF
    C. CAT5e
    D. CAT6a

Answer: **B** is correct. 10GBase SR (short range) uses multimode fiber (MMF), so MMF should be purchased.

A is incorrect. Single mode fiber (SMF) is used for longer distances (such as with long-range 10GbaseLR or extended-range 10GbaseER), but requires more expensive cable, connectors, and equipment.
C is incorrect. CAT5e is twisted-pair, so it wouldn't work with 10GBaseSR, which uses fiber. Additionally, CAT5e is recommended for 1,000-Mbps networks, but will not support 10 Gbps.

D is incorrect. CAT6a is twisted-pair and can be used for 10GBaseT, but not with 10GbaseSR, which requires fiber.

32. You are designing a 10-Gigabit network for a high-speed data center. All of the cable runs will be 10 meters or less. Which of the following cable types provides the BEST choice?
    A. 10GGaseER
    B. 10GGaseLR
    C. 10GBaseSR
    D. 100BaseFX

Answer: **C** is correct. 10GBaseSR (short range) uses multimode fiber (MMF) and is the best choice. MMF is used for shorter distances and has a lower cost for the cable, the connectors, and the lasers used to put the signal onto the fiber.

A is incorrect. 10GBaseER (extended range) uses single mode fiber (SMF) and can be used for the greatest distances, up to 30 kilometers (about 18 miles) using standard materials. SMF has a higher cost for the cable, the connectors, and the lasers.

B is incorrect. 10GBaseLR (long range) uses SMF and has a specified range of up to 10 km (6.2 miles). SMF has a higher cost for the cable, the connectors, and the lasers.

D is incorrect. 100BaseFX has maximum data throughput of 100 Mbps, so it would not meet the needs of a 10-Gbps data center.

33. Which of the following standards would be used within a data center to provide 10 Gigabit Ethernet with the least cost?

    A. 10GBaseR

    B. 10GBaseT

    C. 10GBaseW

    D. 10GBaseX

Answer: **B** is correct. 10GBaseT provides 10 Gigabit Ethernet using CAT6a twisted-pair cable, which is cheaper to install and maintain than fiber.

A is incorrect. 10GBaseR refers to a family of 10 Gigabit Ethernet standards using fiber with specific ranges: 10GBaseSR (short range), 10GBaseLR (long range), and 10GBaseER (extended range).
C is incorrect. 10GBaseW refers to a family of 10 Gigabit Ethernet standards using fiber for wide area networks (WANs): 10GBaseSW, 10GBaseLW, and 10GBaseEW. These work with Synchronous Optical Networking (SONET) equipment.
D is incorrect. 10GBaseX refers to either 10BaseLX4 or 10BaseCX4. 10BaseLX4 uses fiber, while 10BaseCX4 uses copper in a niche market but with a maximum distance of 15 meters.

34. Which of the following is a valid LAN technology that provides the highest data rate?

    A. 10BaseT

    B. 100BaseT

    C. 1000BaseT

    D. 10GBaseT

Answer: **D** is correct. 10GBaseT uses twisted-pair and provides a data rate of 10 Gbps. It is commonly called 10 Gigabit Ethernet.

A is incorrect. 10BaseT uses twisted-pair and provides a data rate of 10 Mbps. It is commonly called Ethernet.
B is incorrect. 100BaseT uses twisted-pair and provides a data rate of 100 Mbps. It is commonly called Fast Ethernet.
C is incorrect. 1000BaseT uses twisted-pair and provides a data rate of 1,000 Mbps (or 1 Gbps). It is commonly called Gigabit Ethernet.

35. Which of the following is a valid LAN technology that can be used for the greatest distance?
    A. 10GBaseT
    B. 10GBaseER
    C. 10GBaseLR
    D. 10GBaseSR

Answer: **B** is correct. 10GBaseER (extended range) uses single mode fiber (SMF) and can be used for the greatest distances. It can be used for 30 km (about 18 miles) with standard techniques, but has been able to reach up to 40 km (about 25 miles) using advanced techniques.

A is incorrect. 10BaseT uses twisted-pair cable and has a maximum distance of 100 meters (about 330 feet).
C is incorrect. 10GBaseLR (long range) uses single mode fiber (SMF) and has a specified range of up to 10 km (about 6 miles). It has been used for distances up to 25 km (about 15.5 miles).
D is incorrect. 10GBaseSR (short range) uses multimode fiber (MMF) and has a specified range of up to 400 meters (about 1313 feet).

Objective: 5.5 Given a scenario, implement the appropriate policies or procedures.

36. Users are reporting errors accessing some websites. You've verified that you can access GetCertifiedGetAhead.com, but you are unable to access websites that require you to log on. What is the MOST likely problem?
    A. TCP port 53 is blocked at the network firewall.
    B. UDP port 67 is blocked at the network firewall.
    C. TCP port 80 is blocked at the network firewall.
    D. TCP port 443 is blocked at the network firewall.

Answer: **D** is correct. Hypertext Transfer Protocol Secure (HTTPS) is used for secure transactions such as when logging on to a website or making purchases. HTTPS uses port 443, so it is likely blocked at the firewall.

A is incorrect. Domain Name System (DNS) uses port 53 by default, but there is not a problem with DNS. It uses Transmission Control Protocol (TCP) port 53 when doing zone transfers between DNS servers and User Datagram Protocol (UDP) port 53 when responding to DNS queries.
B is incorrect. Dynamic Host Configuration Protocol (DHCP) uses UDP ports 67 and 68 by default, but a problem with DHCP isn't indicated.
C is incorrect. HTTP uses port 80 by default, but HTTP is working.

37. Before new employees receive an account and password, they are required to read and sign a document acknowledging they understand their responsibilities. Which of the following BEST describes this document?
    A. AUP
    B. MOU

C. SLA

D. SOW

Answer: **A** is correct. An acceptable use policy (AUP) outlines user responsibilities. New employees are typically required to read and acknowledge an AUP before being given an account, and periodically afterward.

B is incorrect. A memorandum of understanding (MOU) expresses an understanding between two or more parties, such as two or more organizations. It indicates their intention to work together toward a common goal and is unrelated to employee responsibilities.
C is incorrect. A service level agreement (SLA) is an agreement between a company and a vendor that stipulates performance expectations, such as minimum uptime and maximum downtime levels. It is unrelated to employee responsibilities.
D is incorrect. A statement of work (SOW) identifies the scope of work for a contractor. It is not used for employees.

38. An organization wants to ensure that employees understand the guidelines related to their use of network resources. What is used to describe this?

A. ACL

B. DoS

C. Incident response

D. AUP

Answer: **D** is correct. An acceptable use policy (AUP), sometimes called an acceptable usage policy, describes the rules and guidelines related to using information technology (IT) systems. It is common to require employees to sign the AUP when hired and periodically afterward.

A is incorrect. An access control list (ACL) is a list of rules for a router or firewall that identifies traffic allowed through a network or blocked at the device.
B is incorrect. Denial of service (DoS) refers to an attack that attempts to stop a system from providing regular services to legitimate users.
C is incorrect. Incident response refers to the procedures an organization takes after a computer security incident. AUPs help prevent security incidents caused by employees.

39. Your organization has contracted with a service provider to provide connectivity between headquarters and several remote locations. The connections should meet minimum speeds, but after measuring it, administrators discovered the speeds are significantly lower. Which of the following documents is MOST likely to allow the organization to hold the service provider responsible for providing higher speeds?
    A. MLA
    B. MOU
    C. SLA
    D. AUP

Answer: **C** is correct. An organization can hold a service provider responsible for providing minimum service levels using a service level agreement (SLA). The SLA is an agreement between a company and a vendor that stipulates performance expectations, such as minimum uptime and maximum downtime levels.

A is incorrect. A master license agreement (MLA) is typically used with software, but does not specify performance expectations. The license authorizes organizations to use the software as long as they comply with the requirements in the agreement.
B is incorrect. A memorandum of understanding (MOU) expresses an understanding between two or more parties, such as two or more organizations. It indicates their intention to work together toward a common goal and is unrelated to ensuring minimum performance requirements.
D is incorrect. An acceptable use policy (AUP) outlines user responsibilities; organizations typically require employees to read and acknowledge an AUP annually.

40. Your organization has hired a contractor to review your network with a goal of improving availability of the internal network and running applications. Which of the following will document the scope of work for the contractor?
    A. MLA
    B. MOU
    C. SLA
    D. SOW

Answer: **D** is correct. The statement of work (SOW) identifies the scope of work for a contractor.

A is incorrect. A master license agreement (MLA) is typically used with software. The license authorizes organizations to use the software as long as they comply with the requirements in the agreement.

B is incorrect. A memorandum of understanding (MOU) expresses an understanding between two or more parties indicating their intention to work together toward a common goal.
C is incorrect. A service level agreement (SLA) is an agreement between a company and a vendor that stipulates performance expectations, such as minimum uptime and maximum downtime levels.

Objective: 5.6 Summarize safety practices.

41. Your company recently purchased another company. Several administrators have inspected the server room at the new company and raised safety concerns. Specifically, they state that the server room has a system that can remove all oxygen from the room and threaten the lives of anyone in the room. What is the purpose of this system?
    A. ESD prevention
    B. Safety of personnel
    C. Temperature control
    D. Fire suppression

Answer: **D** is correct. This scenario describes a fire suppression system.

A is incorrect. An electrostatic discharge (ESD) prevention system includes tools and techniques to prevent ESD damage, but does not include the ability to remove oxygen from a room.
B is incorrect. Removing oxygen from a room does not preserve safety of personnel. A Material Safety Data Sheet (MSDS) provides personnel with safety information about potentially hazardous materials, such as cleaning agents. The MSDS for a cleaning agent will provide the best information, such as first aid treatment.

C is incorrect. Heating, ventilation, and air conditioning (HVAC) systems maintain proper temperature and humidity. They do not remove oxygen from a room.

42. A technician has had prolonged contact with a cleaning agent and is getting a rash. Which of the following will provide the best information in this scenario?
    - A. SLA
    - B. MOU
    - C. SOW
    - D. MSDS

Answer: **D** is correct. The Material Safety Data Sheet (MSDS) for the cleaning agent will provide the best information, such as first aid treatment.

A is incorrect. A service level agreement (SLA) stipulates performance expectations, such as minimum uptime and maximum downtime levels.
B is incorrect. A memorandum of understanding (MOU) expresses an understanding between two or more parties indicating their intention to work together toward a common goal.
C is incorrect. A statement of work (SOW) identifies the scope of work for a contractor.

Objective: 5.7 Given a scenario, install and configure equipment in the appropriate location using best practices.

43. Which of the following identifies where you would connect equipment from an external service provider with an organization's equipment?
    A. 110 block
    B. 66 block
    C. MDF
    D. IDF

Answer: **C** is correct. A main distribution frame (MDF) is a frame (or rack) used to connect cables from external sources to internal equipment.

A and B are incorrect. A 110 block is a connection point for telephone wires and computer connections and is replacing the 66 block. Both are used internally and are not exclusively used to connect to an external service provider.
D is incorrect. An intermediate distribution frame (IDF) is internal to a company and includes cross connects for cables. It will often be an intermediate point between the MDF and other devices that need the connection.

44. Bart is troubleshooting a problem and he determines the problem is with a switch. The switch is connecting multiple office computers on the second floor and north side of the building. All switches terminate in the server room. Which of the following will make it the easiest for Bart to locate the switch?
    A. Connecting via a 110 block
    B. Using cable trays

C. Using naming conventions

D. Using patch panels

Answer: **C** is correct. A consistent naming convention would make it the easiest to identify the switch. For example, the switch could be named (and labeled) as "sw15_2_n" with *sw15* indicating switch 15, *2* representing the second floor, and *n* representing the north side of the building.

A is incorrect. A 110 block is a connection point for telephone wires and computer connections. However, just using a 110 block won't make it easier to locate a specific switch.
B is incorrect. Cable trays can keep cables protected, but they don't necessarily help locate specific switches.
D is incorrect. Patch panels are used in almost all network installations. Labeling patch panels would be helpful, but just the use of patch panels doesn't make it very easy to locate a switch.

Objective: 5.8 Explain the basics of change management procedures.

45. You are tasked with implementing an approved change to a server. Users have been notified that there will be an outage of approximately 1 hour long, which is the approved maintenance window. What should you do if you are unable to complete the change within the allotted time?

A. Roll back the drivers.

B. Test the change on the test server.

C. Roll back the changes.

D. Increase the maintenance window.

Answer: **C** is correct. Approved changes should include a rollback procedure to implement if it isn't possible to implement the changes within the allotted time.

A is incorrect. If the change updated drivers, then you would roll back the drivers. However, the scenario didn't indicate what would be changed.
B is incorrect. Testing the change on a test server is appropriate. However, that would be done before approving the change.
D is incorrect. It is not appropriate to increase the maintenance window. Personnel will expect the server to be available after an hour.

46. After a recent software update, a user is no longer able to access a 3D printer through a company-created application. After investigation, you discover that the update installed incompatible drivers on the user's system. Of the following choices, what will MOST likely restore the user's system capabilities?
    A. Install a new operating system on the user's system.
    B. Roll back the drivers.
    C. Test the drivers on a test system.
    D. Request authorized downtime for the printer.

Answer: **B** is correct. Because the update installed incompatible drivers on the user's system, the solution is to roll back the drivers to the previous version.

A is incorrect. It is not necessary to install a new operating system.
C is incorrect. Testing the drivers on a test system will prevent a similar incident, but won't restore the system affected in this scenario.
D is incorrect. The problem isn't with the printer, but instead with the user's system.

47. Which of the following scenarios is a valid reason to request authorized downtime?

    A. A major upgrade for a test server

    B. To reboot a desktop system

    C. To test drivers on a test system

    D. A minor upgrade for a production server

Answer: **D** is correct. You should request a maintenance window for authorized downtime when performing any modifications for a production server.

A and C are incorrect. It is not necessary to request downtime for test systems.

B is incorrect. It is not necessary to request downtime to reboot desktop systems.

Objective: 5.9 Compare and contrast the following ports and protocols.

48. An organization wants users to be able to access websites for research and to make purchases. What ports must be opened on the firewall? (Choose all that apply.)

    A. 22

    B. 80

    C. 143

    D. 443

Answer: **B** and **D** are correct. Websites use Hypertext Transfer Protocol (HTTP) for typical web pages and HTTP Secure (HTTPS) for secure transactions such as when making purchases. HTTP uses port 80 and HTTPS uses port 443.

A is incorrect. Secure Shell (SSH) uses port 22.
C is incorrect. Internet Message Access Protocol (IMAP) uses port 143.

49. Which of the following protocols provides the highest level of security for traffic sent over a network?

    A. HTTP
    B. Telnet
    C. SIP
    D. HTTPS

Answer: **D** is correct. Hypertext Transfer Protocol Secure (HTTPS) uses Secure Sockets Layer (SSL) or Transport Layer Security (TLS) to secure HTTP traffic with encryption.

A is incorrect. Hypertext Transfer Protocol (HTTP) data is sent in cleartext unless it's encrypted as HTTPS.
B is incorrect. Telnet data is sent in cleartext and Secure Shell (SSH) is often used as a secure replacement.
C is incorrect. Session Initiation Protocol (SIP) is used to manage Voice over Internet Protocol (VoIP) sessions, but it does not provide security.

50. A user is accessing the Internet with a web browser. What port does a web browser use by default?

    A. 67
    B. 80
    C. 143
    D. 3389

Answer: **B** is correct. Web browsers use Hypertext Transfer Protocol (HTTP) and HTTP uses port 80. During secure transactions, web browsers use HTTP Secure (HTTPS) over port 443.

A is incorrect. Dynamic Host Configuration Protocol (DHCP) uses port 67 (and port 68).
C is incorrect. Internet Message Access Protocol (IMAP) uses port 143.
D is incorrect. Remote Desktop Protocol (RDP) uses port 3389.

51. Which of the following protocols does NOT retransmit lost packets?
    A. TCP
    B. UDP
    C. HTTP
    D. FTP

Answer: **B** is correct. User Datagram Protocol (UDP) does not retransmit lost packets but instead uses a "best effort" to deliver the packets.

A is incorrect. Transmission Control Protocol (TCP) tracks packet delivery and will retransmit lost packets. TCP provides guaranteed delivery.
C and D are incorrect. Both Hypertext Transfer Protocol (HTTP) and File Transfer Protocol (FTP) use TCP, so they will retransmit lost packets as a part of the TCP functionality.

52. Which of the following ports are used for email? (Choose all that apply.)
    A. 25
    B. 53
    C. 143
    D. 3389

Answer: **A** and **C** are correct**.** The Simple Mail Transfer Protocol (SMTP) uses port 25 to send email and Internet Message Access Protocol (IMAP) uses port 143 for email.

B is incorrect. Domain Name System (DNS) uses port 53 and it performs name resolution by resolving host names to IP addresses.
D is incorrect. Remote Desktop Protocol (RDP) uses port 3389.

53. Which of the following identifies a valid difference between IPv4 TCP and UDP?
    A. The TCP header uses flags, but the UDP header does not use flags.
    B. The UDP header uses flags, but the TCP header does not use flags.
    C. UDP is connection-oriented, but TCP is connectionless.
    D. UDP provides guaranteed delivery, but TCP only makes a best effort to deliver traffic.

Answer: **A** is correct. The User Datagram Protocol (UDP) header has only four fields: source port, destination port, length, and checksum. In contrast, the Transmission Control Protocol (TCP) header has many more fields, including several flags such as SYN and ACK, which are used when establishing a session.

B is incorrect. The UDP header does not use flags.
C is incorrect. TCP (not UDP) is connection-oriented, and UDP (not TCP) is connectionless.
D is incorrect. TCP (not UDP) provides guaranteed delivery. UDP (not TCP) makes a best effort to deliver traffic.

Objective: 5.10 Given a scenario, configure and apply the appropriate ports and protocols.

54. What port needs to be opened on a firewall to allow outgoing DNS traffic through?

    A. 25

    B. 53

    C. 80

    D. 443

Answer: **B** is correct. Domain Name System (DNS) uses port 53 for DNS traffic. DNS is used for resolving names to IP addresses and to locate specific servers using resource records. For example, an MX (Mail Exchanger) record is used to locate mail servers.

A is incorrect. Simple Mail Transfer Protocol (SMTP) uses port 25.
C is incorrect. Hypertext Transfer Protocol (HTTP) uses Transmission Control Protocol (TCP) port 80.
D is incorrect. Hypertext Transfer Protocol Secure (HTTPS) uses TCP port 443.

55. Which port is used by DNS?

    A. 21

    B. 22

    C. 25

    D. 53

Answer: **D** is correct. Domain Name System (DNS) uses UDP port 53 for DNS queries. DNS is used for resolving names to IP addresses.

A is incorrect. File Transfer Protocol (FTP) uses port 21 (and port 20).

B is incorrect. Secure Shell (SSH) uses port 22.

C is incorrect. Simple Mail Transfer Protocol (SMTP) uses port 25.

56. Which of the following ports are commonly used for FTP traffic?

A. 20 and 21

B. 25 and 143

C. 67 and 68

D. 80 and 443

Answer: **A** is correct. Ports 20 and 21 are the default ports used for File Transfer Protocol (FTP) traffic.

B is incorrect. Ports 25 and 143 are used for email. Port 25 is used for Simple Mail Transfer Protocol (SMTP) and port 143 is used for Internet Message Access Protocol (IMAP).

C is incorrect. Ports 67 and 68 are used by Dynamic Host Configuration Protocol (DHCP) by default.

D is incorrect. Port 80 is used by Hypertext Transfer Protocol (HTTP) and port 443 is used by HTTP Secure (HTTPS).

57. What port does RDP use?

A. 22

B. 67

C. 143

D. 3389

Answer: **D** is correct. The Remote Desktop Protocol (RDP) uses port 3389 by default.

A is incorrect. Secure Shell (SSH) uses port 22.

B is incorrect. Dynamic Host Configuration Protocol (DHCP) uses ports 67 and 68.

C is incorrect. Internet Message Access Protocol (IMAP) uses port 143 by default for email.

58. You need to connect to a remote system using RDP. Which of the following ports must be opened on the firewall?

    A. 53

    B. 3389

    C. 67

    D. 445

Answer: **B** is correct. The default port for Remote Desktop Protocol (RDP) is 3389, so this port needs to be opened on the firewall to allow RDP traffic.

A is incorrect. Domain Name System (DNS) uses port 53.

C is incorrect. Dynamic Host Configuration Protocol (DHCP) uses ports 67 and 68.

D is incorrect. Server Message Block (SMB) uses port 445.

59. Which of the following protocols uses port 22?

    A. FTP

    B. SSH

    C. SMTP

    D. RDP

Answer: **B** is correct. Secure Shell (SSH) uses port 22.

A is incorrect. File Transfer Protocol (FTP) uses ports 20 and 21 by default.
C is incorrect. Simple Mail Transfer Protocol (SMTP) sends email over port 25 by default.
D is incorrect. The Remote Desktop Protocol (RDP) uses port 3389 by default.

60. Administrators have stored small text files on a server, which hold router and switch configuration scripts. They use TFTP to connect to the server and download the scripts when necessary. However, they can no longer connect to this server using TFTP. Which of the following is the MOST likely reason?
    A. Port 67 is blocked on a router.
    B. Port 161 is blocked on a router.
    C. Port 20 is blocked on a router.
    D. Port 69 is blocked on a router.

Answer: **D** is correct. Trivial File Transfer Protocol (TFTP) uses User Datagram Protocol (UDP) port 69. If port 69 is blocked, it will block TFTP traffic.

A is incorrect. Dynamic Host Configuration Protocol (DHCP) uses port 67, so if port 67 was blocked, it would affect DHCP, not TFTP.
B is incorrect. Simple Network Management Protocol (SNMP) uses port 161, so if port 161 was blocked, it would affect SNMP, not TFTP.
C is incorrect. File Transfer Protocol (FTP) uses port 20, so if port 20 was blocked, it would affect FTP, not TFTP.

61. You are checking a firewall and see that port 161 is open. What protocol would be using this port?

    A. IMAP

    B. SNMP

    C. DNS

    D. SSH

Answer: **B** is correct. The Simple Network Management Protocol (SNMP) is used to administer and monitor network devices on port 161.

A is incorrect. The Internet Message Access Protocol (IMAP) uses port 143 for email.

C is incorrect. Domain Name System (DNS) is used to resolve host names to IP addresses on port 53.

D is incorrect. Secure Shell (SSH) encrypts some protocols and it uses port 22.

Appendix A—Acronym List

This acronym list provides you with a quick reminder of many of the different Network+ related terms along with a short explanation.

Numeric–Topics in Acronym List

802.2—Logical Link Control. A specification that defines how the Data Link layer interacts with the Network layer of the OSI model.

802.3—Ethernet. A group of standards used to define a wide range of cables and connections.

802.3af—Power over Ethernet (PoE). A standard that delivers power to devices over an Ethernet cable. Compare to 802.3at.

802.3at—Power over Ethernet plus (PoE+). A standard that delivers power to devices over an Ethernet cable. 802.3at provides up to 25.5 W of power. In contrast, 802.3af provides up to 15.4 W of power.

802.5—Token Ring networks. A type of network that uses a special 3-byte frame as a logical token. The logical token is passed around to devices in the ring and devices can only transmit data when they have the token.

802.11—Group of wireless technologies. Network+ focuses on 802.11a, 802.11b, 802.11g, 802.11n, and 802.11ac.

802.11a—An early wireless standard with a maximum speed of 54 Mbps using the 5-GHz frequency range. It has the shortest range compared with other 802.11 standards.

802.11ac—The newest wireless standard with a theoretical maximum of 1 Gbps, which can use the 2.4-GHz and 5-GHz frequency ranges. It's an update over the 802.11n standard.

802.11b—An early wireless standard with a maximum speed of 11 Mbps using the 2.4-GHz frequency range. It has a relatively short range.

802.11g—A wireless standard with a maximum speed of 54 Mbps using the 2.4-GHz frequency range and range slightly better than 802.11b.

802.11n—A new wireless standard with a maximum speed of 600 Mbps, which can use the 2.4-GHz and 5-GHz frequency ranges and has a longer range than 802.11g. 802.11n uses MIMO.

A–Topics in Acronym List

A record—IPv4 host name record. This isn't actually an acronym, but it looks like one. It identifies a specific type of record used in DNS servers to resolve host names to IPv4 addresses. Compare to AAAA, CNAME, MX, and PTR DNS records.

AAA—Authentication, authorization, and accounting. Authentication verifies a user's identification. Authorization determines if a user should have access. Accounting tracks a user's access with logs. AAA protocols are used in remote access systems. For example, TACACS+ is an AAA protocol that uses multiple challenges and responses during a session.

AAAA record—IPv6 host name record. This isn't actually an acronym, but it looks like one. It identifies a specific type of record used in DNS servers to resolve host names to IPv6 addresses. Compare to A, CNAME, MX, and PTR DNS records.

AC—Alternating current. Power received from a commercial power company. Compare to DC.

ACL—Access control list. A group of rules on routers and firewalls that define what traffic the router or firewall will allow or deny.

ADSL—Asymmetric digital subscriber line. A specific type of DSL line typically used for Internet access. ADSL lines have different speeds for the upload and download links. The download link is normally faster than the upload link. Compare to DSL and SDSL.

AES—Advanced Encryption Standard. A strong encryption algorithm used to encrypt data and provide confidentiality. AES is quick, highly secure, and used in a wide assortment of cryptography schemes.

AH—Authentication Header. IPsec includes both AH and ESP. AH provides authentication and integrity, and ESP provides confidentiality, integrity, and authentication. AH is identified with protocol number 51.

AP—Access point. A device used to connect wireless devices to a wired network. A wireless router includes an AP and additional capabilities. Sometimes called a wireless access point (WAP).

APC—Angle polished connector. A connector used with fiber cables. The fiber is polished at an 8- or 9-degree angle to prevent the fiber core from capturing reflections.

APIPA—Automatic Private Internet Protocol Addressing. Used by some DHCP clients to automatically assign an IP address when the client does not receive a response from a DHCP server. APIPA addresses start with 169.254 such as 169.254.3.4.

APT—Advanced persistent threat. A group that has both the capability and intent to launch sophisticated and targeted attacks. APTs are typically sponsored by a government.

ARIN—American Registry for Internet Numbers. A Regional Internet Registry (RIR) that manages the distribution of IPv4 and IPv6 addresses in the United States, Canada, and several islands. It is one of five worldwide RIRs.

ARP—Address Resolution Protocol. Resolves IP addresses to MAC addresses. Compare this to DNS, which resolves host names to IP addresses. ARP operates on the Network layer (Layer 3) of the OSI model.

The arp command-line tool is different than ARP (the protocol). You can view the ARP cache with the arp command.

AS—Autonomous system. A collection of connected Internet Protocol (IP) routing prefixes. Regional Internet Registries manage the distribution of AS prefixes along with IPv4 and IPv6 addresses.

ASCII—American Standard Code for Information Interchange. A standard used to define codes for specific characters. ASCII is defined on the Presentation layer (Layer 6) of the OSI model.

ASIC—Application-specific integrated circuit. Hardware used in Layer 3 switches to mimic the functionality of a router.

ASP—Application service provider. A business that provides a software application to one or more organizations. An organization providing Software as a Service (SaaS) cloud-based applications is an ASP.

ATM—Asynchronous Transfer Mode. A group of telecommunications standards used to transfer voice, data, and video signals. ATM uses small, fixed-size cells. ATM operates on the Data Link layer (Layer 2) of the OSI model.

AUP—Acceptable Use Policy. An AUP defines proper system usage. It will often describe the purpose of computer systems and networks, how users can access them, and the responsibilities of users when accessing the systems.

B–Topics in Acronym List

BERT—Bit-error rate test. A testing tool that measures the number of bit errors as a percentage of the total bits transmitted.

BGP—Border Gateway Protocol. A protocol used on the Internet and with WANs that maintain multiple links. Replaced EGP.

BLE—Bluetooth low energy. Also called Bluetooth Smart. It is a Bluetooth technology that uses less power than traditional Bluetooth, but has enough range for a personal area network (PAN).

BNC—British Naval Connector/Bayonet Neill-Concelman. A twist-on connector used with coaxial cable.

BootP—Boot protocol/Bootstrap protocol. The predecessor of DHCP. It assigns IP addresses to clients after they boot. Some imaging systems still use BootP.

BPDU—Bridge protocol data unit. Data sent to switches with information about the Spanning Tree Protocol (STP). Data is sent on Layer 2 as frames.

BRI—Basic rate interface. Part of an Integrated Services Digital Network (ISDN) configuration. BRI contains two bearer channels (B channels) of 64 Kbps and one data channel (D channel) of 16 Kbps.

BSSID—Basic service set identifier. The MAC address of an access point. The BSSID identifies individual access points within a wireless network that includes multiple access points. Compare to SSID and ESSID.

C–Topics in Acronym List

CA—Certificate Authority. An organization that manages, issues, and signs certificates and is part of a PKI. Servers configured to issue certificates are also referred to as a CA. Certificates include public keys along with details on the owner of the certificate and on the CA that issued the certificate. Certificate owners share their public key by sharing a copy of their certificate.

CAM—Channel access method. A method used to allow multiple systems to share a single transmission media. CDMA and CSMA are examples.

CAN—Campus area network. A network that connects multiple buildings in a small geographical area, such as a university campus. Compare to LAN, MAN, PAN, and WAN.

CARP—Common Address Redundancy Protocol. A protocol that allows multiple hosts on a network to share a set of IP addresses for failover redundancy. It is used with firewalls and routers and provides functionality similar to VRRP and HSRP.

CAT—Short for category. Used to identify various twisted-pair cable categories, such as CAT5 and CAT6. CompTIA objectives list this as an acronym for computer and telephone, but this isn't common usage.

CCTV—Closed-circuit TV. This is a detective control that provides video surveillance. Video surveillance provides reliable proof of a person's location and activity. It is also a physical security control and it can increase the safety of an organization's assets.

CDMA—Code division multiple access. An access method used for radio communications. CDMA is used by some mobile phone standards such as 3G.

CHAP—Challenge Handshake Authentication Protocol. Authentication mechanism where a server challenges a client. More secure than PAP and uses PPP. MS-CHAPv2 is an improvement over CHAP and uses mutual authentication.

CIDR—Classless Inter-Domain Routing. Method of allocating IP addresses used in place of classful IP addresses. CIDR notation uses a slash and a number (such as /24) to indicate how many bits are a 1 in the subnet mask. For example, /24 indicates the subnet mask is 255.255.255.0. The CompTIA objectives list this as Classless Inter-Domain Routing, but RFCs include a hyphen showing it as Inter-Domain.

CNAME—Canonical Name. This isn't actually an acronym, but it looks like one. It identifies a specific type of record used in DNS servers as an alias. It allows DNS to provide the same IP address for different host names. Compare to A, AAAA, CNAME, MX, and PTR DNS records.

COS—Class of service. A 3-bit field in some Ethernet frames used to identify specific types of traffic. Traffic shaping mechanisms manipulate these bits to assign class levels from 0 to 7 and use these levels to give priorities to certain types of traffic. Compare to TOS and DSCP.

CPU—Central processing unit. The primary chip that controls processing within a computer.

CRAM-MD5—Challenge-Response Authentication Mechanism-Message Digest 5. An alternative to transmitting passwords in plaintext. It provides a level of confidentiality for passwords.

CSMA/CA—Carrier Sense Multiple Access/Collision Avoidance. An access method used with 802.11 wireless networks. Devices attempt to avoid collisions by monitoring transmissions on the frequency channel.

CSMA/CD—Carrier Sense Multiple Access/Collision Detection. An access method used with wired networks. Devices are able to detect collisions and resend data after waiting a random amount of time.

CSU—Channel Service Unit. Provides the digital interface connecting the network device (such as a router) to the digital circuit (such as a T-1). You will often see this paired as CSU/DSU, but the CompTIA acronym list shows them separately. The DSU provides the digital interface connecting the digital circuit back to the network device.

CWDM—Course wave division multiplexing. Wave division multiplexing transmits multiple channels of data over a single fiber-optic cable using different wavelengths (or colors) of laser light. CWDM uses up to eight channels.

D–Topics in Acronym List

dB—Decibel. A measurement unit for electronics and sound.

dBi—Decibel isotropic. Identifies the gain of an omnidirectional antenna. References the hypothetical isotropic antenna, which can theoretically transmit signals equally in all directions at the same time.

dBm—Decibel milliwatt. Refers to the power ratio of decibels referenced to 1 milliwatt (mW). It is often used to identify the signal strength of a WAP.

DC—Direct current. Power created by power supplies. Power supplies receive AC power and provide DC power as an output. Compare to AC.

DCS—Distributed computer system. An application system that has components distributed among multiple networked computers. For example, a two-node DCS can have one node running one subroutine while the second node runs a second subroutine. A DCS can have hundreds, thousands, or even millions of nodes.

DDoS—Distributed denial of service. An attack on a system launched from multiple sources intended to make a computer's resources or services unavailable to users. DDoS attacks are often launched from zombies in botnets. DDoS attacks typically include sustained, abnormally high network traffic. A performance baseline helps administrators detect a DDoS. Compare to DoS.

DHCP—Dynamic Host Configuration Protocol. Provides clients with IP addresses and other TCP/IP configuration information such as the address of a DNS server and the default gateway. DHCP issues a range of IP addresses in a network (called a scope). It can reserve specific IP addresses for specific clients based on the client's MAC address. DHCP uses ports 67 and 68.

DLC—Data link control. The service provided by the Data Link layer of the OSI model.

DLP—Data leak prevention or data loss prevention. A network-based DLP system can examine and analyze network traffic. It can detect if confidential company data or any PII data is included in email and reduce the risk of internal users emailing sensitive data outside the organization. End-point DLP systems can prevent users from copying or printing sensitive data.

DMZ—Demilitarized zone. Area separating the Internet and an internal network with one or more firewalls. A DMZ provides a layer of protection for Internet-facing servers. It allows access to a server or service for Internet users while segmenting and protecting access to the internal network.

DNAT—Destination Network Address Translation. A form of NAT that changes the destination IP address for incoming traffic. It is used for port forwarding.

DNS—Domain Name System. DNS uses port 53 and resolves host names to IP addresses. The CompTIA objectives also spell DNS out as Domain Name Service and Domain Name Server, but these aren't commonly used. A DNS server runs the DNS service.

DOCSIS—Data-Over-Cable Service Interface Specification. An international telecommunications standard used for high-bandwidth data transfer over cable TV.

DoS—Denial of service. An attack from a single source that attempts to disrupt the services provided by another system. Examples include SYN Flood, smurf, and some buffer overflow attacks. Compare to DDoS.

DS3— Digital Signal 3. Also known as a T-3 leased line.

DSCP—Differentiated services code point. A method of classifying services for a quality of service (QoS) solution. DSCP uses 6 bits in the IP header to classify the data. Compare to COS and TOS.

DSL—Digital subscriber line. A family of technologies used for Internet access. Many small networks use a DSL modem to access the Internet through a local phone company. It is much faster than traditional dial-up modems, but not as fast as broadband cable modems. Most DSL Internet lines are asymmetric (ADSL), with the download link much faster than the upload link. Compare to ADSL, SDSL, and XDSL.

DSSS—Direct sequence spread spectrum. A wireless standard that transmits data over the spectrum of the channel. DSSS isn't as efficient as OFDM and doesn't support faster speeds. 802.11b uses DSSS and only supports speeds up to 11 Mbps. Compare to DSSS and OFDM.

DSU—Data Service Unit. Provides the digital interface connecting the digital circuit back to the network device. You will often see this paired as CSU/DSU, but the CompTIA acronym list shows them separately. The CSU provides the digital interface connecting the network device (such as a router) to the digital circuit (such as a T-1).

DWDM—Dense wavelength division multiplexing. Type of multiplexing over fiber-optic cable. Wave division multiplexing transmits multiple channels of data over a single fiber-optic cable using different wavelengths (or colors) of laser light. DWDM typically supports up to 40 channels. Compare to CWDM.

E–Topics in Acronym List

E-1—E-Carrier Level 1. Similar to T-1, but for countries outside the United States, Canada, and Japan. E-1 provides 2.048 Mbit/s of bandwidth.

EAP—Extensible Authentication Protocol. An authentication framework that provides general guidance for authentication methods. Variations include EAP-TLS, EAP-TTLS, LEAP, and PEAP.

EAP-TLS—Extensible Authentication Protocol-Transport Layer Security. An extension of EAP sometimes used with 802.1x. This is one of the most secure EAP standards and is widely implemented. EAP-TLS requires certificates on the 802.1x server and on each of the wireless clients.

EAP-TTLS—Extensible Authentication Protocol-Tunneled Transport Layer Security. An extension of EAP sometimes used with 802.1x. It allows systems to use some older authentication methods such as PAP within a TLS tunnel. It requires a certificate on the 802.1x server but not on the clients.

EBCDIC—Extended Binary Coded Decimal Interchange Code. A standard used to define codes for specific characters. It is defined on the Presentation layer (Layer 6) of the OSI model.

EDNS—Extension mechanisms for Domain Name System (DNS). A method that allows extending DNS as needed. As an example, EDNS supports increasing DNS security such as with DNS Security Extensions (DNSSEC).

EGP—Exterior Gateway Protocol. An obsolete routing protocol previously used on the Internet. Replaced by BGP.

EIA/TIA—Electronic Industries Alliance/Telecommunication Industries Association. Organizations that help create telecommunications standards. For example, TIA/EIA-568 defines cabling standards.

EMI—Electromagnetic interference. Interference caused by motors, power lines, and fluorescent lights. STP cables help protect signals from EMI. Fiber-optic cable is immune to EMI. Compare to RFI.

ESD—Electrostatic discharge. Release of static electricity. ESD can damage equipment and low humidity causes a higher incidence of electrostatic discharge (ESD).

ESSID—Extended service set identifier. Another name for the SSID. An extended basic service set includes all of the basic service sets (the access points identified by their MAC addresses) in a wireless network.

ESP—Encapsulating Security Payload. IPsec includes both AH and ESP. AH provides authentication and integrity, and ESP provides confidentiality, integrity, and authentication. ESP is identified with protocol number 50. The CompTIA objectives list this as Encapsulated Security Packets, but RFCs define it as Encapsulating Security Payload.

EUI—Extended unique identifier. Refers to EUI-64.

EUI-64—Extended Unique Identifier-64. A 64-bit hardware address used with IPv6 instead of the 48-bit MAC address used with IPv4. EUI-64 is defined on the Data Link layer (Layer 2) of the OSI model.

F–Topics in Acronym List

FC—Fibre channel. High-speed standard commonly used in storage area networks. Fibre channel originally used only fiber cable, but upgrades to the standard allowed the use of copper cables. Fibre looks like a typo but was selected to differentiate it from fiber cable.

FCoE—Fibre Channel over Ethernet. A lower-cost alternative to traditional SANs. It supports sending Fibre Channel commands over an IP network.

FDDI—Fiber Distributed Data Interface. A type of ring network topology using fiber-optic cable. FDDI networks use a logical token and two rings. Data travels in opposite directions for each of the rings providing fault tolerance.

FDM—Frequency division multiplexing. A standard that transmits data over several different frequencies at the same time. For example, cable TV transmits multiple television channels over the same cable.

FHSS—Frequency hopping spread spectrum. A wireless standard that transmits data over the spectrum of the channel, but in a pseudorandom pattern. Bluetooth uses a sub-type of FHSS. Compare to DSSS and OFDM.

FM—Frequency modulation. The process of encoding information by varying the frequency of the carrier wave.

FQDN—Fully qualified domain name. An FQDN includes the host name of a system and the domain name. For example, a computer named Server1 in the domain GetCertifiedGetAhead.com has a FQDN of Server 1.GetCertifiedGetAhead.com.

FTP—File Transfer Protocol. Used to upload and download files to and from an FTP server. FTP uses ports 20 and 21. Secure FTP (SFTP) uses SSH for encryption on port 22. FTP is defined on the Application layer (Layer 7) of the OSI model.

FTPS—File Transfer Protocol Security. An extension of FTP that uses TLS to encrypt FTP traffic. Some implementations of FTPS use TCP ports 989 and 990.

G–Topics in Acronym List

GBIC—Gigabit interface converter. A transceiver used to connect twisted-pair Ethernet cables with fiber cables.

Gbps—Gigabits per second. A data transfer rate indicating how many billions of bits are transferred each second. If the *b* is capitalized (as in GBps), it indicates how many billions of bytes are transferred. A byte is 8 bits.

GPG—GNU Privacy Guard. Free software based on the OpenPGP standard and used to encrypt and decrypt files. It is similar to PGP, but avoids any conflict with existing licensing by using open standards.

GRE—Generic routing encapsulation. A tunneling protocol developed by Cisco Systems.

GSM—Global System for Mobile Communications. A standard used for digital cellular networks. Commonly called 2G.

H–Topics in Acronym List

HDLC—High-level data link control. A synchronous Data Link layer protocol based on IBMs Synchronous Data Link Control (SDLC). The current standard is ISO 13239.

HDMI—High-definition multimedia interface. A connector for high-quality audio/video cables. TVs and computer monitors commonly include an HDMI interface to provide quality audio and video.

HIDS—Host detection system. An IDS used to monitor an individual server or workstation. It protects local resources on the host such as the operating system files, and in some cases, it can detect malicious activity missed by antivirus software.

HIPS—Host intrusion prevention system. An extension of a host-based IDS. Designed to react in real time to catch an attack in action.

HSPA—High Speed Packet Access. A combination of High Speed Downlink Packet Access and High Speed Uplink Packet Access. HSPA improved 3G cellular networks.

HSRP—Hot Standby Router Protocol. A Cisco proprietary protocol that allows multiple routers to appear as a single virtual router. One router is active and one or more other routers are standby routers. If the active router fails, a standby router can take over automatically. RFC 2281 describes HSRP.

HT—High throughput or high throughput computing. Refers to using multiple computing resources to perform a task over a long period of time.

HTML—Hypertext Markup Language. Language used to create web pages served on the Internet. HTTP/HTTPS transmits HTML documents over the Internet and web browsers display HTML documents.

HTTP—Hypertext Transfer Protocol. Used to transmit web traffic on the Internet and in intranets. HTTP uses TCP port 80.

HTTPS—Hypertext Transfer Protocol Secure. Encrypts HTTP traffic with TLS using TCP port 443.

HVAC—Heating, ventilation, and air conditioning. HVAC systems regulate temperature and humidity within an area.

Hz—Hertz. A standard defining a unit of frequency. 1 Hz is one cycle per second.

I–Topics in Acronym List

IaaS—Infrastructure as a Service. A cloud computing technology that allows an organization to rent access to hardware. It provides customers with access to hardware in a self-managed platform. Customers are responsible for keeping an IaaS system up to date. Compare to PaaS and SaaS.

IANA—Internet Assigned Number Authority. Part of ICANN. IANA oversees Internet IP address allocation, autonomous system number allocation, well-known ports, protocol number assignments, and management of the DNS root zone.

ICA—Independent Computing Architecture. A Citrix Systems proprietary protocol used for serving applications to systems remotely. CompTIA lists this as Independent Computer Architecture, but this isn't common usage.

ICANN—Internet Corporation for Assigned Names and Numbers. An organization that coordinates and manages Internet namespaces, IP addresses, and Internet Protocol identifiers. Compare to IANA.

ICMP—Internet Control Message Protocol. Used for diagnostics such as ping. ICMP is defined on the Network layer (Layer 3) of the OSI model. Ping sends ICMP echo requests and receives ICMP echo replies.

ICS—Industrial control system. Refers to a system used to control production equipment. Supervisory Control and Data Acquisition (SCADA) systems are a type of ICS.

ICS—Internet connection sharing. Process of sharing a single Internet connection with multiple computers. As an example, you can create a hot spot with an iPhone and share the connection with other systems.

IDF—Intermediate distribution frame. A signal distribution frame used to connect equipment within an organization. Compare to MDF.

IDS—Intrusion detection system. A detective control used to detect attacks after they occur. Monitors a network (NIDS) or host (HIDS) for intrusions and provides ongoing protection against various threats. IDSs include sniffing capabilities.

IEEE—Institute of Electrical and Electronics Engineers. International organization with a focus on electrical, electronics, and information technology topics. IEEE standards are well respected and followed by vendors around the world.

IGMP—Internet Group Management Protocol. Used for multicasting. Computers belonging to a multicasting group have a multicasting IP address in addition to a standard unicast IP address. IGMP is defined on the Network layer (Layer 3) of the OSI model. The CompTIA objectives list this as Internet Group Multicast Protocol, but this isn't a common usage.

IGP—Interior Gateway Protocol. A routing protocol used to exchange routing information within a private network. OSPF, RIP, and IS-IS are examples of IGPs.

IKE—Internet Key Exchange. Used with IPsec to create a secure channel over port 500 in a VPN tunnel.

IMAP4—Internet Message Access Protocol version 4. Used to store email on servers and allow clients to manage their email on the server. IMAP4 uses TCP port 143.

InterNIC—Internet Network Information Center. An organization that was previously responsible for domain name allocations and X.500 directory services. ICANN has assumed InterNIC responsibilities.

IP—Internet Protocol. A core protocol within the TCP/IP protocol suite. Both IPv4 and IPv6 are in use today. IP is defined on the Network layer (Layer 3) of the OSI model.

IPS—Intrusion prevention system. A preventive control that will stop an attack in progress. It is similar to an active IDS except that it's placed in-line with traffic. An IPS can actively monitor data streams, detect malicious content, and stop attacks in progress. It can be used internally to protect private networks, such as those holding SCADA equipment.

IPsec—Internet Protocol security. Used to encrypt traffic on the wire and can operate in both tunnel mode and transport mode. It uses tunnel mode for VPN traffic. IPsec is built in to IPv6, but can also work with IPv4 and it includes both AH and ESP. IPsec is defined on the Network layer (Layer 3) of the OSI model.

IPv4—Internet Protocol version 4. A popular version of IP that uses 32 bits to identify hosts. Addresses are typically displayed in a dotted decimal format such as this: 192.168.1.5. Each decimal is separated by dots and represents 8 bits. IPv4 is defined on the Network layer (Layer 3) of the OSI model.

IPv6—Internet Protocol version 6. A newer version of IP that uses 128 bits to identify hosts. Addresses are represented in hexadecimal format with eight groups of four hexadecimal characters similar to this: FE80:0000:0000:0000:20D4:3FF7:003F:DE62. The same address can be shortened as: FE80::20D4:3FF7:3F:DE62. IPv6 is defined on the Network layer (Layer 3) of the OSI model.

ISAKMP—Internet Security Association and Key Management Protocol. A protocol used to establish Security Associations. It provides a framework for authentication and key exchange.

ISDN—Integrated Services Digital Network. A set of standards used to transmit voice, video, and data over a public switched telephone network (PSTN). Two types of ISDN configurations are Primary Rate Interface (PRI) and Basic Rate Interface (BRI).

IS-IS—Intermediate System to Intermediate System. A link-state routing protocol commonly used in large service provider backbones. Compare to RIP and OSPF.

ISP—Internet Service Provider. A company that provides Internet access to customers.

IT—Information technology. Computer systems and networks used within organizations.

ITS—Intelligent Transportation System. Provides information about various forms of transportation to improve safety and promote a smarter use of transportation methods.

IV—Initialization vector. An IV provides randomization of encryption keys to help ensure that keys are not reused. WEP is susceptible to IV attacks because it uses relatively small IVs and IVs are sent in the clear.

K–Topics in Acronym List

Kbps—Kilobits per second. A data transfer rate indicating how many thousands of bits are transferred each second. If the *b* is capitalized (as in KBps), it indicates how many thousands of bytes are transferred. A byte is 8 bits.

KVM—Keyboard video mouse. Administrators use a KVM switch to share a single keyboard, video display, and mouse among several different servers.

L–Topics in Acronym List

L2F—Layer 2 Forwarding. An early tunneling protocol created by Cisco Systems for use with VPNs. It was later combined with Microsoft's Point-to-Point Tunneling Protocol (PPTP) to create the Layer 2 Tunneling Protocol (L2TP).

L2TP—Layer 2 Tunneling Protocol. Tunneling protocol used with VPNs. L2TP is commonly used with IPsec (L2TP/IPsec). L2TP uses port 1701. L2TP is defined on the Data Link layer (Layer 2) of the OSI model.

LACP—Link Aggregation Control Protocol. A protocol used to bundle multiple links together. This is also called port bonding. Defined by 802.3ad.

LAN—Local area network. Group of devices connected within a network. Compare to CAN, MAN, PAN, and WAN.

LC—Local connector or Lucent Connector. A type of connector used with fiber cable.

LDAP—Lightweight Directory Access Protocol. Language used to communicate with directories such as Microsoft Active Directory. Identifies objects with query strings using codes such as CN=Users and DC=GetCertifiedGetAhead. LDAP uses TCP port 389. Secure LDAP encrypts transmissions with SSL or TLS over TCP port 636.

LEC—Local Exchange Carrier. Refers to the local telephone company.

LED—Light-emitting diode. Small components that emit light. NICs have LEDs used to indicate a link with a network and activity when the NIC transmits or receives data.

LLC—Logical Link Control. Part of the Data Link layer on the OSI model. It defines how the Data Link layer interacts with the Network layer of the OSI model. The MAC sublayer is also part of the Data Link layer and it defines how the Data Link layer interacts with the Physical layer.

LTE—Long Term Evolution. A wireless standard for smartphones and mobile devices. It is the successor to 3G and commonly referred to as 4G, though it doesn't meet the specific requirements of 4G.

LWAPP—Lightweight Access Point Protocol. Used to configure multiple wireless access points, which reduces administration time. CompTIA lists this as Light Weight Access Point Protocol in the acronyms list, but this isn't common usage.

M–Topics in Acronym List

MAC—Media access control. A 48-bit address used to uniquely identify network interface cards. It is also called a hardware address or a physical address, and is commonly displayed as six pairs of hexadecimal characters such as 1A-2B-3C-4D-5E-6F. Switches, routers, and wireless access points can limit access to a network with MAC address filtering. The CompTIA Network+ objectives also list this as medium access control, though this usage isn't common.

MAN—Metropolitan area network. A computer network that spans a metropolitan area such as a city. Compare to CAN, LAN, PAN, and WAN.

MAU—Multistation access unit. A central device used in some ring topologies. Devices transmit data to and from the MAU instead of with neighboring devices in the ring. The MAU monitors devices on the network and ensures the network continues to operate, even if one of the devices fails.

Mbps—Megabits per second. A data transfer rate indicating how many millions of bits are transferred each second.

MBps—Megabytes per second. A data transfer rate indicating how many millions of bytes are transferred each second. Notice that the *B* is capitalized in MBps. A byte is 8 bits.

MDF—Main distribution frame. A signal distribution frame used to connect equipment within an organization to a subscriber carrier outside of the organization. Compare to IDF.

MDI—Medium Dependent Interface. The interface used to transmit data. It is used when devices are connected with a normal straight-through cable. Compare to MDI-X.

MDIX—Medium Dependent Interface Crossover. An interface used to transmit data to a similar device by simulating a connection with a crossover cable. Many devices use auto-MDIX, which can automatically configure the port as MDI or MDIX based on the connection. Compare to MDI.

MGCP—Media Gateway Control Protocol. A protocol that controls the functions between Voice over IP (VoIP) devices. Replaced SGCP.

MIB—Management Information Base. A hierarchical database of devices using a specific syntax. SNMP uses a MIB.

MIMO—Multiple-input, multiple-output. A smart antenna technology used with 802.11n designed to achieve faster speeds. It uses multiple antennas and transceivers, which provide diversity gain and improved reliability. Data is sent in separate streams in a process called spatial multiplexing.

MLA—Master license agreement. Typically used with software. The license authorizes an organization to use the software as long as they comply with the requirements in the agreement.

MLA—Multilateral agreement. An agreement between three or more parties.

MMF—Multimode fiber. A type of fiber used in short range cable runs such as with 10GBaseSR and 10GBaseSW. MMF has a larger core than SMF and is less expensive. Compare to SMF.

MOU—Memorandum of understanding. Defines responsibilities of each party, but it is not as strict as an SLA.

MPEG—Moving Picture Experts Group. A group that had defined several compression methodologies used for audio and video. These methodologies operate on the Presentation layer (Layer 6) of the OSI model.

MPLS—Multiprotocol Label Switching. A type of WAN topology. MPLS supports multiple protocols such as ATM and frame relay and operates on multiple layers of the OSI model. It uses labels to identify paths instead of IP addresses used with TCP/IP. The CompTIA objectives lists it as Multi-Protocol (with a hyphen), but RFCs do not use a hyphen.

MSA—Master Service Agreement. A contract between two parties that applies to future transactions and agreements. It streamlines the process of creating agreements in the future without requiring the parties to create new contracts from scratch.

MS-CHAP—Microsoft Challenge Handshake Authentication Protocol. Microsoft implementation of CHAP. MS-CHAPv2 provides mutual authentication.

MSDS—Material Safety Data Sheet. Provides personnel with safety information about potentially hazardous materials, such as cleaning agents. It often includes first aid treatment instructions.

MT-RJ—Mechanical Transfer-Registered Jack. A connector used with fiber-optic cable. It is used with duplex multimode connections.

MTU—Maximum transmission unit. The MTU identifies the largest size of a packet or frame that can be sent across a network.

MU-MIMO—Multi-user multiple-input, multiple-output. The use of MIMO technologies for multiple wireless devices. 802.11n introduced MIMO. 802.11ac introduced MU-MIMO.

MX—Mail Exchanger. A type of record used in DNS servers to local mail servers. Compare to A, AAAA, CNAME, and PTR DNS records.

N–Topics in Acronym List

NAC—Network access control. Inspects clients for health and can restrict network access for unhealthy clients to a remediation network. Clients run agents and these agents report status to a NAC server. NAC is used for VPN and internal clients. MAC filtering is a form of NAC.

NAS—Network attached storage. A server or computer appliance used to store and serve files over a network. NAS units can have one or more drives and can support different RAID configurations.

NAT—Network Address Translation. A service that translates public IP addresses to private IP addresses and private IP addresses back to public IP addresses. It is often used on wireless routers and proxy servers.

NCP—Network Control Protocol. A component within the Point-to-Point Protocol (PPP).

NetBEUI—Network Basic Input/Output Extended User Interface. An older networking protocol originated by IBM. It is not routable and is rarely used today.

NetBIOS—Network Basic Input/Output System. A service operating on the Session layer of the OSI model for connectivity over a network. Its use is dwindling in today's networks.

NFS—Network File System. A file system protocol that allows users to access files over a network. Sun Microsystems created it, but it is now an open standard. It is commonly used with Unix and Unix derivatives. CompTIA lists this as Network File Service in the objectives, but this isn't common usage.

NIC—Network interface card. An expansion card or built-in hardware that is used to connect a device to a network. NICs commonly have RJ-45 jacks and twisted-pair cables plug into the RJ-45 jack. NICs operate on both the Physical and Data Link layers (Layers 1 and 2, respectively).

NIDS—Network intrusion detection system. A NIDS is installed on network devices, such as routers or firewalls and monitors network traffic. It can detect network-based attacks.

NIPS—Network intrusion prevention system. An IPS that monitors the network. An IPS can actively monitor data streams, detect malicious content, and stop attacks in progress.

NIU—Network interface unit. A device marking the demarcation point between the customer's wiring and a carrier's local loop. Also called a network interface device.

nm—Nanometer. One billionth of a meter.

NNTP—Network News Transport Protocol. Protocol used to host newsgroups. Many newsgroups are now referred to as forums, or simply groups and can be accessed using HTTP instead of, or in addition to, using NNTP.

NTP—Network Time Protocol. Protocol used to synchronize computer times. NTP operates on the Application layer (Layer 7) of the OSI model.

O–Topics in Acronym List

OCx—Optical Carrier. Represents the various Optical Carrier specifications such as OC-1, OC-3, and so on. SONET fiber-optic networks use OC specifications.

OFDM—Orthogonal frequency-division multiplexing. A wireless standard that splits the signal into multiple subcarriers and transmits the data on each subcarrier simultaneously. Used by most wireless standards, including 802.11a, g, n, and ac. Compare to DSSS and FHSS.

OS—Operating system. Includes Windows, Linux, and Apple iOS systems. OSs are hardened to make them more secure from their default installation.

OSI—Open Systems Interconnection. A seven-layer model that provides a general framework for network communications. Layers are Physical (Layer 1), Data Link (Layer 2), Network (Layer 3), Transport (Layer 4), Session (Layer 5), Presentation (Layer 6), and Application (Layer 7). Compare to TCP/IP model. The CompTIA objectives list this as Open System Interconnect, but this isn't common usage.

OSPF—Open Shortest Path First. A link-state routing protocol. Routers share information with each other using OSPF. Compare to RIP and ISIS.

OTDR—Optical time domain reflectometer. A tool used to measure the length of a fiber-optic cable and identify any anomalies along the cable. Compare to TDR.

OUI—Organizationally unique identifier. A 24-bit number that uniquely identifies a vendor or manufacturer. 48-bit MAC (or hardware) addresses include the OUI as the first 24 bits.

P–Topics in Acronym List

P2P—Peer-to-peer. A type of topology where computers share information directly with each other instead of through a central server. P2P applications (also called file sharing applications) allow users to share files such as music, video, and data over the Internet.

PaaS—Platform as a Service. A cloud computing technology that provides cloud customers with a preconfigured computing platform they can use as needed. PaaS is a fully managed platform, meaning that the vendor keeps the platform up to date with current patches. Compare to IaaS and SaaS.

PAN—Personal network area. A network of devices close to a single person. Compare to CAN, LAN, MAN, and WAN.

PAP—Password Authentication Protocol. An older authentication protocol where passwords or PINs are sent across the network in cleartext. CHAP is more secure. PAP uses PPP.

PAT—Port Address Translation. A form of NAT that translates public IP addresses to private IP addresses, and private IP addresses back to public IP addresses. PAT uses a single public IP address. Compare to DNAT.

PC—Personal computer. Any type of computer used by an end user. Typically refers to a desktop computer or a laptop computer.

PDF—Portable Document Format. A file format originated by Adobe Systems that is now an open standard. A PDF document includes a description of exactly how the text and graphics appear within the document.

PDU—Protocol data unit. A generic name for data formatted at the Application, Presentation, and Session layers (Layers 7, 6, and 5, respectively) of the OSI model. In contrast, the Transport layer (Layer 4) identifies data as segments, the Network layer (Layer 3) identifies data as packets, the Data Link layer (Layer 2) identifies data as frames, and the Physical layer (Layer 1) identifies data as bits.

PGP—Pretty Good Privacy. Commonly used to secure email communications between two private individuals but is also used in companies. It provides confidentiality, integrity, authentication, and non-repudiation. It can digitally sign and encrypt email. It uses both asymmetric and symmetric encryption.

PKI—Public Key Infrastructure. A group of technologies used to request, create, manage, store, distribute, and revoke digital certificates. Certificates include public keys along with details on the owner of the certificate and on the CA that issued the certificate. Certificate owners share their public key by sharing a copy of their certificate. Certificates can be used for authentication such as when WPA2 Enterprise is used with a RADIUS server.

PoE—Power over Ethernet. A standard that delivers power to devices over an Ethernet cable. Defined by 802.3af. 802.3at defines PoE+, which provides up to 25.5 W of power. In contrast, 802.3af provides up to 15.4 W of power.

POP—Post Office Protocol. Used to transfer email from mail servers to clients. The current version is POP3. POP3 uses TCP port 110.

POTS—Plain old telephone service. This refers to voice-grade telephone service and can be used with simple dial-up modems. DSL modems use upgraded digital lines. The CompTIA objectives list this as plain old telephone system, but this isn't a common usage.

PPP—Point-to-Point Protocol. Tunneling protocol used with VPNs to create remote access connections. PPTP uses TCP port 1723.

PPPoE—Point-to-Point Protocol over Ethernet. A network protocol used to encapsulate PPP frames within Ethernet frames. Commonly used with DSL.

PPTP—Point-to-Point Tunneling Protocol. Tunneling protocol used with VPNs. PPTP uses TCP port 1723.

PRI—Primary Rate Interface. A standard used with ISDN. Two types of ISDN configurations are Primary Rate Interface (PRI) creating a T-1 in the United States and Canada, and an E-1 in Europe.

PSK—Pre-shared key. A secret shared among different systems and commonly used with WPA Personal and WPA2 Personal on wireless networks. In contrast, Enterprise mode uses a RADIUS server for authentication.

PSTN—Public switched telephone network. The combination of components used in telephone networks. It includes all the different links, such as telephone lines, fiber-optic cables, cellular networks, microwave links, satellite links, and undersea telephone cables.

PTP—Point-to-Point. A network connection between two systems. Within telecommunications, PTP refers to connections between two parties using telephones.

PTR—Pointer record. This isn't actually an acronym, but it looks like one. It identifies a specific type of record used in DNS servers to resolve IP addresses back to host names. Compare to A, AAAA, CNAME, and MX DNS records.

PVC—Permanent virtual circuit. A type of connection used within ATM and frame relay networks. A PVC provides a dedicated link. Compare to SVC.

PVC—Polyvinyl chloride. Type of cable covering used in cables. PVC cable is not plenum safe and should not be run through plenums. Instead, plenum safe cable is used within plenums. Plenum safe cable is fire retardant and does not emit dangerous chemicals if it burns.

Q–Topics in Acronym List

QoS—Quality of service. Refers to the overall performance of a network. Traffic shaping policies limit certain types of traffic, such as streaming audio and video, to increase the overall performance of the network.

R–Topics in Acronym List

RADIUS—Remote Authentication Dial-In User Service. Provides central authentication for remote access clients and can be used for authentication with WPA/WPA2 Enterprise. RADIUS encrypts the password packets and uses UDP.

RARP—Reverse Address Resolution Protocol. An older protocol used by computers to request an IPv4 address. BootP and DHCP have replaced RARP.

RAS—Remote access service. Provides access to an internal network from an outside source location using dial-up or a VPN.

RDP—Remote Desktop Protocol. Microsoft protocol used to provide connection to a remote system over a network. RDP connections use port 3389.

RF—Radio frequency. A wireless signal that transmits over the air. Common RF ranges are 3 kHz to 300 GHz.

RFC—Request for Comments. A formal publication from the Internet Engineering Task Force. Many RFCs define a standard such as RFC 793, which defines TCP. Some RFCs are informational to provide background information such as RFC 6101, which documents historical information about SSL.

RFI—Radio frequency interference. Interference from RF sources such as AM or FM transmitters. STP cables help protect signals from EMI. Fiber-optic cable is immune to EMI. Compare to RFI.

RG—Radio Guide. Refers to a type of cable such as RG-6 coaxial cable.

RIP—Routing Information Protocol. A distance-vector routing protocol. It is used by routers to share information with each other so that each router can determine the shortest number of hops (routers) between two systems. Compare with OSPF and IS-IS.

RJ—Registered Jack. A type of connection plug used with twisted-pair cables. Phone lines use smaller RJ-11 connectors and network cables use larger RJ-45 connectors. They are formally known as 6P6C, 6P4C, or 6P2C for RJ-11 and 8P8C for RJ-45 connectors.

RSA—Rivest, Shamir, Adleman. An asymmetric algorithm used to encrypt data and digitally sign transmissions. It is named after its creators, Rivest, Shamir, and Adleman. RSA uses both a public key and a private key in a matched pair.

RSH—Remote Shell. A Unix command-line utility used to connect to a remote computer.

RSTP—Rapid Spanning Tree Protocol. An improvement over Spanning Tree Protocol (STP). Both help prevent broadcast storms caused by switching loops. Often replaced by Shortest Path Bridging (SPB).

RTP—Real-time Transport Protocol. A standard used for delivering audio and video over an IP network. The CompTIA objectives list this as Real Time Protocol, but RFCs identify it as Real-time Transport Protocol.

RTSP—Real-time Streaming Transport Protocol. A protocol used to establish and control media sessions between media servers and clients.

RTT—Round trip time. This identifies how long it takes a packet to get to a remote system and return. Ping and tracert/traceroute both show round trip times. The CompTIA objectives also list this as Real Transfer Time, but this isn't common usage.

S–Topics in Acronym List

SA—Security Association. Communication between systems over a network used to securely share security information such as cryptographic methods and an encryption key. The framework for an SA is provided by ISAKMP.

SaaS—Software as a Service. A cloud computing technology that provides applications over the Internet. Web mail is an example of a cloud-based technology. Compare to IaaS and PaaS.

SCADA—Supervisory Control and Data Acquisition. Typically used in industrial control systems within large facilities such as power plants or water treatment facilities. SCADA systems are often contained within isolated networks that do not have access to the Internet, but are still protected with redundant and diverse security controls. SCADA systems can be protected with NIPS systems and VLANs.

SC—Standard Connector/Subscriber Connector. A square-shaped fiber-optic connector using push-pull coupling. Sometimes called square connector.

SCP—Secure Copy Protocol. Based on SSH, SCP allows users to copy encrypted files over a network. SCP uses TCP port 22.

SDLC—Software Development Life Cycle. A software development process. Many different models are available.

SDP—Session Description Protocol. Used to describe initialization parameters for streaming media sessions.

SDSL—Symmetric digital subscriber line. A specific type of DSL line. The upload and download links have the same speed in an SDSL line. Compare to DSL and ADSL.

SFP—Small form-factor pluggable. A transceiver used to connect twisted-pair Ethernet cable with fiber cable. Also called a mini-GBIC. It has replaced the GBIC in most implementations.

SFTP—Secure File Transfer Protocol. An extension of Secure Shell (SSH) using SSH to transmit the files in an encrypted format. SFTP transmits data using TCP port 22.

SGCP—Simple Gateway Control Protocol. Used with Voice over IP (VoIP). Superseded by MGCP.

SHA—Secure Hash Algorithm. A hashing function used to provide integrity. SHA-1 uses 160 bits, and SHA-256 uses 256 bits. As with other hashing algorithms, SHA verifies integrity.

SHA-3—Secure Hash Algorithm version 3. Hash function formally known as Keccak. NIST selected this as the standard to replace earlier versions of SHA.

SIEM—Security Information and Event Management. A security system that attempts to look at security events throughout the organization.

SIP—Session Initiation Protocol. A protocol used for signaling and controlling multimedia sessions such as voice and video calls and instant messaging sessions.

SLA—Service level agreement. An agreement between a company and a vendor that stipulates performance expectations, such as minimum uptime and maximum downtime levels. Organizations use SLAs when contracting services from service providers such as Internet Service Providers (ISPs).

SLIP—Serial Line Internet Protocol. A legacy protocol used to encapsulate Internet Protocol data so that it can be sent over serial connections.

SMF—Single mode fiber. A type of fiber used in long and extended range cable runs such as with 10GBaseLR, 10GBaseER, 10GBaseLW, and 10GBaseEW. SMF has a smaller core than MMF and is more expensive. Compare to MMF.

SMS—Short Message Service. A text messaging service used with smartphones and mobile communication systems.

SMTP—Simple Mail Transfer Protocol. Used to transfer email between clients and servers and between email servers and other email servers. SMTP uses TCP port 25.

SNAT—Static Network Address Translation/Source Network Address Translation. These are various types of NAT and their definition varies by vendor. Static NAT uses a single public IP address in a one-to-one mapping. It maps a single private IP address with a single public IP address. Compare to DNAT.

SNMP—Simple Network Management Protocol. Used to manage network devices such as routers or switches. SNMP agents report information via notifications known as SNMP traps, or SNMP device traps. SNMP is defined on the Application layer (Layer 7) of the OSI model.

SNTP—Simple Network Time Protocol. A simplified version of NTP. Applications that don't require detailed accuracy sometimes use SNTP instead of NTP.

SOA—Start of authority. One of the records in a DNS zone. It includes information about the zone such as an authoritative server for the zone, the email address of a domain administrator, and information DNS servers use to periodically update and refresh the zone.

SOHO—Small Office/Home Office. Indicates a small office typically supporting between 1 and 10 users. A SOHO network indicates a small network.

SONET—Synchronous Optical Network. A group of protocols used with fiber cable. Some SONET networks use ring topologies. Sometimes spelled out as Synchronous Optical Networking.

SOW—Statement of work. A document that identifies the scope of work that a third party will perform.

SPB—Shortest Path Bridging. A standard that combines multiple network functions into a single protocol. It supports multipath routing and replaces spanning tree protocols such as STP and RSTP.

SPI—Stateful packet inspection. A method used by firewalls to allow or block traffic based on the state of the traffic within a communication session. The firewall allows traffic that is part of a known session. It blocks traffic that isn't part of a known session or active connection, unless it is initiating an active session.

SPS—Standby power supply. A type of uninterruptible power supply (UPS).

SSH—Secure Shell. An encryption protocol used to secure a wide variety of traffic such as Telnet and Secure File Transfer Protocol (SFTP). SSH uses port 22.

SSID—Service set identifier. The name of a wireless network in human readable form. Disabling SSID broadcast can hide the network from casual users, but an attacker can easily discover it with a wireless sniffer. It's recommended to change the SSID from the default name. Compare to BSSID and ESSID.

SSL—Secure Sockets Layer. A legacy protocol used to encrypt traffic on the wire. It was used with HTTPS to secure HTTP traffic on the Internet as

HTTPS. SSL uses port 443 when encrypting HTTPS traffic. TLS is the replacement for SSL.

ST—Straight tip or snap twist. A type of connector used with fiber-optic cable. Typically used with multimode fiber.

STP—Shielded twisted-pair. Twisted-pair cable commonly used in Ethernet networks that require protection against EMI, RFI, or cross-talk. The shielding around the pairs provides the protection. Compare to UTP.

STP—Spanning Tree Protocol. A protocol that protects against switching loops. A switching loop can be created if two ports of a switch are connected together. Often replaced by Shortest Path Bridging (SPB).

SVC—Switched virtual circuit. A type of connection used within ATM and frame relay networks. An SVC is a temporary connection, typically set up on a per-call basis. Compare to PVC.

SYSLOG—System log. A message logging standard that delivers event notification messages. Typically, many devices send event notifications to one or more data collectors. For example, several devices can be configured to send real-time notifications to a syslog server. Note that while the CompTIA objectives list this with all caps (SYSLOG), source documents such as RFC 5424 list it as syslog.

T–Topics in Acronym List

T-1—Terrestrial Carrier Level 1. A copper-based transmission system. T-1 provides 1.544 Mbit/s of bandwidth. Compare to E-1.

TA—Terminal adapter. A device that connects a terminal to an ISDN device. The CompTIA objectives list this as terminal adaptor (with an *o*) but this isn't common usage.

TACACS—Terminal Access Controller Access-Control System. An older remote access authentication protocol.

TACACS+—Terminal Access Controller Access-Control System+. Access control protocol that can be used for the management of network devices (including routers). It provides authorization, authentication, and accounting (AAA) services and can be used for remote access solutions. TACACS+ uses TCP port 49.

TCP—Transmission Control Protocol. Provides guaranteed delivery of IP traffic. Uses a three-way handshake to establish a connection. TCP is defined on the Transport layer (Layer 4) of the OSI model. Compare to UDP.

TCP/IP—Transmission Control Protocol/Internet Protocol. Represents the full suite of protocols used on the Internet and most internal networks.

TDM—Time-division multiplexing. Multiplexing transmits multiple signals on the same media. Time-division multiplexing does this by transmitting different signals at different times. For example, when transmitting two signals, the signals take turns transmitting.

TDR—Time-domain reflectometer. A tool used to measure the length of a copper cable and identify any anomalies along the cable. It can identify cuts, breaks, and nicks. Compare to OTDR.

Telco—Telephone company. Sometimes refers to a telecommunications company.

TFTP—Trivial File Transfer Protocol. Used to transfer small amounts of data with UDP port 69. In contrast, FTP is used to transfer larger files using TCP ports 20 and 21.

TKIP—Temporal Key Integrity Protocol. Wireless security protocol introduced to address the problems with WEP. TKIP was used with WPA, but many implementations of WPA now support AES.

TLS—Transport Layer Security. Used to encrypt traffic on the wire. TLS is the replacement for SSL. Like SSL, it uses certificates issued by CAs.

EAP-TLS uses TLS to encrypt the authentication process and can be used with WPA2 Enterprise and RADIUS servers.

TMS—Transportation management system. Part of a supply chain. It controls procurement processes (inbound transportation) and shipping processes (outbound). Compare to WMS.

TOS—Type of Service. An 8-bit field in the IPv4 header. This field has been used differently over the years. Currently, the most common usage is as a 6-bit DSCP code, and a 2-bit Explicit Congestion Notification (ECN) field. ECN provides notification of a busy network without dropping packets. Compare to COS and DSCP.

TTL—Time to Live. Refers to the number of hops (routers) that a packet will pass through before it "dies." For example, if the TTL is 64, each router (hop) will decrement the packet by 1 before sending it on. When the TTL reaches 0, the router no longer forwards it. This prevents a packet from traveling over a network indefinitely.

TTLS—Tunneled Transport Layer Security. An extension of TLS commonly used with Extensible Authentication Protocol (EAP). EAP-TTLS encrypts data within a TLS tunnel. It requires a certificate on the server.

U–Topics in Acronym List

UC—Unified Communications. Refers to the integration of multiple communication technologies. It includes Voice over IP (VoIP), instant messaging services for online chat, video conferencing, desktop sharing, integrated voice mail, email, Short Message Service (SMS), and more. Often used as a marketing buzzword for sales.

UDP—User Datagram Protocol. Used instead of TCP when guaranteed delivery of each packet is not necessary. UDP uses a best-effort delivery mechanism. UDP is defined on the Transport layer (Layer 4) of the OSI model.

UNC—Universal Naming Convention. A Microsoft format that identifies the network path of a folder shared on a server. It takes the form of \\computerName\sharedFolder. For example, a folder named data shared on a server named Server1 is identified as \\Server1\Data.

UPC—Ultra polished connector. A connector used with fiber cables. The polish supports better physical contact between the fiber-optic cable and the connector. Sometimes called an ultra physical contact connector.

UPS—Uninterruptible power supply. A battery backup system that provides fault tolerance for power and can protect against power fluctuations. A UPS provides short-term power giving the system enough time to shut down smoothly, or to transfer to generator power. Generators provide long-term power in extended outages.

URI—Uniform Resource Identifier. Used to identify the name of a resource and always includes the protocol such as *http://GetCertifiedGetAhead.com*.

URL—Uniform Resource Locator. A type of URI. Address used to access web resources, such as *http://GetCertifiedGetAhead.com*.

USB—Universal Serial Bus. A serial connection used to connect peripherals such as printers, flash drives, and external hard disk drives. Data on USB drives can be protected against loss of confidentiality with encryption. Attackers have spread malware through Trojans.

UTM—Unified threat management. A security appliance that combines multiple security controls into a single solution. UTM appliances can inspect data streams for malicious content and often include URL filtering, malware inspection, and content inspection components.

UTP—Unshielded twisted-pair. Twisted-pair cable commonly used in Ethernet networks. It does not have any shielding and does not protect against EMI, RFI, or cross-talk. Compare to STP.

V–Topics in Acronym List

VDSL—Very-high-bit-rate digital subscriber line. A type of DSL that provides faster transmission speeds than ADSL. CompTIA lists this as Variable Digital Subscriber Line, but this isn't common usage.

VLAN—Virtual local area network. Defined on a switch at the Data Link layer (Layer 2) of the OSI model with 802.1q. A VLAN can logically group several different computers together, or logically separate computers without regard to their physical location. It is possible to create multiple VLANs with a single switch.

VNC—Virtual Network Computing. A system that allows users to connect to a computer remotely and take control of the desktop. Some organizations implement VNC for helpdesk technicians, allowing them to provide remote technical support to users. CompTIA lists this as virtual network connection in the objectives, but this isn't common usage.

VoIP—Voice over IP. A group of technologies used to transmit voice over IP networks.

VPN—Virtual private network. Provides access to a private network over a public network such as the Internet. VPNs can be host-to-gateway VPNs or gateway-to-gateway VPNs. VPN concentrators provide VPN access to large groups of users.

VRRP—Virtual Router Redundancy Protocol. A protocol used to provide high availability for routers. It groups multiple physical routers as a single virtual router. If one router fails, VRRP automatically assigns another router.

VTC—Video teleconference. A group of interactive telecommunication technologies that allow people in two or more locations to interact with two-way video and audio transmissions.

VTP—VLAN Trunk Protocol. A Cisco protocol that transmits VLAN definitions to switches on the network. It reduces administration requirements for these switches.

W–Topics in Acronym List

WAN—Wide area network. A network connecting two or more networks over a large geographical distance. Compare to CAN, LAN, MAN, and PAN.

WAP—Wireless access point. A device used to connect wireless devices to a wired network. A wireless router includes a WAP and additional capabilities. Often called an access point (AP) to differentiate it from Wireless Application Protocol.

WAP—Wireless Application Protocol. A standard for creating web content dedicated to mobile devices.

WEP—Wired Equivalent Privacy. An early wireless security protocol. WEP has significant security flaws and was temporarily replaced with WPA, and permanently with WPA2. WEP used RC4 incorrectly making it susceptible to IV attacks.

WINS—Windows Internet Name Service. A Windows service hosted on WINS servers to resolve NetBIOS names to IP addresses within a private network. WINS is not used on the Internet. The Internet and most internal networks use host names and host names are resolved to IP addresses by DNS servers.

WLAN—Wireless local area network. A network used to connect wireless devices together.

WMS—Warehouse management system. Part of a supply chain. It controls movement of material within a warehouse during receiving, storage, and shipping processes. Compare to TMS.

WPA—Wi-Fi Protected Access. Replaced WEP as a wireless security protocol using legacy hardware. WPA has been superseded by WPA2. WPA can use TKIP or AES and AES is more secure. In Enterprise mode, it can use RADIUS to support authentication. In Personal mode, it uses a pre-shared key (PSK).

WPA2—Wi-Fi Protected Access II. Security protocol used to protect wireless transmissions. It supports CCMP for encryption, which is based on AES and is stronger than TKIP, which was originally released with WPA. It uses an 802.1x server for authentication in WPA2 Enterprise mode and a pre-shared key for WPA2 Personal mode, also called WPA2-PSK.

WPS—Wi-Fi Protected Setup. Allowed users to easily configure a wireless network, often by using only a PIN. WPS brute force attacks can discover the PIN.

www—World Wide Web. Information space where data is shared over the Internet using hypertext links.

X–Topics in Acronym List

XDSL—Extended digital subscriber line. Refers to all DSL technologies such as SDSL and ADSL.

XML—Extensible Markup Language. A set of rules used to define how to describe data. As a comparison, HTML is a set of rules used to define how to display data. XML is often used to create formatted reports, and by databases for inputting or exporting data.

Z–Topics in Acronym List

Zeroconf—Zero configuration. A set of technologies with the goal of automatically configuring hosts on a network with TCP/IP information. The goal is zero touch requirements by administrators or users.

»Get Certified »Get Ahead

After the Network+ Exam

What's next for you after passing the Network+ exam? Many people pursue the CompTIA Security+ certification. It builds on your Network+ knowledge and helps show employers that you have a solid understanding of basic security issues that threaten the confidentiality, integrity, and availability of an organization's IT resources.

The CompTIA Security+: Get Certified Get Ahead: SY0-401 Study Guide has helped thousands of people pass the Security+ exam the first time they take it. If you plan to pursue any of the advanced security certifications, the SY0-401 Security+ Study Guide will also help you lay a solid foundation of security knowledge. Learn the material, and you'll be a step ahead for other exams.

Many people have taken and passed the Security+ certification within 30 days after passing the Network+ exam and you can too. If you're interested, check out this blog post: *http://blogs.getcertifiedgetahead.com/pass-the-security-exam-in-30-days-or-less/*.

»Get Certified »Get Ahead

Made in the USA
Columbia, SC
01 July 2021

41295732R00222